Ann Widdecombe

RIGHT

FROM

THE

BEGINNING

Ann Widdecombe by Laura Lehman-Kochan

Ann Widdecombe

Right from the Beginning

Nicholas Kochan

Frontispiece Illustration by Laura Lehman-Kochan

First published in Great Britain 2000
Published by Politico's Publishing
8 Artillery Row
Westminster
London
SW1P 1RZ

Tel 020 7931 0090
Fax 020 7828 8111
Email publishing@politicos.co.uk
Website http://www.politicos.co.uk/publishing

First published in hardback 2000

A catalogue record for this book is available from the British Library.

ISBN 1 902301 55 2

Printed and bound in Great Britain by St. Edmundsbury Press.

CONTENTS

To Julius Martin Kochan

ACKNOWLEDGEMENTS

A large number of people have given generously of their time to assist the writing of this book. Many serving and retired politicians have cooperated and talked at length. Some have spoken for quotation, and that has been noted in the text. Others have preferred to speak for background, and that wish has been respected. My thanks to them all.

I would like to thank members of Ann Widdecombe's family, notably her mother Rita Widdecombe and her brother Canon Malcolm Widdecombe, for their cooperation. I am also indebted to Caroline Gregg and Adam Newton.

Many colleagues have supported me in the course of a sometimes frenetic period of writing and research. Judith Crosland has been a resourceful and immensely willing researcher and I would like to acknowledge her particular contribution to the chapter on Ann Widdecombe's fiction.

David O'Leary has been a source of characteristically sound advice and diligent textual reading. His policing of cliché-ridden prose has been necessarily severe, but much appreciated. Any clichés that survive are the sole responsibility of the author. Iain Dale, the publisher, has gone beyond the call of duty in encouraging the author to be fair but bold. My thanks too to Sean Magee, John Berry and Gillian Bromley. Other valuable contributions to the text and to research have been made by Miriam Kochan, Lawrence Joffe and David Paul. I would like to thank Tracey McAuliffe-Duffy for her immensely patient and enthusiastic transcribing of tapes too numerous to mention.

Finally, I would like to acknowledge the immense patience of my wife, Laura Lehman-Kochan. While I was hard at work in my loft, she has borne the brunt of a demanding young child. It has been very much appreciated.

NICHOLAS KOCHAN
17 August 2000

INTRODUCTION

POLITICIANS rarely admit that they are virgins. They criticize their opponents in the fiercest language, but they do not demonize them. They fight their corner but they do not get so involved that they are moved to tears. They may observe religion in their private lives but they don't publicly proclaim it. Ann Widdecombe is, in short, no ordinary politician. In language, in appearance and most significantly in belief, Ann Widdecombe is different. No wonder some hate her and others love her.

This book deals with that rare phenomenon, a multi-faceted personality in contemporary politics. When Widdecombe was seen to support the shackling of pregnant women prisoners five years ago, she was called Doris Karloff. When she denounced Michael Howard three years ago, she was seen, in the media at least, as the justified avenging angel. Her rise to the top of her party in 1999 caught many by surprise. That transformation from darkness to light, from fringe player to star of the show, has been in part achieved by exploitation of the media's hunger for pictures and shocking phrases. But in part it is the result of the maturing of a genuinely interesting political character.

The withering of star quality in the Conservative Party, which undoubtedly began with the departure of Margaret Thatcher, but gathered pace during John Major's latter years and culminated in the massacre of May 1997, has been Widdecombe's opportunity. But it was a long time coming. Widdecombe fought two general elections before she was given the safe seat of Maidstone. She waited three years before even getting a foot on the ministerial ladder. She was never given a position that qualified her for entry into the Major

Cabinet. This was probably due less to any lack of administrative ability than to the perception she created of ferocity and lack of compromise. Yet such an image, as those who got to know her well became aware, was but skin deep. This book shows the many areas where Widdecombe has had doubts within herself. It also shows her capacity to listen to ordinary constituents and colleagues. Her willingness to show the author all sides to her personality has made this account the more complete, though it remains far from comprehensive. Nor are its conclusions always those Widdecombe would have expected.

The moralizing scourge of abortionists, homosexuals, unmarried mothers and scroungers might deserve the stigma of 'heartless Tory', or 'Doris Karloff', were she not also a 'secret' supporter of the homeless of Westminster, a promoter of better care for prisoners and a sponsor for African schools. Some would call this mere religious pretence; but others would see evidence of someone who looks at the sadder sides of contemporary life and does not turn away. These two aspects of Ann Widdecombe are in fact two sides of an individual for whom conscience plays an unusually large part in life. Those private actions and public concerns suggest a Toryism somewhat removed from the hard-nosed materialism that was introduced in 1979. Her belief in public service, private probity and the primacy of Parliament hark back to an earlier period when Tories believed in One Nation and the role of politicians as models for the multitude.

The devotion to public service was at the root of the most painful issue in her political life. This concerned her response to the mistreatment of a civil servant by her secretary of state. The decision not to resign from the Major government but later publicly to denounce Michael Howard put Widdecombe at the centre of British politics. It also fuelled an argument over her personality and judgement which is aired in the relevant chapters of this book.

Those seeking the source of Widdecombe's energy, ambition and brashness need look no further than her father. Murray Widdecombe was a rude and aggressive man, but he also had an absolute compulsion to push out of the way obstacles to his own promotion.

He achieved such a place of pride in Ann's life and career that it was unlikely any other man could match it. She tried to find one only once, but, although disappointed, she was not surprised it did not work. As she realized that 'Mr Right' would not come along, she channelled her passion and aggression into an all-consuming political life. Without the complications and demands of a private life Ann was able to give full vent to her desire to become a public persona. This would win her fame, but also notoriety. Her very public conversion to Catholicism, her language about sex, her abuse of Michael Howard would win as many brickbats as plaudits.

Conservatives, asked to make a judgement at some future time as to Ann Widdecombe's suitability for high office, will have no reason to doubt her energy. In fact, she drives herself so hard, some worry about her health. But colleagues may have more reason to ask what she stands for. While she considers herself right-wing, she supports the rehabilitation of young offenders. Her passion is for moral lobbies – on questions such as abortion and euthanasia – rather than the biggest issues of the day. She is more interested in the economics of the small business than the running of the national economy, although she can speak to the party line on both. Somewhat paradoxically, she supports both the return of capital punishment and the protection of foxes. Supporters in some leadership contest yet to come will believe her public following and her media persona are worth votes.

She will, however, win few votes from the women's lobby. Although Widdecombe's progress through the Tory party was probably held back by discrimination against women candidates, Widdecombe has no patience with the upsurge of interest in women's issues, which she regards as both trendy and indulgent. She would argue that her own success in breaking through the many glass ceilings in the Tory party proves what women can do in all walks of life, if they have the ability and the will.

Ann Widdecombe has said she dreams of being Prime Minister; but then, she also dreams of going to the moon. Once there, she says she would relish the opportunity to look down on the earth, admire its beauty and observe its follies. Her chance of passing the fitness requirement to walk on the moon must be slim. Her fitness to make the walk to Number Ten Downing Street must be considerably greater. Whether that is what her God, and more particularly the Tory party, have in mind is something she would neither consider nor discuss. The important thing, she declares, is to enjoy the present. That entails wearing what she wants, speaking colourfully and powerfully, and grabbing every available opportunity to say her piece to the media.

This book describes a woman who is riding high. But it comes at a particular time in a career which is far from finished. Readers will have to wait for Ann Widdecombe's autobiography for the full story. But they may have to wait a very long time indeed!

ONE

A Victualler's Daughter

'IT was the only time anyone called me beautiful,' Ann Widdecombe joked some fifty-two years later. Her long eyelashes cast dark shadows on her peach-like cheeks on the morning of Saturday 4 October 1947, and the nurses who carried the newly born baby looked at her and said how beautiful she was. But when she was taken home to be introduced to her brother, all he could say was 'Oh, damn!' Malcolm had wanted a brother, and now he would be stuck with a sister. That 'damnable' sister was christened Ann Noreen after her mother, Rita Noreen. Noreen was actually a fallback middle name for the little girl, whose father rejected his wife's suggestions, which included Georgina, Kathleen or Brionie. Noreen has never appealed to Ann, and she has also always hated her first name. But, like her much-vaunted lack of beauty, she has got used to it.

The families of both Rita Plummer and her husband Murray Widdecombe were of west country stock, from the area around the borders of Cornwall and Devon. Generations of Widdecombes had lived in the small town of Saltash, in the east of Cornwall, while the Plummers came from St Budeau, a village to the west of Plymouth in Devon, just across the River Tamar from Saltash.

The recent history of the Widdecombe family begins with a colourful character called Charles who enjoyed hunting and drinking but made money by baking bread for sailors based at Plymouth during the First World War. Having made a small fortune, more by chance than design, he lost it again, leaving his son, Ann's father Murray, with little to build a life on, and a lot of relatives to support. Charlie was not a 'sensible individual', recalled his grand-daughter, with a strong sense of disapproval. Ann's mother gave a more sympathetic explanation for his downfall, saying he lost his money because he was priced out of the market by a Co-operative store that set up next door to his bakery. The dislike of socialists that seems to have existed in Ann's branch of the Widdecombe family had its origins in part in this raid on the family wealth.

Grandfather Charlie was very ambitious for his four children, and while he still had his money, he sent his eldest son Murray (named, incidentally, after his Scottish mother Alice Murray) to the fee-paying Devonport High School in Plymouth to give him the best possible education. Murray took and passed the examination to study natural sciences at Cambridge University – the country's best academic scientific institution; but by this time the family's financial plight was such that he had to turn down the opportunity and go out and get a job, denied the chance to be the first Widdecombe to attend university. Murray took and passed the Civil Service entrance examinations and chose to enter the Admiralty, embarking on a career that led him to the very heart of the defence establishment. His headmaster is reported to have comforted him for the loss of his university place by saying that the able young man would earn as much in his first year working in the Admiralty as he earned today as a headmaster.

The Admiralty administered the Royal Navy, and attended to the needs of the sailors and ships employed within it. At the time, the Navy was the 'Senior Service' and Murray was attracted by the Admiralty's prestige; it was also very close to home at Plymouth, and he had schoolfriends whose fathers were in the Service. They would ensure the youth was well supported. To have gone to Cambridge would have been a great triumph, but the Admiralty offered a respectable and dependable career.

Murray went into the Admiralty as an 'executive officer', the first rung on the Civil Service ladder. But from the day he entered the administration, at the age of eighteen, he was determined that he would make the most of his career. In fact it became a ruling obsession, set the framework for his entire family life and was the most profound influence on the life and works of his daughter.

The other increasingly significant part of life at this time was his friendship with Rita Plummer.

Murray was only sixteen when he met the girl who would be his partner for life. Family legend has it that Rita, then fifteen and attending the local council school, spotted the callow youth on the opposite side of the platform at Plymouth railway station – he was going back home to Saltash, she was going to St Budeau – and was so struck by the prefect's stripe on his cap that she wanted to know who he was. Perhaps Rita already saw the ambition and ability in the lad who had won responsibility at school. But a friend told her not to waste her time on him: 'Oh, that's Murray Widdecombe. You can forget it: he's not interested in girls!' Rita regarded Murray's indifference as a challenge, and as they met regularly on the commuter trains taking them to and from their schools, the friendship flourished, although they would not marry for ten years.

The Plummer family were in more modest circumstances than the Widdecombes. Rita's father, James Henry, was one of thirteen children of an Irish Catholic family who lived in County Cork. He was a mariner, and when on one voyage his ship stopped off at Plymouth, he decided to stay. In due course, he met a tough Devonshire lady called Florence Susan Doyle, and the two married. They later set up a sweetshop in the small town of St Budeau outside Plymouth. Mrs Plummer was known to the family as Susie or Gran Plum. The couple's only child, Rita, quickly made herself useful around the shop and learnt to do book-keeping in her parents' little business. After her husband died, Susie continued running the sweetshop until her house was bombed in the Blitz on Plymouth, when she moved in with her daughter, by then married to Murray Widdecombe. Gran Plum would be an important influence on her grand-daughter.

Rita's parents bridged the two poles of Christianity, her father a Roman Catholic of Irish extraction, her mother a Baptist (though she had, incidentally, been educated at a convent). Her mother, being the dominant partner, sent Rita to a Baptist church 'so that I wouldn't be contaminated by the Roman Catholics'. The origins of Ann's complex relationship with the low and high elements in the Christian church may be seen to have their origins here.

Having got to know Murray, Rita was impatient to get married and start a family, but he wanted to make further progress in his career before making the commitment. Ann recalled a different, and slower, style of life: 'In those days you didn't rush into things. My father had to be able to establish himself. He had to be able to afford a proper home. It was a different world: people were slower paced. They had duties here, there and everywhere. No harm in it for that.' The other complicating factor in the couple's early life was the career path of an Admiralty civil servant. While the Admiralty had its headquarters at Bath and Whitehall, its staff were spread around the key naval outposts of the British Empire, and Murray's progression up the ranks would inevitably involve regular foreign postings which would be disruptive to a secure family existence.

But eventually Murray took the plunge, and he and Rita were married in June 1936. In September 1937, at which point the family was based in Gibraltar, they had their first child, Malcolm. Two years later, when war was declared, Murray was co-opted into the uniformed forces with the rank of captain. This put a temporary halt to Rita's plans to have a sibling for Malcolm, as Murray had decided that, in the face of so much uncertainty, it would be very unwise to add to the family. In Ann's words, 'My father refused point blank to have children during the war.' A contributory factor to the decision was the complications that had been involved in Malcolm's birth – the survivor of twins, he weighed only three pounds at birth, and was a sickly child until the age of two; Murray may have been concerned that his wife could not be sure in wartime of the necessary specialist treatment being available should she need it. So Malcolm had to wait ten years for the sibling Rita had wanted to have much earlier. By that age, he was a rumbustious boy, who understandably wanted an equally robust brother to keep him company. Instead he got this tiny little girl; hence his initial displeasure.

Malcolm was not the only Widdecombe who wanted another boy in the family, as Ann was well aware: 'He had wanted a brother. My mother wanted a son and it's not recorded what my father wanted. My grandmother who lived with us wanted a son and the other grandmother wanted a daughter. So I was outnumbered. My mother wanted four sons. I can't tell you why.' In any event, as sister Ann grew she became more fun for Malcolm, and as soon as she was capable of walking he dragooned her into joining his games and pursuits. However, he did not have as much chance of playing with his sister as he would have liked. To protect his education from the disruption of Murray's overseas postings, he had been put into a local boarding school called Monkton Combe. At weekends, though, he came home, and the two embarked on their rowdy games. Malcolm, by this stage a burly teenager, has happy memories of pushing his little sister around in a small home-made cart, called the 'covered wagon', which Gran Plum had made up, and from which Ann regularly tumbled to Malcolm's enormous delight. Ann recalled that as she rolled round the garden in the wagon, she pretended to be 'in the Wild West' and would shoot all the Indians in sight. Malcolm remembers her as 'quite tomboyish, because she had a brother. We used to have rough and tumble games.' As Malcolm grew up, however, he changed from robust playmate into protective elder brother, who would visit his sister at her schools.

The family lived in Hampshire, between Fareham and Gosport, in a house reserved for Admiralty officials called Ordnance House; Ann recalls the sundial in the garden and the long lawn which gave ample room for the young girl's play and antics. The house had several staff to look after the occupants, including two gardeners, local men called Grayall and Compton. Grayall won his way to Ann's young heart by pushing her to the local sweetshop on his bicycle to buy sweets, become a rarity with postwar rationing; Compton she remembers as a surlier character. Murray was concerned that Ann might become too familiar with these men and told her to mind her language. Ann resented his intrusion into her private existence, and waited her moment to get her own back. The cheek of a girl so young was breathtaking. Rita recalled: 'She used to go out and play in the garden with the gardeners. Every time she wanted to go to the loo, she used to say to them, "I'm going into the lavatory now." And her father said to her one day, "Ann, when you're talking to men, you do not talk about knickers or lavatories, will you remember that?" And we thought that was that, you see. And nothing happened for ages.

'One day we had a luncheon party and the table was packed and she was awful. Her father said to her, "Ann, if you don't behave yourself you'll have to leave the table." She stood up in her chair and said, "I won't, I shan't, knickers and lavatory to you!" Of course everybody went into shrieks of laughter, so he couldn't do anything about it. But we all laughed about it afterwards. That was typical of Ann.'

The young girl was not just cheeky, she was also curious about the puffed-up naval officials who doubtless made up much of the family's social circle. Rita again: 'When we had visitors she was awful. One day Murray said to me, "You must keep Ann in the kitchen because the Admiral is coming for lunch, and I don't want her near him." I thought, "That's all right, the gardeners will look after her." Anyhow, this wretched Admiral came early. He was wearing his formal dress. She rushed to the door, and she looked him up and down, and she said, "What's all that nonsense on your sleeve?" So Dad said, "Well, that's my promotion gone." '

Ann received the undivided attention of many members of her family, not to mention the staff; but the one family member who was already a very important presence in her life was ironically the one who had very little time or overt affection to give her. Murray doted on his daughter with a passion he never showed to his son Malcolm. Murray did not hold his daughter in his arms, and he would certainly not smother her with kisses, but he would be interested in her opinions and watch her progress eagerly. Ann was not merely clever and quick to speak her mind; she was also gritty, and utterly infuriating – qualities which her father had in spades. There was as much rivalry as there was love between father and daughter in this household. Murray succeeded in offending almost everyone he met with his lack of patience and his bad temper. But his loyalty to his family was absolute, and his decency never questioned. Ann affectionately describes him as an 'irascible old cuss'. Malcolm is more blunt and says he was 'hard, grumpy, aggressive and a terribly dangerous driver . . . he was very determined and bossy, and had great strength of character and complete single-mindedness.' Malcolm also jokes that 'Murray's favourite sport was watching hedgehogs: he was just as prickly. I think my sister is quite rough and tough like him.' Murray, like his daughter, had a passion for animals, and Malcolm quotes one of his favourite expressions: 'The more I see of people, the more I love my animals!'

Even the most innocent who got in the way of Murray were not spared his rudeness. Much later, when Helen Williams, a schoolfriend of Ann's, went on a short holiday to the Widdecombes' house, she inadvertently upset Murray and paid the price. She recalled: 'He came home to his routine, his dinner and his relaxation, his bedtime and his writing time, and his golf. Once or twice I got in the way of this routine . . .' The ensuing fracas was such that her stay was cut short. Ann has no memory of this event, but says she herself argued incessantly with the girls who came home to her family. Despite these good-natured arguments, there was no shortage of friends visiting.

Leisure time *en famille* involved playing games like Monopoly and Totopoly; the children teased each other using nicknames. Malcolm (who later became a strong-minded evangelical vicar) acted like a 'pugnacious dictator' at the time, and acquired the name Joe after the dictator Josef Stalin. The ferocious daughter, on the other hand, was given the milder nickname of 'Baba Wid'. 'Everything was Baba at that point,' Malcolm explains. 'We had a kitten and called it Baba cat. We had a lot of fun, loads and loads of laughs.' Those nicknames have stuck, and Rita Widdecombe calls Ann 'Babs' to this day. When Ann was at her convent, she introduced nicknames to her fellows, calling each of them 'something bean'.

Murray's work and other commitments did not leave him much time for entertainment or other frivolity, but he once took Ann to a circus which had come to town. She later recalled that when she returned home at an unusually late hour – bedtimes for the little girl were regular and early – her mother had thoughtfully prepared a warming plate of chips. On Sunday outings to Portsmouth in the summer, Murray taught Ann to swim – and, typically, he was not going to give his daughter any quarter, however much she complained. He thought water wings were 'the biggest blinking bore on earth', so Ann had to learn to swim the hard way: she went under water until she could paddle hard enough to stay afloat. But the teaching worked well, as Ann later became a very good long-distance swimmer and was taking that form of exercise long after she gave up anything else. Her father also taught her to ride a bicycle using exactly the same approach. She had to fall off again and again until she could keep her balance.

But even when Murray was with his family, he regarded himself as on call for his work. On one occasion when he heard late at night that there had been a food-poisoning scare at a naval base, he rushed out to go to the scene of the problem. Calls from departmental colleagues at all hours were commonplace, and given top priority. Malcolm observes that while 'he would work all hours, he enjoyed a lie-in at the weekend so he could catch up'. The habit was inherited by Murray's daughter, whose barrier between private and public time is no less porous, and who works at a similarly relentless pace to her father. For Murray, the hard work and commitment certainly paid off, for he became the head of his department and under-secretary in the Admiralty with responsibility for naval supplies and transport.

The patience required to live with such a preoccupied and irascible man was enormous, but Rita had it. Malcolm describes his mother as 'gentle and soft'; Ann depicts her as a 'soft-hearted, nice, kind person. I'm more like my father. He said I should have been the boy, not Malcolm.' Rita, a slender and elegant woman, with a profile which has remained powerful into her old age, is in fact a firm and determined personality who is at the same time much more low-key and subtle than the other members of her family. When she tried to discipline her troublesome daughter, it never had quite the intended effect. Ann recalls how she 'chased me with a brush, saying she was going to hit me – but never catching me! I take it utterly for granted that children should be smacked. I smacked my nephews.'

Ann's unpublished short story 'Sower, Upon what ground?' gives a child's eye view of discipline, but the extent to which it reflects her own experience is unclear as the roles have been swapped round, with the father the gentle and humorous one, while the mother is harsh. Her fictional hero says:

> As with most, my earliest lesson in self-preservation was to know the extent of parental tolerance so even before I could speak I knew my mother to be a fiercer disciplinarian than my father. When my small hand quested for some forbidden object my father would remove the source of temptation but my mother preferred to remove my hand by dealing it a sharp, stinging smack. When I spilled food down my clothes my father rubbed it off with a wink while my mother would treat the garments with impatient vigour, then hold the spoon herself for the rest of the meal, her angry eyes daring me to spill more. If I coughed or developed hiccoughs she would sit wearily with the food poised while my father made faces to make me laugh doubtless being under the erroneous impression that I could not laugh and cough at the same time . . . Later as I walked rather than crawled into mischief the lesson was always the same – it was wiser to try the patience of my father than of my mother.

Murray's absolute commitment to work and Rita's obligations as a service wife placed a great responsibility on the shoulders of the extended family, in particular the grandmothers. Gran Plum, Rita's mother Florence Susan, was a permanent resident with the family after her husband's death, and Charlie's wife Alice, who was called 'Granny Wid', came every so often, as she circulated round her four children once she was widowed. Much domestic authority in the Widdecombe home rested with these formidable women. Ann: 'I had one permanent grandmother and one rotating grandmother. But I had no grandfathers. I never had a grandfather.' The family tradition of widowed mothers living with their children has continued: when Murray died in 1999, Rita moved into Ann's London house.

Susan Plummer was both a support for the household and a most important influence on Ann. She made sure the house was kept shipshape and she taught her grand-daughter to do her multiplication tables, to read and to write. She also sang to the little girl to entertain her and looked after her basic physical needs. Gran Plum pushed Ann around in her pram for so long as she could, remembered Malcolm, although she had a deteriorating arthritic hip. Malcolm recalled that, 'She doted on both of us,' while Rita remembered her 'terrific sense of humour'. 'We often think of her sayings; they weren't always polite.'

Ann's interest in religion was largely cultivated by Gran Plum. At night, the two knelt down beside Ann's bed and said the Lord's Prayer together. 'I knew the Lord's Prayer when I was about four . . . "Gentle Jesus meek and mild" . . . We said that every single night. And then "Please bless Mummy," "Please bless Daddy," and "Tibby the cat", and everybody else – all of that.'

But Gran Plum was also a practical woman and completely unaffected by the family's improving circumstances which came with Murray's rise in status. She liked to peel her own potatoes, do her own cooking and see for herself that the house was well kept. Ann was allowed to fool around with her adoring Gran Plum by pulling her apron string and undoing the knot until the old lady was fuming. But both her grandmothers and her mother never tired of seeing that the needs of the little girl were cared for, and with Malcolm away so much of the time, she felt (in her own words) 'the Queen Bee. It was an immensely happy and privileged childhood.'

Murray had neither time nor interest to devote to domestic matters – nor indeed was there much call for him to do so, as they were so well catered for by the women of the household. But as soon as Ann started attending school, he was all ears and eyes. His frustration at being unable to pursue his own education to degree level made him especially keen that she should succeed. As he saw evidence of Ann's growing academic ability, the pressure he placed on her to excel only intensified – especially after Malcolm, in whose educational progress he had taken an equally close interest, disappointed him greatly by deciding to enter the church, a decision that caused considerable turmoil in the family.

Ann's first experience of school was not, in fact, particularly enjoyable. Her parents had been notified that they would shortly be posted to Singapore, and there was some debate whether the child should start school before they went or wait until they arrived. The die was cast in favour of school sooner rather than later, and Ann trudged wretchedly to Bridge St Mary where 'there were some really horrible children who used to pinch me and punch me.' She had yet to learn how to get her own back surreptitiously, so when she retaliated overtly, she was punished. The shock to the little girl's already highly developed sense of justice was acute. 'This really offended me,' she remembers. She was rescued from one scrape by an older girl called Lyn ('God bless her, wherever she is now'). School lunches at Bridge St Mary were another torment. On an early occasion she was served cherry pie and bit on 'the huge, vile stones in the cherries'. Lunchtimes after that were haunted by the fear that pudding would be cherry pie.

Ann recalled that at the time of the Coronation of Queen Elizabeth II she was presented with a Coronation mug containing a bag of sweets. She was also taught patriotic songs, in which Malcolm coached his sister, sitting on her bed and teaching her 'God Save the Queen'.

The steady family life and support system that had been developed with the help of the grandmothers was suddenly shattered when Ann was five, with Murray's promotion to the job of head of the armament depot at the British naval base in Singapore. It was an opportunity he could not turn down, but the dislocation for the family was severe and painful. The worst part was the discovery that Gran Plum, who had contributed so much to Ann's early development, was deemed unfit to travel. 'She didn't pass the medical,' Ann explains, 'and the doctor said she wouldn't survive the Red Sea.' So the strong family network was brought into play, and

Susan Plummer moved to live with Ann's father's cousin, 'despite', Ann recalls, 'the fact that she was my mother's mother. That was how families then operated.'

The next casualty was the decision to leave Malcolm in England. 'My mother must have been devastated,' says Ann. 'But in those days there were no assisted passages for children in their school holidays and there was totally inadequate education in Singapore for senior boys. So my parents did what most parents did then if they could afford it, and they sent him to public school.' Malcolm changed from being a weekly boarder at Monkton Combe to being a full boarder, and stayed at the school for three years. Brother and sister were separated from each other from the time when Ann was five and Malcolm was fifteen. Malcolm did not even see his closest family in the long summer holidays, spending them with schoolfriends or one or other of his many relations.

The last members of the Widdecombe household to be left behind in England were the family pets. Quarantine restrictions meant that new temporary homes had to be found for the much-loved cat and dog. It was decided the dog would go to stay with Murray's brother, a vicar, in Dorset; but the cat, which was supposed to be left with some neighbours, ran away.

The loss of these very dear members of Ann's family was felt acutely by all those departing, Ann in particular; but this was not a household that believed in overtly showing or discussing their feelings, and it was simply accepted that some members of the family had to stay behind. Ann tucked the sadness away in her unconscious and buckled down to the task of living a new life with new characters around her. 'I was shielded,' she said. 'In the modern day and age, all this would have been talked over and agonised over and explained in detail. I didn't realise they were all staying behind until we were going, then I was told. But I wasn't invited to dwell on it.' The thick Widdecombe skin she had inherited from her father also protected her, and she got on with things.

In any case, once the break had been made, there was much to distract her. Ann was quickly absorbed by the prospect of a long journey on the cruise liner that would take them to Singapore. This would now, of course, seem a very considerable luxury; but in 1953 air travel for private individuals was not common, while travel by sea was replete with the sense of adventure. This was particularly so for children, as the grand ships of those days were equipped with excellent amenities like swimming pools and children's enter-tainments like fancy dress parties. But social life had only limited appeal for the young Ann, and she often looked for ways to escape the buzz, curling up in a chair on the ship's deck or in her bunk and pondering the new life she was about to start. She thought about the splendid house where the family would live and the new people who would look after her. The mystery was all the greater as she was leaving the country for the first time, and had no idea what foreign people would look like. The only clue she had was given to her by her father: 'My father had told me that the Chinese were yellow, and I envisaged a bright, sunshine yellow, like the colour of butter.' I genuinely believed I was going to see bright yellow people – and I was so disappointed. I said, "They're not yellow, they're not yellow!" '

The colour might not have met her expectations, but the people exceeded them. The moment she arrived at the family's new house, she met someone she would still know forty-seven years later. She tells the story as it happened: 'At the back of the house there was a little low hut structure where the servants lived. Out of this structure emerged A Moi, who was the daughter of my amah. I was so taken aback because she had this black curly hair and black slit eyes (I hadn't seen slanted eyes before). I was so excited I pulled her up the steps leading from the kitchen to the hut, charged into the dining room and said, "Look who I've found." I was wildly excited and, of course, A Moi was very embarrassed and held back, because she didn't want to meet these strange Europeans.'

The house itself, 300 Kloof Road, HM Naval Base, Singapore 27, was a huge official residence, overlooking the naval base. The small child found it spectacular, and quite different from anything she had ever known: to her, it seemed to consist entirely of white and green shutters. Stilts protected the residence from floods or snow, but all the verandahs were open to the elements; the bedrooms were behind the verandahs. A Moi, whose full name is Chew Soon Moi, was only one of a bevy of servants who lived in the hut at the back of the house. A Moi's mother did all the housework and the ironing as well as looking after Ann. Meng the houseboy and A Hoon the cook, 'the fattest man I'd ever seen', completed the staff. The amah also had two other children who were older than A Moi and, as Ann discovered later, by a different father.

A Moi quickly became part of Ann's life and a very close friend for the vibrant little girl. There was no sense of masters and servants, said Ann. 'Apart from the fact that we [the Widdecombes] were in the house and they were in the hut, we lived together in the same household.' A Moi was four years older than Ann, but the girls played together nearly every day. When Ann had children's parties A Moi headed the guest list. At the weekends Rita Widdecombe used to take the pair to Seletar Island, where they went out in small, glass-bottomed boats to see the marine life.

Relations with Meng were initially cooler. He was dubious about working in a house where there was a child, as the previous occupants had not had children. But the idea grew on him, and by the time the Widdecombes left three years later, 'he was terribly upset to see us go. He was utterly devoted to me; he thought I was hilarious.' Ann later admitted she was 'an absolute terror' to Meng. She pestered him incessantly, as she described. 'It was polite to take your shoes off if you went into a house. When Meng went up the steps which ran from the hut to the house, he used to leave his slippers at the bottom of the steps. As soon as he disappeared, I would grab these slippers and hide them. I used to hide them in the most extraordinary places, which my mother would then force me to reveal.'

The servants in the house were frequently Ann's only companions as Murray and Rita were required to attend a lot of official functions. Often she had to spend long evenings on her own, without her parents, and understandably felt somewhat neglected. A short story she wrote much later called *The Knugle* (after the ghost that haunts the young boy hero), describes the loneliness and the fears conjured up by a child left behind at night.

> The child sat up in bed straining his ears to hear each sound of his parents' departure. He heard the front door close, the garage door rolled back while a few brief words which he could not distinguish, exchanged between his parents, floated up to his bedroom window through the crisp night air. The voices emphasised his loneliness: his parents were talking together. They had forgotten him. Car doors banged, the engine was started and the child's heart sank. This was always the point at which he gave up hoping that something would happen to prevent his parents going out. Until he heard the engine revving hope grew green that they would not go. Maybe his mother would 'feel tired' or his father 'fancy a quiet evening'. Perhaps it would be foggy or icy. His parents, both late learners, hated driving in difficult conditions. But always as it became apparent that none of these circumstances would obviate their departure his final hope was that the car would go wrong and when he heard the engine come to life that hope withered and finally died.
>
> The child felt fiercely resentful that his parents should be going out so happily to their own mysterious grown-up enjoyments apparently so little concerned that he was left behind. The headlights swept the room as the car moved off, its sound growing fainter and fainter till he heard it no longer. After the headlights, darkness . . .

For the most part, the little girl adapted well to the life of an expatriate and enjoyed the amenities available to the children of service personnel. She joined the Brownies and became 'quite an avid Brownie person'. She also swam in the sea every day, getting very fit and bronzed. Even school was exciting, not least because it lasted only from eight-thirty in the morning until lunchtime. Ann attended the Royal Naval School at Singapore, which was built, like the houses, on stilts, and had an excellent reputation. Children who took their eleven-plus or Common Entrance examinations there obtained excellent results. Ann later regretted having to leave before she had taken her Common Entrance.

The homeward journey on SS *Asia* was no less exciting than the outbound voyage, and Ann, now eight years old, was able to take advantage of more of the facilities on the liner. She also remembered the ship stopping at some exotic and mysterious places. 'I remember calling at Aden. We saw the Hanging Gardens at Bombay. We saw Pompeii. We docked at Genoa. I still didn't appreciate it was a luxury.' At Genoa the sea journey came to an end and the family completed the trip by train. On arrival at England they had to go through customs, and Murray, then a grand Admiralty official, suffered the indignity of having his declaration challenged by the customs officer. 'Come on, sir,' said the customs officer, 'you've been in Singapore three years, you're the head of the armament depot, and this is all you've bought in that time!'

Murray Widdecombe replied: 'I've got a son at public school.'

'Ah, yes, sir, I see. Sorry,' said the customs officer.

Ann explained: 'I think in those days it was the standard joke among people who were stretching their income to buy education.'

The Widdecombes were not poor, but they were frugal. Rita, in particular, watched the way the family's money was spent, and kept a tight grip on the purse strings. Ann: 'I had all the things I wanted, and so did the rest of us. I think the word is careful – having to be careful.' Ann recalled that in Singapore she wore the cast-off clothing of a girl who had returned to England. 'Those clothes were terribly exciting to me because they were all new and different to me. It didn't matter to me that we hadn't been to the shops to buy them.'

Once back in England, the Widdecombe family went to pick up the relatives they had left behind. Three years had now elapsed since the Singapore contingent had left, and Ann's mother could not wait to see the rest of her family again. But Ann had scarcely noticed the time pass, or the absence of some of her closest childhood sweethearts. The first reunion was with Gran Plum. 'She was emotional. She thought it was wonderful. To me, it was just another adventure.' Then they went to see Malcolm. Rita was emotional after three years' separation from her son, but Ann was again detached. Her mother, she says, 'was wildly excited. She was seeing her son for the first time in three years. I had a mild curiosity.' Malcolm was no more excited about seeing Ann than she was about seeing him, and greeted his sister with the words, 'Hello, muggins!' The warmth of Rita's welcome for Malcolm rankled with his sister. Malcolm noticed how Ann was suddenly downcast. 'She did feel a little bit threatened and a little bit jealous because, of course, my parents hadn't seen me for three years and they wanted somehow to make those three years up to me. And so she did feel as though she was getting a little bit less attention.' Ann later admitted she was extremely jealous of the attention Rita devoted to Malcolm at that time.

The reunions complete, the family had then to sort out their living accommodation. Murray would now be working in London, and had arranged to rent a cottage called The Quell on the Surrey/Sussex borders; but it was not ready when they arrived, and so they had to make do with temporary quarters. These consisted of a large house on Blatchington Road, Tunbridge Wells, left by the owner with his own possessions locked away in rooms which were out of bounds. Ann recalled peeking through the keyhole of the locked attic and seeing a rocking horse; she resisted the temptation to try to get in. Knowing that they would be in Tunbridge Wells for only a few months, Rita Widdecombe was characteristically 'careful' and refused to buy her daughter a full school uniform. Fortunately, St Mark's School on Roedean Hill had a uniform that was brown check, and by coincidence Ann had one brown check dress which she could wear, which looked like the authentic uniform. But when the brown check dress was in the wash, Ann had to wear her school uniform from Singapore, a little white tunic. She hated it. 'I used to put a brown jersey over the top. I absolutely hated the days when I didn't have my brown check dress. It was not that I minded having a different dress from the rest of the girls, it was that the teachers used to complain. They used to say, "Where's your uniform?" They knew very well I was only there for a few months.' That little brown check number is engraved on her memory for another reason too: on one occasion, at a funfair, the dress caught on a piece of machinery underneath the 'train' she was riding. 'My mother nearly had a fit because she thought I was going to be strangled. But all I was worried about was my brown check dress!'

When the family were at last able to move in to The Quell, six months after their arrival in England, they found that the wait had been worthwhile. The cottage was 'in the middle of nowhere' in an idyllic setting, bordered on three sides by woodland; their nearest neighbours were 'ages away'. Admiral Elkins, the cottage's owner, had allowed Murray to rent it on the understanding that he would maintain the garden, which was truly magnificent. Ann waxes lyrically on the subject: 'The garden was terraced in that it went down in steps. We had an apple tree, daffodils (just like Wordsworth's "host of golden daffodils"), and a pond beside it full of lilies, and a little white gate, and then a stream outside with primroses all along it. Then just the wood beyond, nothing more. And up beside the house, another tiny little pond which used to trickle and make the most wonderful pondy noises. It really was fantastic.'

'Of all the houses I've lived in', says Ann, 'including bigger and more luxurious ones, Quell with its tiny rooms and its Aga and its wonderful garden was undeniably the happiest time.'

She and her friends used to go exploring in the woods and play 'adventure' games. One day they saw a badger; on another occasion, a deer. While they were at the cottage they acquired another wire-haired terrier called Tim (Ann at the time was much enamoured of Enid Blyton's *Famous Five* books in which the family has a dog called Tim). They also had a smoky grey cat called Monty which chummed up with a cat called Fluffer belonging to some friends from a neigh-bouring cottage called The Coombes. 'These two cats used to wait for each other at the top of the drive. And then they would walk off together with their tails in the air. Sadly, after we left, Fluffer Coombes used to spend hours just waiting for Monty. When I was a child, this made me want to cry.'

During the week, Ann went to the local primary school, Shottermill, five miles away down the winding Fernden Lane. Each morning Rita Widdecombe drove Ann there in the family's new Austin after she had dropped Murray off at the station to catch the train to London. Later she fetched them after their respective days at school and work. On one occasion Ann wanted to upset the system because a friend had invited her back to her home after school. Rita was having none of it. 'I've come all this way, used all this petrol, and you've really got to come home.' Ann replied with a clear-minded logic, 'But you've used all the petrol anyway, so you might as well leave me here. It doesn't actually un-use the petrol if you take me home.' The issue was particularly acute at the time: it was 1956, and petrol rationing had been introduced as a result of the Suez crisis.

The idyll at The Quell lasted for two years. Then Murray Widdecombe was re-posted from London to Bath. Rita Widdecombe had revelled in country living and its freedom from the endless social round and gossip that took place on a naval base. So, rather than move into Bath city centre, she found a country house in the village of Batheaston, three miles from the city near the area called St Catherine's. It was called The Mead and was situated up a very small winding lane lined with farms, two miles from the nearest bus stop. This was the prompt for Ann to acquire her first bicycle and she rode out over fields and woods for days on end. But this period, which she would later was particularly happy, was rudely interrupted by the recurrence of the whooping cough that she had contracted in Singapore and thought over and done with. Whooping cough is an infection which can only be caught once, so the sickness shocked the family.

As Ann approached the age of ten, a place had to be found at a preparatory school where her academic education could begin in earnest. In fact, her parents had anticipated that they would be living in Bath at this juncture in their daughter's life and had put her name down for Bath High School before they had gone to Singapore. But they had not anticipated that at the time when Ann reached an eligible age, Bath High would be full, with no vacancies in prospect. Faced with these obstacles, Rita Widdecombe started to examine the other local schools, undertaking her investigations with a degree of thoroughness that would now be unthinkable. To see how the girls were dressed and how they behaved, she waited outside the school gates and watched them as they came out.

All the schools but one were found wanting. Girls from Bath Convent, properly called La Sainte Union Convent, were well turned out; they also had a good academic record, and Rita knew enough parents of children who had been to the school to know that it was both respectable and educationally proficient. Ann was given a place at the Convent's preparatory school.

Ann missed the autumn and most of the spring terms of school as a result of the whooping cough and, as this is a highly infectious disease, she had to be kept out of the way of friends and visitors. Seven months later, when Ann was diagnosed free of the illness, she was understandably hugely relieved, and as a special treat her family took her out to see the film *The Ten Commandments*. The content, for the little girl who had long loved and prayed to Jesus, was undoubtedly most appropriate.

Ann took the eleven-plus while she still had the illness and failed a test that most students of her ability would have sailed through. The plans so carefully worked out by her mother now looked to be in jeopardy, and Ann recalled the consternation: 'My parents were obviously very worried about the whole situation. I took the eleven-plus that January and failed it – which had not been expected. So there was the most tremendous performance about should I take it again, what should actually go on?'

The school raised doubts about their new student. But Ann was given an interview, in which she was asked to read and answer questions on *The Wind in the Willows*. She impressed the interviewers and was admitted to the Convent's preparatory school. The Convent would never regret the decision to admit her, and Ann would later say that this institution shaped not just her education, but also her thinking and her life.

TWO

Schooled in Rome

WHEN Ann started life at La Sainte Union Convent she was a serious and pale girl, old before her time, and thin to the point where she gave concern to the nuns who taught her. Her slight figure, milky complexion and well-formed cheekbones were offset by short black hair which Rita had ensured had been well brushed every day. But the penetrating dark eyes were slightly disturbing to the nuns, who sensed Ann's intelligence.

Ann's schoolmates were also unnerved by the new arrival. 'She was never like a child, she was never silly,' said Linda Seale, who later occupied the neighbouring bed to Ann's in the dormitory. A friend remembered her as 'always looking a bit frail', and needing friends to help her sort out some of the more practical aspects of living.

The school, which was run by Irish nuns belonging to the French order of the Sisters of La Sainte Union de Sacré Coeur, believed that 'order was heaven's first law'. Its Catholic charism (guiding principles) was milder, and included hospitality, simplicity and union. Some 500 girls between the ages of five and eighteen attended the school, and although most were day pupils, some thirty attended as boarders. In the French style, the girls called the nuns 'Madame'; the nuns called each other 'Sister'. Most of the nuns were strict, but Sister Bernard Xavier (known to the girls as BX), the headmistress, was a particularly severe disciplinarian and instilled fear into the hearts of her pupils.

Ann, herself a rather austere young girl, made every effort to fit in with the rigid culture. 'It was phenomenally strict, like the army –

almost military,' she remembers. The rigours of the regime were exacerbated by the school's location, for the Bath Stone and corrugated iron buildings were close to the River Avon, and when the river broke its banks in the winter, as it frequently did, some school rooms were flooded. So, while the setting was picturesque, the atmosphere was damp – 'a little bit like Colditz, very bleak,' says Linda Seale.

Ann joined the Convent as a day girl, and her mother drove her there every morning from their home in Batheaston. But after a couple of years, Murray Widdecombe was posted from Bath back to London, where he took up a job at Admiralty headquarters, and the family moved back to Surrey, this time to Guildford, from where Murray could commute to his office in Whitehall. Rita wanted her daughter to come with them and attend the neighbouring Guildford High School; but Ann wanted to stay at the Convent as a boarder, and live the regimented life she now knew well. She felt she had at last settled down in a school, after the many changes of earlier years, and wanted to stay put. 'It was her choice to board,' said Rita.

A boarder's life was quite different from and much harsher than a day girl's. Religion was one particularly difficult area, and Ann, as a Protestant girl, never disguised the fact that she found the round of Catholic services a chore. 'The school prayed all the time. You were woken up with prayers in the morning, you prayed after breakfast, you prayed before you went to bed. There was just a sort of continual emphasis on it.' She had to be up for mass at six-thirty in the morning three days a week and on Sundays; rosary was on Saturday night. Benediction, which immediately followed mass on Friday morning, felt a particular imposition for personal reasons: 'My abiding memory of Benediction is that the incense used to upset my stomach because we also had cold cereal on that day – I always hated cereal with cold milk (I used to have hot milk at home). The combination of incense and the cold milk always made me feel ill.'

There was no escape from the devotion or the discipline. The girls' entire lives were carefully circumscribed. The pupils lived with the nuns in the convent; each dormitory, which held twelve beds, had little cubicles at the top in which the nuns slept. The individual beds did, however, have curtains which could be drawn round them to give the girls a modicum of privacy. Furniture and decoration in the dormitory were minimal: each girl was supplied with a basin, a water bottle and a jug on a side table. A piece of butter was given to boarders for the week's consumption. Great emphasis was placed on tidiness. The school's dress code was strict, with rules prescribing not only the school uniform for summer and winter, for weekdays and Sundays, but even the angle at which the straw boater (summer) or the felt hat (winter) should be worn. The nuns, for their part, were never seen in anything other than the long black gowns which covered them from head to toe. A white piece of linen, called by the girls a 'white biscuit paper', framed the face.

Cleanliness was regarded as very close to Godliness, and it was ordained that girls should wash their hair every fortnight and bathe twice a week at prescribed times. There were time limits on bathing to ensure it did not become an excessive indulgence. Tidiness, for pupils and nuns alike, was all-important, and obedience to the code of living absolute. Drawers in bedside tables were subject to regular inspection, and even the way the covers on the bed were to be folded was prescribed. Here Ann regularly disgraced herself. Sister Evangelista: 'I suppose I was after her to fold the covers properly. It wasn't for her at all. Sure, when I look back on it now it wasn't important really.' To keep the sisters happy, Ann turned to her friend Linda, who was much neater, and Linda folded Ann's thin fleecy coverlet into the regulation envelope-shape for her. In return, Ann helped Linda with her Latin homework, even though she disapproved of the practice. 'She wouldn't approve of that kind of thing because she wouldn't dream of cheating or doing anything slightly dishonest,' says Linda; but Ann helped her out anyway.

The spirit of the school was a long way from that at St Trinian's, but girls living in such a claustrophobic and regulated regime were bound to amuse themselves occasionally; and Ann went along with the spirit of adventure. There was a tradition that on St Cecilia's night, which occurred at the end of November, the ghost of St

Cecilia walked through the corridors of the Convent, and when she was about fourteen Ann thought it would be entertaining to reproduce the experience. So she persuaded a group of friends to wrap white sheets round themselves and walk the Convent's corridors at midnight. Only Ann and a girl called Liz Martin were still awake when midnight struck, but the two duly wound their sheets around their bodies and tiptoed down to the common room. There they played 'ghostly' tunes on the piano – St Cecilia being the patron saint of music. As they crept back to bed, they thought they heard a noise. It was their undoing; they were so frightened that they dashed back to the dormitories, forgetting the need for silence, and were apprehended. The nun who caught them 'jumped six feet out of her skin'. Later Ann discovered that 'the rather grim thing that we could not have known at the time was that actually that night a nun was dying in the Convent.'

As a result of this escapade Ann was gated, and forbidden to go out with her brother the following Saturday afternoon. This was a major blow as boarders were allowed out with a member of their family or an 'approved friend' only on every third Saturday of the month, and having the privilege withdrawn was a draconian penalty. Malcolm would no doubt have been concerned that his little sister might be trouble-making at school. Helen Williams, a day girl who became one of Ann's closest friends, recalls that 'Ann never missed out on the fun,' and reckons that she was involved in all the pranks going 'as long as they didn't hurt anyone'. The nuns were also known to arrange their own pranks at the school to amuse the girls – and there was at least one day when fun was officially endorsed: 17 March, St Patrick's Day, when homework was suspended, and the nuns and girls were allowed to relax. Ann remembers the nuns telling the girls jokes; hymns were sung praising St Patrick; and Ann, like everyone with 'an ounce of Irish blood in them', wore a shamrock.

The St Cecilia's night episode was particularly unfortunate, because Ann had a history of sleepwalking. The phenomenon ran in her family; her father had also sleepwalked when he was younger. Ann told how, on one occasion, 'Madame Evangelista actually followed me because they were worried about the fire escapes and things like that – they would always follow somebody. And apparently I walked down the corridor, turned round and came back again, very eerie.' On another occasion, Ann woke up to see her reflection in her bedside mirror messing about with the carafe of water beside her bed. 'That gave me a slight jolt at the time.' Ann, like her father, stopped sleepwalking as she entered her twenties.

As for Ann's academic aptitude, her prowess at Latin was established early. 'From the moment we did *poeta, poeta, poetam*, I decided this was for me,' she said. 'Sister Evangelista taught us Latin and she was a very wonderful person.' Her ability impressed all around her, says Helen Williams. 'We all fell in love with Latin because of "Vange", but Ann certainly fell in love with the Classics for their own sake.' Ann was also good at history and geography, and her love of English became evident when she read out stories she had written, demonstrating the talent that would produce her later writing. She won school prizes; Murray Widdecombe watched her progress eagerly and with pride, and when she did well he rewarded her. The school had a system whereby marks and position in class in every subject were posted up on the noticeboard every week; when Ann came first Murray produced a pound, 'an old-fashioned green note', she remembers; when she came second, the prize was fifteen shillings, falling to ten shillings when she came third and to five if she were fourth. Theoretically, below that point she had to pay him.

Practical subjects were a disaster area. Ann was incompetent at, as well as profoundly bored by, subjects like sewing, and she frequently asked friends to finish off her work to placate the insistent nuns. Sister Evangelista: 'Practical subjects did not register very high in Ann's achievements, nor did practical chores like a neatly made bed or a tidy dressing table gain her any credit marks as a boarder!' Sport was another activity low on Ann's list of priorities. The girls played hockey on fields at the top of Claverton Down, a hill to the east of Bath, which was bleak and cold. Ann felt the biting wind more than most, because, says Helen, she was 'thin. Her hands were small and not very strong, so were her feet. Her shoes always seemed to be too big. Her clothes were always a bit loose. She was always rounded at the shoulders.'

Science was another black spot. 'I was absolutely lousy at maths and physics and chemistry. I wasn't an all-rounder, but I used to get sufficiently good marks to be able to fight it out with Helen Williams, who was brilliant at science, for top of the class. In the fourth form we used to fight it out every single week – in the nicest possible way – as to who would be first or second and occasionally one of us would go to third or fourth.' Helen remembers 'ongoing very friendly competition, but it got a bit awkward when we chose our Classics versus sciences, because it is very easy to get 10 out of 10 to get your sums right, and very difficult to get 10 out of 10 for history essays. So I think she became a bit miffed that it was easier on paper for my marks to look better than hers, but she always took it in great spirit.'

The two top girls, Ann and Helen, took their competitiveness outside the confines of the classroom. At every available moment, they would be locked in argument over the merits of Catholicism (which Helen promoted and Ann fiercely repudiated) and the merits of Conservatism (which Ann espoused and Helen sought to refute). For hours the peace of the school library would be disturbed by their serious and passionate argument. 'We were arguing for the sake of trying to win arguments,' remembers Helen. But the two also talked about lesser subjects, and Ann moaned about the bother of having to look after her very fine and largely uncontrollable hair.

Later in life, as the arguments about religion and politics sank in, the two women were converted, in rather fine symmetry, to each other's beliefs. So Helen (who, true to her earlier form, spent many years in a convent) became a Conservative, while Ann renounced the Protestantism she had earlier so stoutly defended and accepted the Catholicism she had once reviled. Helen recalls: 'The argument went on and on. Our discussion helped her understand Roman Catholics. After all, she was in school with them all this time. She was very open to reason and, while arguing her point, she was also taking in what was going on.'

Life at the school was not completely harmonious, even for the clearly academically able and self-contained creature with the wild hair. At one stage, when Ann was in the fourth form, she was subjected to bullying by a girl who started making fun of her brother. This hurt Malcolm's young and devoted sister to the quick. 'When my brother came to the school this particular girl would say things like, he wasn't as handsome as she'd expected – he was quite plain really. That sort of thing. It was terribly subtle. Girls are like that – awful. I absolutely hated it.' Ann wrote home to her parents telling her of the pain this gave her, but they told her life carried many unpleasantnesses and she should ignore it. 'Things got to such a pitch that I said to my parents, "I don't know if I can stand this." They said, "You must stick it out – it's part of learning things. You can't just turn around and go when you don't like things." '

Helen also remembers being upset by girls in the Convent who came from society families. 'Some people threw their classy weight around. There was a divide between those people and Ann and I.'

In the upper years, the girls were allowed out of school on Sundays as well as Saturdays. Most of the girls used this time to see boys and flirt; but Ann used it to reinforce her own religious beliefs. 'I used to go to Bath Abbey because we were not allowed to go to our own Church of England services on Sundays,' she explains. 'It was like a protest against the system which stopped me worshipping in my own church. This was pre-Vatican Two and things were very, very restricted. They would not recognize other churches; the tension between the two churches was really quite enormous.' Ann made no secret of this defiance, but the nuns did not object. On at least one occasion, two of them entered the abbey and spotted the young girl. Ann later wondered at her self-confidence: 'My line was, "So this is how I spend my time, this is how they spend their time." I can never remember any pressure from them on me to do otherwise.'

While religion was a burning interest for Ann (and her friend Helen), boys were a bore and an irrelevance to both of them. Ann had shown a complete lack of interest in boys and sex from the moment she joined the school. She viewed them as a temptation to

which she would not succumb, and her belief that the subject was a
distraction to her higher concerns, like religion and Latin and
Roman history, never wavered. Rita wanted Ann to know about the
biology of sex early on, as Ann recalls, but she ignored the whole
subject: 'My mother gave me a book called *The Facts of Life* when I
was eleven. I was bored by it and didn't read it.' She said she was
similarly uninterested in puberty and the effect that had on her body
and her life.

Ann's friend Helen shared her contempt for the other sex: 'Boys
didn't interest Ann or me a scrap. We had all the fun we wanted from
debating, arguing, doing things that we thought were fun. We had this
sort of agreement that we weren't interested in the way most of our
friends were.' Ann was not 'a girlies' girl', remembers Linda; she
dismissed magazines like *Roxy* and *Valentine* as 'drivel'. The other girls
went from reading magazines to putting on cosmetics and flirting
with boys, but Ann and Helen were wholly dismissive. Linda: 'She
would totally frown on all that. Ann would look down on us really.
We were fluffy, according to her – very lightweight.'

Ann treated the whole subject with contempt: 'I must have been
quite mammothly confident, because it didn't worry me that other
people were doing other things. They wanted to go out socially and
meet the boys from the Prior Park Catholic School and they would
come back and the conversation was about nothing but boys and I
used to get sick and weary and tired of it. I wanted nothing to do
with this nonsense at all. I was very off the whole darned thing – it
seemed to me an utter nonsense and to bring out the worst characteristics and silly behaviour in the other girls who were normally
quite sensible individuals and it just had no appeal at all.'

Indeed, boys did not merely bore Ann, they made her very angry.
Linda recalled how, one Saturday afternoon, she had gone with Ann
into Bath to see the film *Cleopatra*. Their motives were quite different,
of course: Linda went to see the glamorous Richard Burton and
Elizabeth Taylor, while Ann was interested in the ancient history. Be
that as it may, on the way back Linda stopped to chat to some boys
who were being familiar. Ann was appalled. 'She stormed off in a

huff,' says Linda. 'She wouldn't even stand and wait while I chatted.'

Ann's academic life, which had been plagued by science and practical subjects, eased up in the sixth form when she was able to concentrate on her first loves, the ancient world and English. In the third year sixth, Ann began to prepare for the entrance examination to Oxford, and this required her to learn ancient Greek as well as Latin. Helen Williams was roped in to help her with the Greek. Helen recalls: 'She started from scratch and had to move on pretty quickly. One thing she needed to do was to be able to translate Greek when it was being read to her. So she taught me how to read Greek. I didn't know a word of what I was reading but I read it to her and she would translate it back to me. I had to learn the letters of the alphabet and how to pronounce them and get some sense into the words even if it didn't make sense to me. It was fascinating!'

The friendship between Helen and Ann lasted as long as the two girls were together at the Convent. Helen recalls: 'Ann was a sub-prefect in the sixth form; I wasn't, that year, but I was still supposed to do duties with Ann, and I found her very encouraging. She didn't make a fuss about not being with another prefect, and we did the duties together, or we did them separately if one of us was away from school. The partnership worked.' Helen also remembers Ann inviting her to help with cleaning up one of the classrooms which had been flooded one winter.

The sixth-form years also saw Ann growing in confidence as a debater. She ran the school debating society and represented the Convent in the Inter-School Debating Contest. Sister Evangelista was impressed by her 'remarkable skill in stating her case clearly, defending her argument cogently and demolishing her opponents decisively . . . She also had a keen interest in politics.' Helen Williams was so impressed she was convinced that her friend 'was going to be the first woman Prime Minister. It just seemed to be the direction she was heading in – she was so strong, so good at it and enjoyed it so much.'

The political creed to which Ann adhered, like her religious view, was established from the day she joined the school. But on one issue she took a liberal view. Like most of her classmates, Ann was opposed to capital punishment, and she remembered a debate at school which coincided with the abolition of capital punishment in Britain (in 1965), when she went with the majority against one girl who supported it. 'I was very anti, I thought it was a very shocking thing and a terrible thing.' Two years or so later she reversed this view, arguing that capital punishment was a deterrent and should be available to the courts.

Her capacity for organizing people, together with her passionate interest in Roman history, led her to start a Roman Society at the school. This mounted a Roman display and exhibition; it also held a toga party when the guests dressed up as senators of the middle Roman period. The costumes were based on the inevitable sheets off the school beds, supplemented by some from Helen Williams's mother's linen cupboard. 'I don't think our food was particularly Roman,' said Helen, 'but we tried to hold conversations that were suitable to the occasion.' Ann also organized a trip for the Roman Society to visit the exceptionally fine Roman villa excavated at Chedworth in Gloucestershire. For a pupil to organize a day out was regarded as a considerable achievement by her peers.

Ann's happiest time at the Convent was her final year. 'You've got your A levels,' she explains, 'you were now in the business of looking forward to university and something new. I had a terrific year.' Her academic ability and her willingness to take responsibility earned her appointments as senior prefect and house captain, while she still had time to follow her debating activities. It was, as she herself says, 'a jolly year'.

There was just one disappointment at this time; but it was a profound one. To the surprise and shock of her teachers and fellow students, Ann failed to win a place at Oxford University. She had stayed on the extra term to take the Classics examinations and had done creditably, but had flunked the interview. So she went through the university entrance procedures and took a place to read Latin at Birmingham.

The love of Latin she had developed at the Convent would stay with her, and the knowledge she had acquired there stood her in good stead for her studies at university. As for the religious impact of the Convent on Ann's life, here the legacy was more complex. The Catholic practice and theology had quite repelled her, and once she had left, and for a long time afterwards, Catholicism played no further part in her life. But it did not disappear forever. The unyielding nature of the nuns and their unbending religious commitment had impressed her at a deep level. In due course she would come to respect their fervour and Catholicism's absolute beliefs. The pain and struggle she underwent at La Sainte Union Convent had been intense, but not in vain.

When her schooldays came to an end, Ann needed to earn some money before she went up to university. Her father was ready to oblige and found her a job as a clerical officer in the Registry department at the Admiralty. There she opened envelopes and despatched the contents to the appropriate recipient. She was 'not ecstatic about the work and left earlier than [she] had intended', going back to the Convent for a few weeks to do some teaching. The call of the Alma Mater was strong and would get louder.

THREE

Latin and Churchill: a Birmingham Education

Ann had hoped to leave school and take the traditional path into national politics, beginning at Oxford, proceeding to law school and ending with a safe Westminster seat. But the first gate on this route was closed in her face when St Anne's College Oxford declined to take her to read law; she had passed their written examinations, but did not do well at the interview. Surprisingly, no one seems to have told her that she could wait another year and try for Oxford again.

Typically, she made the most of her lot. When her papers went through the selection procedures, she came out with a place at both the universitities she had applied for and settled on going to the absolutely respectable University of Birmingham, where she commenced her studies in the autumn of 1966. This was not a centre of academic excellence, nor was it noted for its social or political institutions; but it was solid and traditional in the way that Durham University was, and the newly created and flamboyant Sussex University was not.

There was nothing at Birmingham University like the Oxford Union, which in her dreams she had long aspired to join and even to star in. So the opportunity of maturing, both in personal terms and as a politician, was put on hold while Ann applied herself to her studies with enormous diligence. She had no problem with Latin, which she had studied at school and found straightforward. Greek was harder, but she passed muster. Her contemporary and fellow Classics student Christine Holmes says her ability derived from her logical mind. Roman history was another passion she brought to Birmingham. She would later say that one of her favourite books was Virgil's *Aeneid*, the tale of the mystical founding father of the Roman people.

Ann's rigour was more than Birmingham expected. For a few months she avoided using an English translation of a text. Then she discovered that all the other students were using such props, and there was no need for her absolutist discipline. The discovery may have come as something of a relief, but there must also have been a slight sense of let-down, a feeling that the place was undemanding, and, as she already knew, not the best.

There was no end to her application, although it was expressed in some eccentric ways. Christine Holmes remembers that 'Ann would work long after I'd gone to bed, tapping out her work on her typewriter until the early hours. It was my job to get her up in the morning by threatening her with a cold wet flannel.' These considerable reserves of energy made a great impression on Pat Potts, who was studying physics at the university, and lived close to Ann in the hall of residence. 'We used to be these night birds – she'd stay up half the night. And occasionally (it must have been more than occasionally because I was always tired) we'd have milky coffee. She'd be sitting there having toast at some unearthly hour of the morning, I don't know what we'd be talking about! But she'd be as bright as a button the following day. I'd be going around like death warmed up. She never needed any sleep; she'd do her essays really late at night or very early in the morning.' Potts also recalls munching through packets of Ann's favourite chocolate digestive biscuits as they chatted the nights away.

Ann herself remembers the erratic late hours: 'I was a very late bird, well, students are. Now, when I think my big ambition in life is an early night, students talk all night, till two in the morning . . . I was very late in sleeping habits, I didn't go to bed until about two. We used to have coffee and put the world to rights, yes, that's true. In those days, it was coffee, most students didn't drink.'

The homeliness of the university living arrangements was enhanced by the fact that the women's halls were men-free. Mason Hall, where Ann lived, was strictly separated from the adjoining male hall, called Chad. Girls in the block lived in each other's pockets, passing in and out of their adjoining rooms, but no man got close to their portals at night, although they were allowed visiting rights during the day. Pressures to liberalize the dining situation were beginning while Ann was there, but she sought to resist them, and had a good platform from which to do so in her successful campaign for election as internal affairs officer in the Junior Common Room. She says, 'I don't think I liked the idea of having men in the dining rooms at all. I think the idea of coming back from a hard day's work and being sociable with all the men was absolutely ghastly.' Her fight was, inevitably, a vain one; shortly after she left, dining room and hall of residence alike admitted men. Ann now admits that gender segregation flew in the face of contemporary trends, although for her the seclusion of a women's zone, uncomplicated by men, was very comfortable.

Her campaigns to win the posts of internal affairs officer and then vice president of the JCR were typically uncompromising. The key point was that she was going to 'make sure the books were straight'. She promised to make a major contribution to the JCR. One colleague thought this was 'very eloquent for an eighteen, nineteen year old'. Shades of the row she was subsequently to foment at Oxford surface here; but Birmingham was not the place to spend the energy or the angst waging a big fight when the issues were small, the forum inconspicuous and the people for the most part lacklustre. Nevertheless, however inauspicious the surroundings, Ann's ambition to star on the national political stage was undoubtedly stirring at Birmingham. The evidence for this manifested itself in diverse ways. At one point those girls who shared her floor at Mason Hall were roused by a man's voice loudly emanating from Ann's room. They thought the obvious inference unlikely, given what they knew of Ann's private life; listening more carefully, they realized it was a record of Winston Churchill giving a speech. She was already learning the rhythms of political rhetoric, as well as drawing at the well of a political tradition she hoped to continue. Another political model was Enoch Powell, a brilliant academic and classicist (like Ann) and prophet of the far right, who called up the image of a 'river . . . flowing with much blood' as a consequence of immigration in the 1960s. When Christine Holmes asked Ann what she wanted for her twenty-first birthday, Ann said T.E. Utley's biography of Enoch Powell.

Ann made no secret of her ambitions, nor did she set much limitation on them, as Christine recalls: 'I used to laugh, she said to me she was going to be Home Secretary. We must have been in her bedroom when she told me "My ambition is to be Home Secretary." I laughed and said, "Don't be silly." ' Ann would talk politics with any of her friends who would care to listen, and not mind being rubbished and contradicted. They made no secret of their frustration with her certainty, but nothing could dent her Conservative conviction.

Pat Potts, however, also detected a nuance that mitigated her absolutism: namely, her belief in social justice and the duty to acknowledge the underdog. 'She was into the social justice side,' said Pat, 'she believed that everybody had to contribute to society, and that we all had a role. But she was very much opposed to what she would call "shirking". People had to pull their weight for the benefit of society. We not only had rights, we had responsibilities. She was in some respects supportive of the underdog. She would say, "It's all right to support them but you can't let them sponge off you." You have to give them the wherewithal to move on.'

Ann's political opinions hardened at Birmingham University. Evidence had started to appear that the abolition of capital punishment in 1965 had led to an increase in offences for which the death penalty would formerly have been available, and Ann took this to mean that it had worked as a deterrent. So in 1970, when the government reviewed the figures to assess the impact of the abolition over five years, there was further debate, and Ann supported the re-introduction of capital punishment. She later said, 'In those five years, we still collected capital murder statistics as distinct from all other homicides. We had the figures and they showed that capital murders went up 125 per cent. Armed robbery went up even faster. Had we had it back in 1970, I would have been quite prepared in, say, the mid-1980s to try again to do without it. I think it's desirable that society does do without it, but while it is a real deterrent, I think you've got a moral choice to make. There is a very strong moral imperative to have it. If ever it were to be shown that we've now reached a stage where either it is no deterrent at all or it's such a marginal deterrent that there is a doubt, then I would be quite happy to do without it.'

Ann's certainties at this stage were not only political, but also religious. Her firm belief in Christianity was well established. She was a strict attender at church and met her good friend Pat Potts through membership of the evangelically orientated Christian Union. Pat recalls: 'The Christians there were very emotional, it was an emotional form of Christianity, but she'd go along to quite a lot of Saturday night meetings. Ann used to read her Bible very diligently. She saw things so clearly, that God was there and God was real in her life and it was impossible that somebody didn't believe in Jesus Christ and Christian religion. Again there's this certainty about her convictions.' She remembers Ann going to church every Sunday, 'Bible in hand'. The ethical certainties so prevalent in Widdecombe's later life were already evident at Birmingham; Pat Potts also recalls that she was strongly anti-abortion. She had 'absolutist moral values, and in some respects, at the time, I thought she was self-righteous'.

Set against this moral certainty was the knowledge that her views were unpopular in many student circles. Indeed, the university debating society where Ann was active was very left-wing, her views anathema to the dominant cast of mind of its members; so some trepidation before she entered that lions' den would have been understandable. Jill Edge, another close colleague whose room was on the same floor as Ann's at Mason Hall, remembers such a moment of doubt on an occasion when the motion was 'This House believes that abortion, homosexuality, the pill and pot are the signs of all civilised society.' Ann recalled the event in the following lurid terms: 'The Birmingham Students' Union had the most awful reputation for student filth. You could go along to a debate, and the undergraduates seemed to take a delight in just twisting the motions so that you had the dirtiest possible interpretation. When I saw this particular motion that I was going to have to debate – even though I was on the right side of the motion (I was anti all these things), I really didn't want that debate – it was going to be absolutely ghastly and filthy.

'But in the end, I think that my ambition to get the cup for the best university debater overcame my scruples about what sort of debate it might be. In fact, by their standards, it wasn't a bad one. But it was an unfortunate feature at that time of university debating at Birmingham that it wasn't terribly serious. When I went to Oxford, the difference, not just in quality, but the difference in approach and seriousness and style could not have been greater.'

In fact, however outrageously at variance with the majority Ann's views were, she twice won the McKee Cup for the best woman debater.

Ann's disapproval of the Student Union was only entrenched by its support for demonstrations and sit-ins during 1968. Birmingham came out in support of the activities in France and the London School of Economics, and it had its own sit-in. She recalled the occupation of the university's Great Hall, the assemblies of students in the main quadrangle and the destruction by students of their records. Her disapproval of such direct action confirmed her distaste for the students' radical demands, and her most vivid memory of the episode is of going out to vote to end the sit-in. 'I liked a more old-fashioned branch of student politics,' she asserts.

Her sense of the virtues of individual rebellion, let alone mass rebellion, is severely circumscribed, although it has its place. 'I think no matter how you are brought up, you will eventually accept some of it, modify some of it, and reject some of it. Occasionally people reject it all, but I didn't. I just modified bits and pieces. I think I am a natural Conservative, as well as a conviction Conservative.'

Religious study remained a key part of Ann's life and she
sometimes hosted the Christian Union's early morning prayer and
Bible study meetings. She also attended a Billy Graham rally in
Birmingham – along, incidentally, with Cliff Richard, who 'professed
his faith' at that time. When she came back, she told Christine
Holmes that she had given away all the money she'd saved for her
holiday. 'I must admit I was a bit shocked at why she should have
done that and thought her loopy,' says Christine. 'However, I was even
more surprised when she told me she'd received a cheque from an
aunt or godmother for the exact amount she'd given away.' Ann was
an occasional visitor at the University Centre for Christian Pastoral
Care, called St Francis Hall, where chaplains of many branches of
Christianity were available for discussion with interested students. A
woman chaplain called Marie Isaacs both fascinated her, and made
her feel uneasy. 'I didn't like even in those days the concept of a
woman doing it. I used to chat to her quite a lot, and I liked her as a
person. But also I wanted something much clearer than the sort of
Christian thinking she had to offer.'

The austere life of the devout believer and unflappable politician
and advocate was occasionally interrupted by bouts of physical
activity, rather alien to her later existence. Students were required by
Birmingham University to nominate a sport at that time, as schools
required pupils to do compulsory PE, and Ann selected sailing. She
had enjoyed this with her family during her youth and thought it
would be the same among her fellow students. The reality was not
quite such fun. 'I had done some sailing in Malta when I went out for
a holiday, and I thought it would be absolutely fantastic. Of course
there was a difference between sailing in Malta and sailing on
Birmingham reservoir. And I remember I used to wrap up in these
huge jerseys and this big anorak that I had and gloves. I would be
terrified of falling in – not because I minded water, I'm quite a good
swimmer, but it was just so damn cold. I decided I didn't like the
sport, and I decided on a change.'

Her next choice of sport was horse riding, and this proved a
longer-lasting diversion, albeit a costly one, as the university's subsidy

only lasted for the year of mandatory sports practice. But never-theless, she persevered and went riding most weekends. Her efforts to introduce some friends to the sport met with little success. One vacation, she took two of them down to her parents' home at Haslemere, where, in the course of their stay, they all went riding. Ann was the only experienced rider among them, and Pat Potts, one of the two friends, got kicked by a horse. Potts remembers the episode. 'I can still see it – Ann this midget on this big horse, me on this other horse, and she got her horse cantering, so of course mine followed. I was absolutely terrified. I was hanging on for dear life, I thought I was a goner, I really did.' Ann later admitted her excitement got the better of her. 'I got so enthusiastic about it that I'd clean forgotten how anybody could worry. I used to try to get all my friends up on a horse, quite regardless of the fact that some of them were terrified out of their minds.'

Towards the end of her three years at Birmingham, when examinations loomed, Ann looked to her faith for support. Christine Holmes and Ann would revise for their exams together, and after one long night of study, Ann suggested she should offer a prayer that their hard work would bear fruit in the exam. 'Ann had one last idea to save us from the examiner's discovery of how little knowledge we had acquired. We would pray, or rather she would, and I would add my amen. After that Ann went off confident in her God and her knowledge (more in the latter, I suspect, than the former) and slept. I wasn't too convinced, so I read some more.

'Next day we left together for the exams and when I looked at the papers I was feeling decidedly sick and very tired. We sat near each other and turned the paper to be confronted with questions we had swotted up and others we could pad out. I have never been so relieved and from then on began to believe in the power of prayer and later became a Christian. I acknowledge Ann's part in that, for she planted seeds of interest in our conversations together and demonstrated her faith in her actions and prayers.'

In fact, that prayer might have worked in more mysterious ways than even Ann could have predicted. Christine Holmes recalled that after another late night's studying (this time Ann had been on her own) 'there was a tremendous thud from Ann's room – the bookcase had come off the wall and the books had hit Ann. To be hit by a copy of Liddell and Scott [the Greek–English lexicon] and sundry other tomes caused more than a headache. Ann had to be taken to hospital with suspected concussion and never did sit that exam!'

Ann performed very creditably in her finals, but her hopes for a first class degree were not realized: she only got an upper second. Her mother later said that the accident with the bookshelf was responsible for the lower class, but Ann discounted this as 'absolute rubbish!'

During the final year of studies, most students' thoughts turn to their future, and Ann was no exception. Indeed, she found the Roman traits of planning and certainty more to her taste than most students did. Her evident love of and ability in Latin seemed to make her suitable either for research at Birmingham, which she seriously considered, or for teaching. But there was no avoiding her overwhelming desire, which had grown rather than diminished at Birmingham, to have a political career. She thought that there was only one place where she could work towards this: Oxford, the place denied to her three years earlier. But to go there now would need funding. Delicately, on one occasion when she was with her parents, she broached with her father the problem involved in the cost of her studying for a second undergraduate degree. He was delighted. Ann was the apple of his eye, and her academic progress his deepest wish. Ann's mother Rita remembered: 'She had been at Birmingham three years. It was one morning that Dad was going to work and she said, "Dad, could I have a word with you?" and he said, "Yes, if you're quick, I've got my train to catch." She said, "Could you lend me two thousand pounds?" He said, "Whatever for?" and she said, "I'd like to go to Oxford." He was delighted, of course. She had it all worked out. She wanted to get a good degree at Birmingham, she didn't give tuppence about a degree at Oxford, she wanted to go there for the experience of being in the Union.'

Ann says: 'I came to realize, "This is what I want to do and I don't really want to do anything else." I was already contemplating staying on at university for two or three years for the research. I might just as well in fact go to Oxford instead and do Politics and Economics.'

In her last year at Birmingham, Ann waded through the Classics papers for Oxford entrance with relative ease, given that she had been studying just this material for the last three years. Later she would hear that she had won the coveted place she sought, at Lady Margaret Hall. Her mother recalls the arrival of the telegram, which she placed strategically in the kitchen by a bottle of sherry for Ann to discover. The sherry was consumed amid the celebrations, where joy was mingled with relief.

FOUR

Oxford – Where Fun was a Debatable Point

When you have worked so hard, and waited so long, to get into your dream university as Ann did to get into Oxford, you do not waste the experience. Oxford for Ann was no academic ivory tower; it was an opportunity to socialize, to practise being a grown-up politician and expand her contact book.

Politicians who visited Oxford during these years found someone perhaps old before her time, a slightly over-anxious Westminsterite-in-waiting: Richard Crossman, for example, commented after participating alongside Ann in a Union debate in 1971 that he saw in the twenty-four-year-old debater a future Tory chief whip. The arguments, the ideology, even the panache were already established then, and if accounts by fellow colleagues are true, have changed but little since.

Ironically, for a student so dedicated to achieving high office in that acme of university debating societies, the Oxford Union, Ann never quite made the sought-after position of president. This pinnacle eluded her, as the following account shows, precisely because her sense of responsibility made her no friends among the student members. Widdecombe-style earnestness was little prized in 1969 even among university Tories, although most of her colleagues, even those who opposed her opinions, recognized a doughty and admirable fighter whose political prowess they underestimated.

Of one thing there was no doubt: Oxford was a breath of fresh air for the ambitious young woman. Here she could spread her wings socially, find her political feet and prepare herself for the long climb up the ladder to advancement, an experience beyond her grasp at the provincial Birmingham. She also enjoyed the company of many high-flying students who had set their sights on reaching the top in the worlds of banking, newspaper publishing or the Civil Service, and was determined to make best use of the university's unparalleled social amenities for her own purposes.

Ann's life at Lady Margaret Hall, then a women-only college with an academic bent, bore little relation to that of most undergraduates. She was three years older than most, and had the luxury of one degree — and a good one at that — already under her belt. This allowed her to neglect her course in Politics, Philosophy and Economics, as she reckoned that she only needed one degree to get a job. Indeed, afterwards she would say that, in any event, academic politics not only bore no relation to real politics, it was a positive hindrance to success. Political colleagues who bored her with pompous philosophizing would get castigated for sounding as silly as university essays. Much more important to her than the quality of the degree she might take away from Oxford was full participation in the university's life outside the libraries and tutorials. She wanted both to demonstrate her debating prowess and lead a full social existence. 'Oxford was very liberating. I wasn't overshadowed by work all the time; I wasn't thinking, "Oh, I've got to get a degree!" Also I was discovering things that I'd never done before, and I was mixing with people who had similar ambitions. I felt better fitted in for it and I wasn't saying things that made me sound boastful or different because in fact other people had much bigger ideas than I ever had.'

Nor was Ann confined to Oxford: unlike most students, she had her own car, a redoubtable but ancient turquoise Morris Minor nicknamed Methuselah, or 'Methy', which allowed her to slip home or away to the country at will. But Ann also did what most students who lived slightly out of the centre did, and started using a bicycle again. This was an old and stately machine with flat handlebars which she had owned since she was eleven. For the second year she lived in the suburb of Summertown with Mrs Kidd-May, a formidable but elderly North Oxford lady: 'I was the ideal tenant because I didn't have riotous parties.'

The serious side to Ann's Oxford existence was her performance at the Oxford Union. Generations of those who fancied their chances in grown-up politics had cut their teeth at Oxford's world-famous debating society, where debates had once been seen as barometers of opinion which Westminster politicians needed to take seriously. By the late 1960s, when Widdecombe joined, the Union's reputation had fallen a long way from the 1930s, when it caused uproar after refusing to support a motion that 'This House would fight for King and Country.' Nevertheless, those who participated still took its proceedings and customs very seriously, and Westminster politicians continued to speak at its debates, ensuring that the press were present and that budding student debaters would get noticed.

Even the Oxford Union went through a radical phase in the 1960s, alongside the LSE and other universities that were following the lead of students in France. So in early 1969 the Union overwhelmingly passed motions such as 'This House would dig up the cricket pitch turf to stop a match with the visiting South African side,' and 'This House would ditch the authorities and run its own university.' As late as June 1970 left-wingers including Christopher Hitchens, who subsequently made his mark as a journalist, created a great furore when they disrupted a meeting at the Union on the Vietnam War addressed by the Labour foreign secretary of the time, Michael Stewart. As part of his stunt, Hitchens lowered a noose from the Union's gallery. A future president of the Union, and the man with whom Ann formed a deep personal relationship, Colin Maltby, later commented, 'It was an extremely ugly thing and the debate had to be abandoned, and this seemed horrendous. All this collapsed within a year, and it seemed afterwards the final gasp of the left. Then we were in the boring Seventies, where relatively little of that sort of thing seemed to happen.'

When Ann Widdecombe joined the Union in 1969 the tide was just on the turn: revolution was moving off the agenda, and

Conservatism becoming more acceptable. By this time Conservatives were capable of winning elections to the highest positions in the Union. Gyles Brandreth and Stephen Milligan were presidents in Widdecombe's early terms at Oxford, although the former was better known for his funny speeches than for serious ideas. David Thomas, a fellow Union aficionado, remarked that 'being a Conservative was still a definite minority opinion, not only in the university but also in the Union. But it wasn't a crippling electoral disadvantage in the Union. If you were a good speaker and had a good presence, then your political opinions would not be held against you. If you were a mediocre Conservative you were not likely to get anywhere, whereas the mediocre lefty could do quite well.'

For Widdecombe and her Conservative friends the Union was particularly valued as a bastion of formality, modelled on Westminster, and governed by rules and a sense of status they were committed to upholding. Widdecombe enjoyed the rules of the club, and mastered them like few others, but she also brought to her speeches a political conviction, at odds with the left-leaning trend of the members, but consistently held over her four years as a member. At the time this was little appreciated by her colleagues, one of whom later commented, 'If you'd asked any of her group of contemporaries which one of that group would end up as a very senior frontbench spokesperson for one of the major parties, I don't think many would have chosen Ann.'

Ann was on her way to the Oxford Union within days of arriving at the university in October 1969, accompanied by her college friend Elizabeth Brimelow. The nascent Conservative politician spoke to the motion 'That power tends to corrupt and absolute power corrupts absolutely; great men are always bad.' Patric Dickinson, now the Richmond Herald at Arms at the Royal College of Arms, then an aspiring Union activist (and later president), remembered Ann's unpretentious appearance. 'I watched people's incredulity at this tiny figure. I remember this little midget figure, wearing a rather old–fashioned overcoat and looking very strange, actually got up and spoke in her very first ever debate.' Widdecombe weighed something

like six and a half stone at the time, but her strong voice belied her
flimsy appearance. Moreover, she showed an ability to tailor her looks
to the occasion; so, while she may have been content to be plainly
dressed for the run-of-the-mill weekly debate, for the end-of-term
photographs of officers and members of the standing committee, she
put on her best frocks. These have led some, including Edwina
Currie, who has spoken authoritatively and flatteringly about Ann's
time at Oxford, [even though their periods at Oxford did not
overlap] to suggest that Ann was highly glamorous. In fact, Ann was
generally speaking less interested in appearance then than now, and
certainly not a conventional Tory lady politician adorned with
twinset and pearls.

Two weeks after dipping that initial foot in the debating water,
she made her first public attack on the Labour government of the
day, supporting a motion that 'Her Majesty's Government is
undeserving of the confidence of this House.' It was a standard
motion, called for short 'the confidence motion', repeated each year
and geared to attracting the leading Westminster political lights to the
Union for an exciting showdown. This occasion was no exception,
with Ann speaking on the same side as Nigel Lawson, Stephen
Milligan and Geoffrey Johnson Smith MP, the vice chairman of the
Conservative Party. They were confronting, among many others, two
leading Labour MPs, Gerald Kaufman and Shirley Williams. The
motion was lost, 303–281, and the minutes recorded with a typical
ironic Oxford flourish, 'A reluctant President declared the motion
lost by 22 votes. The Treasurer threw an apoplectic fit and declared
that if this swing of 0.164893% were repeated throughout the
country, he might yet be Prime Minister. The House rose at exactly
midnight.' The minutes were signed by the secretary Stephen
Milligan.

Six months later Stephen Milligan had become president of the
Union, and gave Widdecombe the task of debating against Jack Straw,
at that time president of the National Union of Students, who
proposed the motion that 'Equality in education is more important
than excellence.' Straw won, but Widdecombe had enhanced her

standing as a powerful Conservative voice – a voice she would use to some effect in renewed confrontation with Straw in the House of Commons twenty-five years later. By that time Milligan, who later also became a Conservative MP, had met an unhappy and notorious end.

Widdecombe's ideological stance had rapidly marked her out from the rest of that year's debating group. One fellow student noted, 'In student politics, ideology is much less important than charisma, yet Widdecombe was clearly ideological and driven.' Her colleagues at the Oxford Union also quickly realized that Widdecombe was not driven solely by a passionate Conservatism; she was also fascinated if perplexed by religion. If Conservatism was out of favour at this time, religion was even more anathema to most students, but when the chance to debate the motion that 'God is not Dead. He was never alive' came up on 21 May 1970, Widdecombe leapt to it. Predictably, the motion was carried; but the debate was very poorly attended, and the minutes, which were written in verse, ended:

> So secure in the knowledge we'd all go to Heaven
> The House bade good night at the strike of eleven.

By this time, however, Widdecombe's readiness to support the religious cause in debate was not matched by quite such enthusiasm to practise it in her personal life. Her devotion to Anglicanism was in fact waning, and her attendance at church, and at the Oxford Christian Union, became more sporadic, although it is true she attended a mission in her first year at the University. Her brother, now Canon Malcolm Widdecombe, pinpointed Oxford as the trigger for an extended period of agnosticism that lasted some ten years. Her ability, indeed compulsion, during this period to argue through the agnostic principle proved to some that she did not regard it simply as part of the trendy retreat from religious theory and observance, but rather as a personal stance, just as potent a commitment as her former religious conviction. Indeed, her eagerness to defend agnosticism may be interpreted as a defensive posture, masking a very deep religious core.

In June 1970 Widdecombe was given her first official position at the Union, as the teller for the 'ayes' in the debate on the motion 'Equal rights for women are a dead duck.' It was a particularly appropriate motion for Widdecombe, who relished the paradox of laying into the trendy feminist movement while simultaneously stressing her right and the right of other evidently able women to storm the male bastions by dint of individual effort. Thomas recalled her general attitude: 'She wouldn't have seen it as a matter of positive discrimination; she would have said, "Women should be given the chance to work and take a place in the workplace that is equivalent to men's, and if they work the hours that men work they should be treated the same." She wouldn't say now, and I don't suppose she would have said then, that they could work for shorter hours than men because they had to look after their children, and then still be paid the same rate, given the same status. She would always have said, "No, no, this is not what I mean, what I mean is that women shouldn't be discriminated against, not that the special circumstances of working mothers should be taken into account." '

Friends saw that Widdecombe was as impatient with old-fashioned male courtesy towards women, with its principle of offering protection to the 'weaker sex', as she was towards the women's movement. Thomas told how she responded at Oxford to his efforts to display manners of the old school. 'When we walked down the street I would attempt to get her to walk on the inside of the pavement, so that I took the gutter side of the pavement. She would resist doing this and we would spend time walking down the pavement crossing over between one another; she attempted to get on the gutter side of me and I attempted to get on the gutter side of her. Initially it would have been done unconsciously on my part. After one or two incidences I wasn't doing it naturally, I was doing it as a joke.

'Quite frequently it happened with the men in the party. So when Colin Maltby and I found ourselves walking on a long way in advance she would cry out from the back, "Hold on there, this isn't Arabia you know!" '

Inevitably this feisty and ambitious Union participant received brickbats which today would be construed as 'sexist', a word unknown at the time to the predominantly male Oxford University. When Philip McDonagh, an Irishman who was president of the Union during Ann's time (he went on to join the Irish diplomatic service and became an ambassador) had a disagreement with Ann, he likened her to a cat, cajoling, 'Annie, let's discuss this over a warm saucer of milk.' One observer said, 'It was the sort of jibe that stuck, however unfairly.'

Widdecombe steadily made her way up the Union's tortuous hierarchy of office, winning an election to the Library Committee on 12 June 1970. She received the least number of votes to qualify and her name was incorrectly spelt, suggesting she was little known at the Union. But she was there; and when, the following winter, she won election to the important standing committee of the Union – the committee that oversees the entire organization – she came top of the poll. That same winter she opposed the motions that 'This House would legalise pot' and that 'This House would prefer pornography to censorship.' Later, she supported the motion that 'America is a sick society.'

The Oxford Union had a very definite *cursus honorum*, or series of steps, by which the ambitious could approach the highly prestigious post of president, and the offices had to be contested in a fixed order. The lowest step was the post of secretary, followed by treasurer, then librarian and, ultimately, president. By 5 March 1971 Widdecombe had achieved enough in terms of debating skills and networking with members to win her first office on this trail, that of secretary. The president that term was Susan Richards, later Susan Kramer, and in 2000 the Liberal Democrats' unsuccessful candidate for the London mayoralty.

Real life impinged very little on the rarefied life of the Oxford Union. The active members traditionally spent their time in debate, in social parading in the Union's famous Gladstone Room, in canvassing for votes for the next election to office, or gossiping about each other's gaucheness or lack of originality. These prancing butterflies for the most part would disdain the practical world, or at best treat it with frivolity. But in the course of Widdecombe's term as secretary, a practical issue forced students to become managers, inconsequential debate to turn to matters with a real impact. In the summer of 1971 the Oxford Union turned into a bearpit where Ann Widdecombe could be seen scrapping for all she was worth among leading university bruisers of the day. The apparently trivial decision by the Union committee to sack its steward turned student against student, and committee member against committee member. 'The machinations that went on were phenomenal,' recalls Widdecombe. 'I learnt how some people would just quite cynically adopt a position and take advantage of it.'

The problem was one of finance. As a result of internal politicking, the previous year's subscriptions were down and the Union's officers faced a cash crisis. According to some, the Union's very survival was at stake. David Thomas, now a banker, observed: 'The decisions taken on the standing committee about how to manage the affairs of the society were far more significant than they usually are. Normally speaking, you've simply got to decide the hour of afternoon tea, are you going to open the garden gate, and has the president dished out speeches fairly. But during this period, standing committee was called upon to take decisions which might well impact on whether the Union was going to be in existence the following year.'

The officers looked around to see how they could make some savings, and they decided to tackle a running sore which had worried officers for years, but which none had confronted. For a long time the competence of the Union's longstanding steward Leslie Crawte had been in doubt. Crawte had been with the Union no fewer than forty-two years; he was a fixture, and much loved, in the way that cussed old Oxford servants were loved by undergraduates who could rely on them to slip them a drink after hours or tell a story to the college if they needed some extra supplies for a party and had not got the readies there and then. But that informality and affection may have allowed Crawte to take his eye off the main task. He was a full-time paid official of the Union, responsible for buying the food and drink for the Union's catering and restaurant facilities – areas into which much of the subscription revenue from the members of the Union, many hundreds of students, was channelled – and while the Union's standing committee had nominal control over expenditure, in practice Crawte had been almost entirely left to his own devices. The students also had in their sights the Union's long standing senior treasurer, Maurice Shock, who had been appointed some fifteen years earlier by Michael Heseltine and Anthony Howard. By this time a senior academic of the university, he was now being accused of failing to exercise proper control of the Union's systems and finances.

Widdecombe tends to put a more charitable slant on the problems with the steward, saying he was not prepared to modernize his way of working: 'The steward of the Union was not actually up to the modern age – he had been there a very long time and nobody underestimated what he had done for the Union.' But at the time she did not allow personal sympathy to cloud her view of what had to be done. As secretary, she joined forces with Julian Priestley, the treasurer of the standing committee, and together the pair decided enough was enough. The bank was threatening action against the Union to force it to repay its £50,000 overdraft. Priestley: 'The Union was losing money in great dollops. That needed to be managed as a matter of urgency. He [Crawte] certainly gave the impression that the books were not transparent. She and I decided we had to get rid of him.' Widdecombe and Priestley formed a most unlikely cabal – she, the determined, ideologically committed Conservative; he, a middle-of-the-road Labourite (and later, as Labour candidate, her opponent in the 1983 general election in Plymouth Devonport) who subsequently failed to achieve his political ambitions in the Labour Party but went on to become secretary general of the European Parliament – but, working in secret, with Ann visiting Priestley's parents' house at Plymouth over the Easter vacation in 1971 to plan tactics, they set about assessing in detail the Union's financial problems.

Ann also brought her concerns about Crawte to her own home, and as she discussed the problems with her father, he became increas-

ingly interested in the issues she raised. These were small beer, of
course, to a man who had just retired after a career in the Admiralty,
during which he had introduced greater efficiency into the provi-
sioning of the Navy; but, as he went through the figures, he was sure
he could produce a plan to save the Union a lot of money and put
the management on a more even keel. This seemed very sensible to
his daughter, and her colleagues on the standing committee agreed to
commission her father to make a report (on a pro bono basis) on the
state of the steward's book-keeping.

The 'Widdecombe Report', as the notorious document he
produced was colloquially known, was as forthright and clear as
anything he would have written for the Ministry of Defence.
Although it did not mention the steward by name, it was an uncompromising indictment of Crawte's methods of accounting and
purchasing. Ann Widdecombe recalls: 'What he found was pretty
damning. It was inadequately managed. We didn't even have
nominated suppliers, despite catering on quite a big scale.' But when
she and Priestley insisted that the Union sack the steward
immediately, there was uproar. At the standing committee meeting of
10 May 1971 – one of the most vitriolic in the Union's history – they
were accused of being heartless, even ruthless. The treasurer and
secretary faced attack from colleagues like the broadcaster-to-be
Libby Purves, who would once have been friends. Purves had been a
stalwart of the Union, but now she felt extremely aggrieved. Indeed,
the debate put Widdecombe at odds with Colin Maltby, who was a
fierce supporter of the steward, and their personal relationship would
not flower until the furore had subsided.

Maltby's view of the affair was largely coloured by his suspicion of
Priestley, of whom he said: 'Julian was a fixer of a major sort; he was
very much interested in fixing things in the Labour Party, and in the
Labour Club and in the Union, on behalf of his chums who were all
at Balliol. He was a control-freak, and a deeply authoritarian figure.
And this led to a huge reaction, not just against him but against all
conventional politicians.' But Ann herself seemed to be quite ready to
accept Priestley at the time, and her tough line held. It was decided to

remove Crawte. In Priestley's words, 'We did a putsch and he was ousted.' Widdecombe did not share his relish, but was equally unbending. 'It wasn't the easiest position to come to, particularly at that age; nobody likes sacking middle-aged men when you're only twenty-two.'

The decision provoked uproar among the Union's members. The Widdecombe Report was the talk not just of Union insiders, but also of the wider university community. Two leading members of the Union, Christopher Tookey (who later distinguished himself as a writer of plays and musicals) and Caroline Lewis, mounted a campaign against the sacking of the steward. Former presidents of the Union, including the distinguished broadcaster Robin Day and the journalist (later the British ambassador to the United States) Peter Jay, were canvassed to help the campaign. Edwina Currie had also been an officer of the Union in the past, and she too was canvassed to make her opinions felt about the affair. She showed her lack of familiarity with the new female Union star when she addressed her letter to the secretary 'Dear Sir or Madam'!

Three days later, the dispute went public. The routine debate scheduled for Thursday 13 May was hijacked by the supporters of Crawte, and the scheduled discussion never took place. The row over the steward turned out to be the most highly charged and tense debate for many years. The call went up from the floor demanding the committee 'rescind [the decision to fire Crawte] or resign'. Intense pressure from the assembled multitude – the chamber was packed to the gills with students baying for the blood of the heartless officials prepared to throw a loyal servant to the dogs – persuaded enough members of the committee to reverse their opinion.

Ann Widdecombe did not participate in the debate, feeling perhaps that her father's report brought her too close to the subject. But she was in no doubt as to her opinion. 'I held out actually for not rescinding, but the rest of the committee caved in completely.' David Thomas: 'She never resiled from the position that the standing committee had done the correct thing and that they had faced up to an unpleasant duty. She later said her effort to fulfil an unpleasant duty had been overturned by mob hysteria.'

The episode was terribly serious for student politics, but it had its lighter moments. Eric Parsloe, a Labour man, asked the rhetorical question, 'What is the root cause behind it all?' A drunken Scotsman bellowing in the gallery shouted, 'Power!'

As a result of these dramatic events Crawte was reinstated, but he had seen the writing on the wall, in block capitals, and within a few weeks had handed in his resignation of his own volition. Widdecombe's position was vindicated. She remained determined to oust Maurice Shock, the Union's senior treasurer, and a year later, he was also gone.

The debate left its mark on Union politics for a number of years, creating a particular rift between students from Exeter College, who had mobilized against the Widdecombe Report, and those of Balliol College, who backed the sacking of the steward. 'The Crawte debate created a bitterness inside the Union,' recalls Patric Dickinson. 'There was great factionalism as a result.' For Ann, it had been a scalding experience. She now sees the approach she and the committee took towards the dismissal of the steward as hamfisted, and insists that she would do it differently today. 'These days I'd handle it more subtly, vastly more subtly, than I handled it at the time.'

Widdecombe came out of the Crawte affair a tougher and less naïve operator. The machinations inside the committee showed her how fickle apparently loyal colleagues could be, and there were some painful lessons of public life to be absorbed. 'I learnt how you can't trust your fellow human beings. It was a ghastly business which I never forgot. One lesson is to be wary of other people. The other lesson is to try and find other ways of doing the same thing. It was a massive part of my political education.' The damage to her political position was demonstrated by her failure at the office elections shortly after the Crawte affair ended, when she only came third out of six for the post of treasurer. This was a bad blow to her aspiration to climb the presidential ladder, exacerbated by the fact that the victorious candidate was Caroline Lewis, a persistent thorn in the side of her Union career and a stalwart supporter of the steward.

While the politics went on, in private and in public, Ann Widdecombe continued to star at debating. On 18 May 1971 she appeared beside Norman St John Stevas (now Lord St John of Fawsley) for a televised debate, unsuccessfully opposing the motion 'Equality in education is more important than excellence.' Her adversaries were two of the leading Labour MPs of the day, Richard Crossman and Shirley Williams. Dickinson reviewed Widdecombe's contribution in the university magazine *Cherwell*, describing it as a 'tough little speech'. Ann interpreted this as damnation with faint praise and, Dickinson recalls, 'She rounded on me afterwards, saying "a speech that was so tough, wasn't little!" She didn't mind "tough", of course, but she minded me saying the speech was little. What I meant to say, of course, was "tough little Miss Widdecombe".'

By 1971, two years into her Oxford period, Ann Widdecombe's plain but proper dressing was a hallmark of her public appearances. So when she appeared at the fun debate of 1971, called the Eights Week debate (because it occurred in the same week as the college rowing races), dressed in bright purple hot-pants, no less, the Union regulars were stunned. Ann's decision to dress in something out of the ordinary was not a surprise. Fancy dress was *de rigueur* for the Eights Week debate, although some might have thought that the compulsory white tie and tails for men and long dresses for women worn by officers at the Union's usual weekly debate was pretty extraordinary for a university debating society. The startling thing about Ann's get-up, said one member, was that it was simply so out of character. Colin Maltby, her boyfriend-to-be, was stunned, and perhaps thought the girl could be more fun than he had hitherto suspected.

One can imagine the hot-pants shock continuing to reverberate as Ann returned to more conventional garb for participation in the debates of the ensuing autumn and winter. She showed some early Europhobic credentials when she lined up behind fervent opponents of the EU, including Peter Shore, in a debate in October 1971 opposing 'joining the Common Market on the terms recommended by Her Majesty's Government.' In November Denis Healey, Dick

Taverne and Crossman crossed swords with her over a 'confidence' motion; this was the occasion on which Crossman professed himself so impressed by Widdecombe. *Cherwell* was also enthralled: 'Ann Widdecombe skilfully countered the criticisms of the Government's opponents, parodied Chris Hitchens' sob-stuff and enumerated the advantages of Tory social policy. The material of her argument was better than its delivery.' The report continues: 'Richard Crossman put on a brilliant act, predicting that Ann Widdecombe would be "the first Conservative lady chief whip"'.

National politics was at the forefront of Union politics, and Ann Widdecombe was consistent in her support of the Conservative Party position. In November 1971 she allied herself with the views of the then minister of education, Margaret Thatcher, and unsuccessfully opposed one motion criticizing the abolition of free milk for the over-sevens and a second supporting those who had voted for 'the monumentous and historic decision for Britain to enter the EEC'.

Ann's debating skill won her respect in some unlikely quarters. The scurrilous student journal the *Oxford Free Press*, for example, complimented her on her rhetoric, calling her one of the 'half dozen really good Union speakers these days. She's a party-conference speaker, cementing loyalties rather than being a persuader. Although she seemed content to indulge in socialist bashing, and was hence largely irrelevant, her jokes had class. Consistently underrated, she made a speech which at least earned deserved cheers. Tough without being soulless.' None of this seems to have won her back popular support, and in the December elections of 1971, she failed again to make it to treasurer. In no way deterred, she maintained her hard-right stance, and in 1972 unsuccessfully supported the motion that 'Capital punishment is a unique deterrent and ought to be restored' (against Brian Walden). She also unsuccessfully opposed a motion calling for 'free and unrestricted abortion on demand'.

At the end of the spring term, or in Oxford parlance, Hilary term of 1972, Ann tried yet again for advancement, this time standing for president for the following term. But Crawte continued to haunt her, and she came fourth out of four candidates. The election was not without its element of scandal: the outgoing president, Ann's former ally Julian Priestley, was suspected of rigging the ballot to ensure a political sympathizer was elected. When this attempt was exposed, the runner-up, Patric Dickinson, was installed as president.

When the Eights Week debate came round again that summer, with its fancy dress opportunity, the members were impatient to see Ann's latest proposition. But those who expected another foray into risqué glamour were to be disappointed: she dressed in a decorous seventeenth century costume – though claiming it to be a likeness of Nell Gwynn. At the time she was acting secretary, and wrote the minutes of a debate about the environment in rhyming verse. They give little indication of her subsequent literary flowering, beginning:

> Although it may cause honourable members pain
> Eight weeks (sic) being here again
> I thought that I could do no worse
> Than read the minutes out in verse . . .

The minutes were signed:

> Ann Widdecombe alias Nell Gwynn
> (ex-secretary and acting secretary)

Ann's Union career was bound to be as unconventional as her personality and style. So she bucked the convention that stated that once officers had made an attempt to win election to the presidency, they did not seek any other post. Having failed in her attempt at the top job in spring 1972, she stood for treasurer for the winter term of 1972 – and won. In this term she supported the motion to re-elect President Nixon, and opposed the view that Christianity was a myth. On 7 December she supported a motion to express concern at the low offer made by The Distillers Co. Ltd to the parents of those children deformed by thalidomide, adding in parentheses beside her signature on the minutes: 'How could anyone oppose it?' But Ann's tenure of the treasurer's office was, like her first period in Union power as secretary, extremely controversial. A ferocious war was raging between Simon Walker (editor of the *Oxford Free Press*; later an adviser to John Major when he was Prime Minister and later still, public relations supremo to Buckingham Palace) and Colin Maltby as a result of an earlier internecine rivalry, and Walker used his paper to mount regular personal assaults on Maltby, vicious even by student standards. Widdecombe came to the aid of Maltby's party and appealed to the Union's standing committee to punish Walker, who was removed from the committee and debarred from standing for office for two terms. The issue surfaced in the chamber at one week's debate when Widdecombe shocked many newcomers to the Union by calling the president, Philip McDonagh, a 'liar'. One witness of the event saw comparisons with her much later denunciation of Michael Howard in the House of Commons.

Walker took the case to the proctors, the university policemen, who reviewed the case and took Walker's part; the Union was forced to reinstate Walker as a member of the standing committee. Ann Widdecombe was incensed, seeing this as unwarranted intervention in the Union's affairs. Turning her talents to an essay in spin-doctoring, she secured short pieces in the national press. *The Times* of 8 December 1972 wrote: 'The *Oxford Free Press* was condemned for its personal vilification. It is therefore very damaging for the reputation of the society when people are seen to get away with that.' The *Daily Telegraph* of the same day wrote in similar terms. Ann herself spoke to the *Oxford Mail* in terms of the very highest principle, protesting against the action of the proctors: 'In 149 years, we have never before put up with proctorial interference' and resigned her office in high dudgeon, although she continued to participate in Union affairs.

The issue still rankles with Walker, who remembers Widdecombe in less than complimentary terms. 'She was very judgmental; she made it absolutely clear that she didn't approve of lots of people. It wasn't interfering or wicked. When I was president I tried to have a condom machine installed and you can imagine how Ann reacted to that. When you did provocative things like that, Ann was clearly incensed and infuriated.' Fellow students saw Walker as a mischievous troublemaker, who particularly enjoyed provoking Widdecombe – and, it must be said, largely succeeded.

Attitudes to women members in this largely male club were ambivalent. Few women made outstanding successes of their careers at the Oxford Union, with the notable exception of Susan Richards. Sometimes, the schoolboyishness permeating much of the Union's activity surfaced, and ruffled the ranks of women members and officers; when, for example, on 8 February 1973, the society jokily passed a motion regretting it had ever admitted women, many must have thought the schoolboys were going too far. It later ruled out a motion proposed by Ann in writing (itself looking suspiciously like a schoolgirl prank) which called on the House to adjourn for a token period 'to express its unmitigated disgust at the failure of Mr Willie Hamilton's anti-discrimination bill, and at the unequal treatment of women in the field of employment'. It also instructed the secretary 'to communicate the above disgust to Mr Willie Hamilton and the Prime Minister'. The president ruled the motion out of order on the grounds that (1) Widdecombe was not present, and (2) she was a woman.

Later in the spring term of 1973 Ann and Sally Oppenheim, a quintessentially glamorous Conservative MP, opposed the motion that 'This House would go all the way with Women's Liberation' or 'This House would burn its bra.' The Tory ladies of the day would have no truck with the Monstrous Regiment of Women who were starting to make their voices heard at the Oxford Union. One of them was Barbara Margolis, who went on, as Barbara Roche, to become an MP and a member of the Labour Home Office team whom Ann would oppose; a series of political and personal events would put some distance between these two formidable women. The minutes of the feminism debate recorded that 'Miss Ann Widdecombe opposed the motion in a strangely gamely [sic] speech from such a staunch upholder of human dignity, in which she said she wanted to go to Sandhurst or (second-best) become a political muck-raker; that she was not interested in underwear; and that she would come to contraception and abortion later on (something that seemed to be new to Mr Maltby, the ex-Librarian from Christ Church). From some of the remarks in her speech, the ex-Treasurer would seem to have it in for the Secretary, who responded by revealing further details of her (Widdecombe's) sex life . . .'

Ann's last formal speech to the Union came in May 1973, when she spoke to a motion in favour of the restoration of capital punishment. But she could not keep away from this hub of her Oxford life, and the Union minutes record that on 7 June 'Miss Widdecombe brought forward a private business motion, an amendment was moved by the Secretary, opposed by the Librarian and consequently – or not withstanding – carried by 42 votes to 40 or thereabouts.' The minutes neglect, however, to record what the motion concerned.

Few of Ann's Oxford contemporaries would have guessed that, of all the Oxonians of that year, she would go on to star at Westminster. Many more would have bet on her boyfriend Colin Maltby making the grade. Julian Priestley: 'She was probably underestimated by everybody. To be brutally frank, she didn't have a great physical presence, although she wasn't only small in height, she was actually very thin. She seemed very buttoned up – a form of right-wing Toryism which a softish social democrat like me found off-putting.' But he recognized that she was a 'very effective speaker'. 'She was a speaker who doesn't change people's minds, who doesn't swing votes, but who reinforces people's views. Her speeches were always very well constructed. She would never have the slightest hesitation about taking up an unpopular cause and just arguing it – and to hell with the consequences. Even then the gutsy persona was very clear. Even though she was in a male-dominated institution where there was always a risk of sexist comments from cheap undergraduates, she was not put off at all. She always seemed absolutely certain of what she was doing. She must have known people weren't particularly pleasant or kind about her behind her back. She was never a popular person, but she fairly early on gained respect.'

Maltby tends to patronize her Oxford achievements rather than praise them. 'I suppose you could just about see her in the Cabinet. I think most people at Oxford at that time would probably have said about Ann, first, that she was more naturally at home in opposition than in government, and second, that she wasn't likely to make it to the very, very top of politics, basically for one underlying reason which is that she is not one of life's natural compromisers. Her very forthrightness and in a sense, simplicity, clarity of the views that she expresses, which she feels viscerally as well as intellectually, mean that she's very formidable at dealing with politics in a straightforward way, which you can afford to do if you are a critic, if you are in opposition. If you are somebody of that strength of conviction, in many, many cases you may not find it easy to make the sorts of alliances and deals and compromises that will perhaps facilitate a rise to the top.'

Ann's tireless efforts at the Union took their inevitable toll on her academic achievement, and she received nothing more than a third-class degree. It was irrelevant to her purpose. 'I always wanted to maintain my right to be at Oxford, but that was all. I certainly wouldn't have wanted to come down with no degree at all – that would have been going too far. But that wasn't what I was there for. I was there for the dreamy days and punts on the river, tea on LMH lawn, Commemoration Balls, it was a wonderful time.

'I now rather regret that I didn't do just a bit more because I could undeniably have got a second if I had, as my tutor said at the end. It was a huge achievement that I actually got a third because when I sat down to write those exams I was actually writing blind, and the fact that I managed to con an Oxford examiner into giving me a third, I think was pretty good. My tutor said, "It's quite clear that, but for the Union, you could have got a second." And I thought, yes I know. But I only came to regret that much later – at the time it didn't seem to matter – I'd got the degree.

'I really like Oxford, and mourned leaving. I thought I would never repeat that sort of three years again, and indeed I never have, because life is more serious than that. Those three years were a foretaste of retirement. I was able to indulge in the things I wanted to do, it especially gave me a chance to be with friends who were similarly un-pressured. When I was at Oxford, I felt immensely hopeful about what life was about to deliver. Everything seemed possible. It was a very good life and it was a good period.'

Ann kept many of her Oxford friends. The Oxford clan tended to stay together, she said, and would meet in London after work to reminisce over the ferocious debates at the Union, the bitchiness behind the scenes, who was hating whom now, and where this or that debating performer had ended up. Oxford has continued to feature in Ann's life, and later, as a political celebrity, she made return visits to Lady Margaret Hall to address 'gaudies', college dinners attended by old members.

Ann had now to find new political forums where she could express her views, and build up her contact book. These would be the Conservative think tank, the Bow Group; the National Association of Conservative Graduates; and, quite quickly, local government. The debating skills she honed at Oxford would serve her well at meetings of the Runnymede council she was about to join, and at the numerous constituency selections she would shortly be attending. Oxford had also been a political playground, where Widdecombe experienced the gamut of adult political life, but in a protected cocoon.

The Union prepared her for the backbiting and bitchiness that she would find at Westminster some thirteen years later. It also provided the backdrop for her first and last love affair.

FIVE

Colin

The photo of a young woman with bouffant hairstyle and choker necklace standing next to, but carefully not touching, a bespectacled young man in bow tie and tails has a prewar feel about it. Neither shows any emotion; both look awkward and on their guard. They are too embarrassed to embrace, too stiff to smile, or even to look at each other. The chaperone could be just around the corner.

But the formality of this image of Ann Widdecombe and Colin Maltby tells only part of the story of their relationship. The other part was the deep love that Ann felt for Colin. To this day she finds it very difficult to discuss a relationship which lasted for three years and was Ann's sole experience of powerful affection for a man. It allowed her to be vulnerable and open as she had never been before, as she describes in her unpublished short story, *Rejuvenatae*: 'Only once have I rejoiced in yielding it up, in confiding.' Colin Maltby was the recipient of this confidence, this experience of emotional giving which, to Ann's sadness, would end in rebuff and frustration.

Ann burst on to Colin's notice in the summer term of 1971, when she donned purple hot-pants to participate in the traditional fancy-dress debate at the Union. Three years her junior, he was intrigued and excited by the wearer of this uncharacteristically 'garish and extraordinary' costume – and further fascinated by her departure from the chamber, carried out in the arms of someone else dressed up as a gorilla. It was a flamboyant act, and confirmed Maltby's view that she was, at the very least, 'an individual'.

Ann's hot-pants were the talk of the Union for some time afterwards, especially among those who were accustomed to seeing her plainly dressed. The incident stayed in her mind, too, and she wrote about it in an unpublished short story called 'The Shy Girl'. Here the shy girl herself says: 'Oh, that [the hot pants] had produced interest. She smiled grimly at the recollection. But when the sort of people it appealed to had found she was not such an extrovert after all, they too melted away. As for the others, they were amused or incredulous, but not attracted. They too kept their distance.'

If this was the response of most of Ann's Oxford contemporaries, Colin Maltby appeared to be the exception to the crowd. He was extremely clever, having won a scholarship to Christ Church, and also an unusually able debater who would have appreciated Ann's efforts on the platform. Yet he was something of an academic nerd, with big glasses, a shambolic dress sense and wild hair; he came from an introverted English family and shared with Ann an awkwardness in personal matters which would draw them together.

Politically, on the other hand, they were very different. The young Maltby called himself a 'child of the sixties' and prided himself on having gone through the decade as a hip teenager, admiring his friends who tried soft drugs (although he says he never tried them himself), humming along to the Beatles, Dylan and the Stones, fantasizing about free love, and protesting at the madness of the Americans in Vietnam. When John F. Kennedy and his Camelot culture brought youth into politics, Colin was a youthful admirer from afar. When he got to Oxford, he looked to all intents and purposes like the rebel of his earlier teens. But in fact he was already throwing overboard his youthful radicalism and starting to acquire 'a general liberal Conservative disposition'. Like many students, he was searching for something to believe in, and Ann's absolutist Conservative faith and clear-cut ideas looked attractive.

After that debate in the summer of 1971, Colin Maltby wanted to catch Ann's eye, and he deliberately involved himself in the Union and the Oxford University Conservative Association, where Ann was also making a name. He did not have much difficulty, as his talent as an aggressive debater was quickly recognized. Ann did not go out courting friends, but Maltby pushed himself into her company and she saw in him the potential to be a political ally. Soon they were seen taking coffee together in the Union's Gladstone Room.

While Maltby's intellect was impressive, his ambition attracted Ann more. Here was somebody who knew he would surpass his peers. 'He was terribly ambitious,' remembered Ann. 'He wanted to be president of the Union, president of the Oxford Union Conservative Association and get a first class degree.' Maltby's contemporaries did not take quite such a charitable view of his ambition as did Ann; they found himtoo tense to relax with or open up to.

The student politicos gossiped and bitched mercilessly, while looking to their future careers in the Westminster bright lights, and they loved to poke fun at the dream ticket of Ann and Colin. Simon Walker saw the relationship as 'rather sweet and sort of good for both of them. To be honest I was rather horrid about it – I had two catfish in a bowl in my room in Balliol and I used to call them Colin and Ann. People made ruthless fun of them and in retrospect I think it was rather mean. They clearly were devoted to each other for quite a long time. I suppose we were rather unkind really.'

While Ann saw in Colin the ambition to make it to the top, Colin saw in Ann a degree of conviction and personality the dry physicist completely lacked. 'She was different – she was distinctive. She was always her own person, and still is. She is sensitive and always was, but her sensitivity applies more to other people's feelings than her own. She is not easily wounded or hurt or upset, neither is she self-centred. She reacts to other people's unhappiness and suffering absolutely genuinely.' Colin also began to enjoy Ann's sense of humour, a quality few of her friends discovered or appreciated – but one that helped to defuse their incessant arguments about politics and about the Union. They were particularly sharply at odds over the case of Leslie Crawte, the Union steward, which split the Union down the middle in the summer of 1971; indeed, Ann and Colin never reconciled their differences on this question, and friends said that the relationship only truly flourished once the issue was finally buried.

When they really became good friends, the relationship was based on politics, politics and more politics. Colin: 'We became interested in each other because we were interested in each other's political activity, ambitions and views. And we would debate with each other – over tea, probably in the Union.' They did not risk testing out each other's speeches in advance because their styles of preparation were so completely different. Colin wrote down every word, got immensely nervous before starting and spoke with a cold steeliness that ground listeners into submission. Ann wrote down a few notes, but spoke from the heart and reached out to the audience.

By the time the Christmas holidays of 1971 arrived, Ann and Colin were seeing each other not just for Union debates or political discussions, but as friends 'romantically committed'. Ann: 'We spent more time together and we got to know each other better. By the end of that year we had a relationship which had gone beyond politics. We started to care about each other as people, so we were friends. We were going out.' The Union, of course, was the hub of their social life and the Union 'hacks' their own clique, but during the evenings they went out to Oxford restaurants and cinemas. It was a comfy if conventional student social life, and no one guessed that they could be anything other than debating friends until a Union officer called Andy Popper saw the pair outside Christ Church one evening, in the front seats of Ann's car, Methuselah, kissing, and passed the word around.

Ann knew they had been caught out, but insisted it was chaste. 'We would not do anything as ghastly as sitting in the back seat,' she insists. Further awkwardness followed when Joseph Egerton, a fellow student, knocked on the door of Colin's college room as the two were hugging. She bellowed out to the visitor to come in, and pushed Colin aside before he had a chance to put on his glasses. A political conversation ensued; then, after half an hour, Egerton noticed that Colin did not have his spectacles on, guessed he might be intruding on something, made his apologies and left.

Ann's embarrassment at this mild sexual experiment reflected her lack of previous experience of men. The twin experiences of convent life, with the taboos it placed on male company, and the overwhelming influence of an awesome and driven father, left her with little sense of confidence in her femininity. She had scorned talk of boys at school, and studiously avoided contact with them; and she saw in her mother a helpmate to her father rather than a woman who had developed her own potential to achieve things in the world. So Ann was wary, and, one may assume, kept a very tight rein on Colin's manoeuvres. Colin, for his part, was on the rebound from a previous student affair, and looking for a full relationship. He saw it as 'something natural for young people at that age, who were looking for experience'.

Further embraces during the summer looked possible, when the two planned a dream holiday to Estoril in Portugal. Here they would be free to get to know each other, far from the gossiping and pressures of the Oxford Union. But Ann had already determined that they would sleep separately, and there was no question of accepting the hotel proprietor's offer of a shared room. Maltby recalled: 'We had to insist to the hotel receptionists on arrival that yes, we had booked two rooms, and yes, we really did want two rooms – and no, they couldn't have one of them back.' And I remember the hotel being slightly surprised, but we insisted.'

The holiday experience was unmemorable. Ann: 'We had lots of happy moments. I'm not sure there are any that stand out.' The episode that does stay in her mind, rather sadly, was a visit to a cork factory in Lisbon, where she was particularly impressed by the cork artefacts: not the most romantic of memories. 'They were very good times, they were not the happiest days of my life but they were very good times.' Estoril would surface in Ann's novel *The Clematis Tree*, as the location in which the joyless character Mark tries and fails to win the affection of a German woman called Smith.

The two returned the following autumn to Oxford and to politics at the Union, and resumed the life of political intrigue and mutual backslapping. It suited them. Maltby: 'The things about which we both really cared probably were to do with our various political achievements and successes.' Maltby seemed to need more reassurance than Ann, and when he lost an election to be president, Ann was there to play the feminine supporting role. Maltby recalls, 'It was an important moment to have someone to share that sort of problem with.'

By now the romance of the Union's two rising stars was public property. Ann said they did not try to make a secret of it – indeed, some suspected they actually enjoyed the show; the appearance of being the 'dream ticket' suited them as much as it irked others. When a journalist from *Cherwell* magazine heard that Colin had taken possession of Ann's old Dansette record player and that it had been moved to his room in Christ Church over the spring holiday in 1972, he assumed the two were now in effect living together. A piece in *Cherwell* on 27 April 1972 saying as much brought down the full wrath of the virginal Ann on the editor's head. She demanded an apology and threatened a lawyer's letter. Ann: 'I said to the editor, "Look, you've got it wrong," and he said, "If you want money, we haven't got any, but if you want a retraction you can have it." I said, "I'll have the retraction." '

This duly appeared on 11 May 1972 and read: 'In last week's John Evelyn column we published a story concerning Miss Ann Widdecombe which was completely without foundation. We would like to apologize for the embarrassment caused.' Ann recalls that 'it became a huge joke because when I got my apology Colin said, "When am I going to get my apology?" and now he was going to sue because it damaged his reputation that it wasn't true!' Subsequent doubts cast on her well-attested virginity would be treated with similar robustness. She was quoted as saying in 1998: 'If anyone says I am not a virgin, I will sue. One can easily do without sex, just as one can do without television.' Ann later said: 'I have never proclaimed my virginity. I always say: "mind your own business, but be careful, I may sue."'

The uneasy physical relationship between the couple did not prevent Colin becoming close to Ann's family. Indeed, she wanted to draw him in, and hoped to win their approval of her choice. Ann: 'If you were attached to me you would automatically get involved with my family.' At Christmas 1972 Colin was invited to stay with the Widdecombes. When the family assembled at the Bristol vicarage of Ann's brother Malcolm for the festive season, none of them knew much about Colin; talk about personal matters had never been encouraged in their rather hidebound household. But each member would submit the visitor to his or her individual appraisal, and Ann would be extremely conscious of their reactions. The most important test would be posed by her father, who could be counted on to be totally frank.

All went well. Indeed, Colin and Murray struck up a strong rapport. They were both clever, argumentative and fascinated by physics, which Murray might have studied at Cambridge had events in his early life been different; and the young man enthused the elder with his knowledge. Colin: 'I got on extremely well with him. And he was always extremely kind, courteous and civil to me. But he was certainly formidable. I thought Ann found him intimidating from time to time.' Colin also appreciated the warmth of Ann's mother, and the feeling was reciprocated; Rita thought he was a most suitable partner for her daughter and later regretted it did not work out. Indeed, everyone hoped that Colin would be Ann's man, although Ann's mother later wondered: 'Colin and Ann together were not like Murray and me. That was different.'

Ann made reciprocal visits to Colin's family in Solihull, staying on one occasion with her Birmingham University friend Jill Edge, who remembers: 'Ann needed a bed for the night and she came to stay with us, but it was just briefly. I think it was because of some romantic liaison.' Ann was being cagey and did not enlarge further. She made an equally favourable impression on the Maltbys, so that hopes were high in both households that the relationship would be long-lasting.

Ann actually stayed on in Oxford after graduating to be near Colin, who started a postgraduate degree at the end of 1972. To friends who moved in their highly political circles, they seemed a fixture. But when Ann started contemplating life outside Oxford, the fear that she would lose Colin started to surface. They kept on meeting, mostly at weekends, either in Oxford or in London, throughout 1973 and 1974, and they even went on holiday together again, travelling to Tangiers at the end of 1973 for Christmas and the New Year – a rather odd choice of timing and location, given Ann's religious conviction. Ironically, when they arrived at the Chellah Hotel, where Colin had booked two rooms, the management thought they would be helpful, and again offered them a double room. Once again Colin firmly slapped them down.

On Christmas Eve, when the couple enjoyed the hotel's set meal to the sound of the unlikely named 'Orchestre "The Fingers" ', they reminisced about the previous year's happy Christmas reunion with the Widdecombes in Bristol. Both must have wished they were back there, and had Rita Widdecombe to look after them. To cap it all, Ann went swimming in the cold Mediterranean on New Year's Day and caught a cold. But that was a blip in an otherwise enjoyable trip, during which the two went to Gibraltar, visited Berber markets and took camel rides.

None of this appeared to daunt Ann. She had decided that Colin was someone to whom she felt she could commit herself, and she thought about marriage. She later asked rhetorically: 'Did I want to marry him? At some stage I think I did.' Colin took a more detached view of such discussions. 'If you had a close relationship with somebody for two or three years and you haven't talked and thought seriously about getting married or settling down together on a permanent basis, then there's probably a reason why not and it probably means that it's not going to happen.' In any event, Colin's life was changing. He had also left Oxford, and was travelling widely as part of his job as president of the Federation of Conservative Students. Ann recalls: 'We drifted apart when we left Oxford in our different ways. So long as he was at Oxford there was a sort of anchor there, but as I was beginning to develop a life in Unilever, and he began to develop a life, first of all in the FCS, then in banking – there was no tie there any more. We were brought together by student politics, and those sorts of relationships don't always last.' Colin adamantly refutes the suggestion that he might have got bored with Ann's refusal to become more sexually involved and enthusiastic. 'Sex was never an issue. I don't think it was ever discussed.'

The political bond was finally severed when Colin quit politics for a high-paying job in fund management. Ann's absolute commitment to the ballot box and a parliamentary career may have looked quite unappealing to him as he sought a professional life in the City. Colin: 'Really our lives were just diverging and we saw less of each other for a while. I guess without it being very explicit in my own mind, at some stage I just thought to myself, "Well, you really have to decide whether this is going to go on drifting or whether it's actually sufficiently important that you're going to do something about it, or are you going to draw a line and move on." And it was me who decided that we should part, not that we were together in any physical sense at all by then.'

Colin decided to break with Ann in the weeks before Christmas 1974. He plays down the emotional side of the break-up: 'We didn't part in any angry fashion and we weren't at any stage hostile or bitter or any of those things that can happen at the end of relationships. It was very civilized. But I'm sure there were some tears afterwards. I think it had been going on long enough. We had been drifting apart. It is fairly apparent that we were not getting engaged, things weren't going to go on more positively. She was quite practical about it.'

Ann did not want to break up, and their parting cut her to the quick. But, as always, she put a brave face on it. 'It was mutual, I don't know whether you ever break up harmoniously but it was a mutual decision. I felt pretty awful at the time, but the next day I felt a huge sense of release. I don't think he'd be insulted, and I've told him that since, but it had become a millstone round our necks. He broke it off, but it was very much by mutual consent.' And she was characteristically stoical when she spoke to a newspaper in 1999: 'I probably did want the relationship to persist. I was in love, and it lasted for three years. How it ended is a private matter, but it was perfectly amicable.' And was she heartbroken? 'I compare it now to going into opposition after years in government . . . Terrible on the night, and afterwards I rejoiced in the sheer release from the pressure of red boxes and the freedom of being able to say what I liked. I always compare the two. The release at the end of government was a bit like the release from a wonderful but difficult love affair.'

Ann did not want to upset her parents' Christmas in 1974; so she and Colin went to Bristol for a jolly Widdecombe family gathering and told them nothing about it. The relationship ended with a comic twist. They had been invited together to a New Year's party given by a Union friend at the Barbican, and as they would not now be going as an item they wanted everyone to know the sad news. They decided to tell their mutual friend Barbara Margolis, who was known as a gossip and could in normal circumstances have been expected to pass it on to the fellow guests. Colin: 'If we told her, we expected everyone to know. But Barbara was so shocked, she didn't tell anyone, so we had to do it ourselves.'

A few weeks later, *The Times* carried the news that Colin Maltby was engaged to be married to Liz Bath, a fellow official of the Federation of Conservative Students and a student at Sheffield University. Colin had told Ann a week before the first announcement of the match, which was made very publicly at the FCS annual conference, and it came as a shock to realize that she had been 'two-timed' ('He would never admit that, of course,' she said later); but she took a 'pragmatic view' that that was the way relationships often ended, especially those which failed to progress to an engagement.

Sadly, romance would not again present itself to Ann Widdecombe: Colin Maltby would be her one and only man. Some colleagues at the Union speculated that Ann had hankered after other men, while a student, but Ann denies it. 'I'm not saying that I didn't look around and say, "Isn't so and so attractive?" But not seriously. I would say that now, "Oh, he's an attractive mortal," but it doesn't mean to say I'm after him. Even then I preferred the company of men to women, I had an awful lot of friendships with men that were just friendships. I still tend to make friendships with men more easily than I do with women.' But those friendships were platonic. In later years, Ann forswore passion for men, and instead offered it to her God, and in some sense to her fellow humans. Whether that is the route she would have chosen had a different man come along is pure speculation, to which there is no answer. Some colleagues argue that Ann is lonely, and sad as a result. Others say that she has great inner resources that support her in a way no partner would. Ann herself would say that she is far too idiosyncratic and impatient for a conventional relationship.

An equally speculative question is whether Ann would have been a different politician had she married. For sure, marriage would have exposed her to elements of life, perhaps including child rearing, that might have given her pause for thought about some of her moral and family principles. At the very best, she would have personal experience to answer her many critics. But critics also respect her authenticity. No one doubts that her views come from the heart and are deeply felt. The part of themselves that most politicians put into their families or their extra-political activities, Widdecombe puts into her politics and her religion. Such devotion comes at a high personal price. It is rare, and respected by even her hardest political foes.

SIX

Turning Burnley Blue

By the time she left Oxford, Ann had been part of academic institutions for some six years and had enjoyed almost every minute of them. Joining the world of real politics and real work turned out to be something of a wrench; and her first job proved particularly awkward.

Lever Brothers, the international food and consumer goods company, had taken her on as a marketing assistant because a company director had seen her performance in the televised Oxford Union debate on education and been impressed. She was flattered only to be deceived. Writing advertising copy for shaving soaps and deodorants quickly bored her, and she found the process of trying to sell detergents to people who did not need them pointless and extremely disagreeable. She could not wait to escape, and by all accounts the company was not disappointed to lose her. She later wrote: 'I thought it was totally false – everything washed whiter and we spent hours wondering which colour to wrap a bar of soap in.' Her experience bore some relation to that of Graham Greene, an author with whom Widdecombe would have certain similarities, who went from Oxford to British American Tobacco. He also found it excruciatingly boring and quit fairly rapidly, writing: 'I feel I've earned my salary today by the utter boredom of things. The new people have got literally nothing to do but sit on stools and look through months' old balance books, which convey nothing.'

The two and a half years Ann Widdecombe worked at Levers

were also destabilizing from a domestic point of view. When she left Oxford, university friends invited her to join them in expensive flats in the smarter parts of central London. But she declined, as she had no wish to live in close quarters with other people, however clever and congenial: most emphatically, she wanted a room of her own, and until one should be found, she stayed with her parents at Haslemere. The drawback to Haslemere was not the presence of her parents – quite the contrary; Rita was always at hand to furnish daily necessities – but the state of its railway line into central London. The journey to Fetter Lane, where Levers was based, was a nightmare. 'It was still in the days where you would get disruption; you would get strikes; you would have derailments – it was still that sort of time.' She used this experience to create a powerful passage early in *The Clematis Tree*, where Mark, the book's irascible anti-hero, is delayed at Waterloo station.

> He glared contemptuously at the seething throng who stood staring expectantly at the departures board which was still as bare of information as when they had entered the station. Some read their *Evening Standard*, turning back to the beginning when they had finished in the forlorn hope of finding something vaguely interesting that they had missed the first time. Others stood chatting either because they knew each other or because they were strangers temporarily united by misfortune. Mark merely indulged a loathing of them all, which he knew to be as unreasonable as it was uncharitable. 'Due to emergency engineering works on the Effingham and Cobham line . . .' explained the announcer. 'Effingham just about sums it up,' growled someone and those near enough to hear laughed.

Ann took the opportunity of an office move to Kingston to start searching for a flat both away from home and situated on a better train line. She looked for a suitable location, and found 36 Moat Court, in the village of Ottershaw, a 'sweet little place, now destroyed by roundabouts, between Woking and Weybridge'. Moat Court provided a 'room of her own', and it suited Ann perfectly. She moved in during the winter of 1974, and stayed there five years. 'This was my first taste of independence. I absolutely loved having my own routine – as young people do. I loved being able to wash my hair at two in the morning if I wanted to. I was able to have my own pictures, choose my own wallpaper.'

Moat Court was on the first floor of a modern block and had a large lounge, two 'quite small rooms', a kitchen, a bathroom and a garage. Ann used one of the small rooms as her study, and she gave some considerable thought to the decor. One wall would be painted, and the other three wallpapered, with cinnamon the unifying colour theme. She went down to the DIY store Brighter Homes to buy the materials. She did the painting herself, but left the wallpapering to Rita. 'My mother came up and did most of it. I did all my own emulsion in those days, my mother used to do the wallpapering – I had no patience at all for wallpapering.'

But shortly after Ann Widdecombe moved into Ottershaw she changed jobs and went to University of London where she would stay until she was elected to parliament in 1987. Widdecombe was an administrator to the University Court in the department that distributed funds for the University's medical schools. The University was a particularly accommodating employer and Ann's colleagues made great allowances for the time she spent on political duties. All were fully aware that the University work came very much second to her political aspirations.

One of these was her involvement with the local Conservative Association of Chertsey and Walton, and in due course she was elected treasurer of the Ottershaw Ward, and councillor for the neighbouring village of Addlestone. Conservative authorities, like Runnymede District Council, were already promoting policies for the sale of council houses, and Ann was a pioneer. In her capacity as vice chairman of the housing committee she wrote a booklet called *Do You Want to Own Your Own Home?* and devised a scheme to attract council house occupants to the idea of buying. She recalls: 'We devised various scales. If you'd been in your home for five years you got such and such a discount, but if you'd been in your home for twenty years – our line was, "That home is always going to be yours." We were never going to benefit from the start, we practically gave them away – not entirely, but the discount was enormous.'

The cut and thrust of council debating was entertaining, but much of the work was mundane and Widdecombe had not got the patience for campaigns to introduce Belisha beacons and zebra crossings. She made no secret of the fact that she was not a natural local government politician. But central government was a different matter. There the big lights shone, and fame was the reward for success. The first time she saw an MP in action was during the October 1974 general election campaign, when she assisted Michael Ancram, now the chairman of the Conservative Party, in his unsuccessful campaign to seek to retain the seat of Berwick and East Lothian. Ann was on a list of Conservative Party activists and her name was given to Ancram as a possible helper. She became his personal assistant and warmed up audiences before he came on as the prime billing. Ancram called her 'a young livewire' and noted that she was not intimidated by the hostile miners and fishermen. 'On one occasion I had to say to her that a warm-up speech was supposed to warm people up and not make them incandescent. She took on all-comers.'

She came out of the election infused with enthusiasm for politics, and determined to find a constituency of her own. She applied to the Conservative Party to join their list of candidates and was rejected. She wanted to know why and went to Marcus Fox, who ran the party's candidate selection process. This early brush with the party hierarchy would be the first of many. Widdecombe: 'I said, "What's the problem?" And he said, "We think you need some more experience." So I said, "Yeah, that's why you fight unsafe seats – to get experience," and "It's not as if I'm looking for Surrey South West or something." Anyway, he said, "Oh, you haven't done enough local work." I was later told that he had a policy at that stage of refusing most people under thirty – which I was at that time.'

If the slightly over-eager woman (as no doubt Fox regarded her) was to make her breakthrough into politics and become a candidate, she would have to work outside the party's machine, rather than with

its support. This meant finding the lists of vacant seats. To her aid
came her Bow Group friend Ian Clark, who had been admitted to
the list: he passed on to her his lists, and Ann wrote off her own bat to
party chairmen asking to be considered as a candidate. Many
selection processes came and went before she passed the initial test
and got on to a shortlist. Then two shortlistings came together,
placing Ann in an awkward dilemma. Both Burnley and Anglesey
wanted Ann to return for an elimination contest; but if she won
Burnley's selection contest, party etiquette would prohibit her from
going on to Anglesey. This was unfortunate, as Anglesey was a
Conservative marginal whereas Burnley was rock-solid Labour. To
add to the dilemma, Ann had been informally told by the Anglesey
committee that she was in with a very good chance of winning the
selection. In the end she went for the safe option and took Burnley.
Anglesey went Tory in 1979, but reverted to Labour in 1987.

Even the Burnley selection process had its hiccups. Some of the
more traditional Tories in the local party hierarchy expressed their
doubts about choosing a woman candidate. This was nothing
unusual, recalls Widdecombe, who had long encountered ingrained
male suspicion and prejudice against female involvement in professional politics. 'When I was first trying there was a huge amount of
quite overt prejudice, in fact it happened with me many, many times
in many constituencies. I was asked questions about "Did I think it
was a job for a woman?" and that sort of thing. It really was there. I
would certainly be asked questions about "Did I intend to marry?"
and "What if I had children?" '

David [now Lord] Hunt, who became a leading Conservative
politician under John Major, confirmed the existence of party
prejudice: 'A lot of the selectors who were choosing candidates were
women. For some reason they seemed always to decide that they
were looking for a young and happily married man, preferably with
small children or with the prospect of small children, who would
then be in the constituency for a number of years building up a
personal vote. It was difficult to persuade them that the right
candidate, however able, should be a woman.' Particular victims of the

prejudice, said Hunt, were Linda Chalker, Virginia Bottomley and Ann Widdecombe. As one Burnley constituent remembered: 'You always get some old codgers saying: Oh, this constituency is not yet ready for a woman! But I always think that with a woman fighting a man, you are going to get publicity. And usually of the right kind.' There were inevitably doubters on the selection panel. Widdecombe herself remembers one member observing with some surprise: 'So you are not a snob?' as if it was a great revelation to her. Another member of the selection committee said to her, 'You're rather small, are you sure you're up to it?' But the doubters were vanquished; and after all, in selecting a woman the Burnley Conservatives were only following the successful practice of the Labour Party in the north of England, which had put into Parliament doughty fighters like Bessie Braddock and Barbara Castle.

The fight at Burnley was to draw more heavily on Ann's patience than her stamina. The town's massive Labour majority, its seemingly endless rows of terraced working men's houses, and its impoverished Conservative organization tested even her indomitable spirit. Every weekend during the eighteen long months between her selection as parliamentary candidate and the 1979 general election, Widdecombe plodded those streets, cheered on the local troops and sought to plug her name among the Tory great and good who were within shouting distance of Burnley. The experience was formative, although the end result predictably negative.

The length of Widdecombe's period of electoral gestation at Burnley was due to the precarious state of the Callaghan government, which was declining fast as a result of trade union activity and the notorious intervention of the International Monetary Fund in the national economy. An election was expected at any moment from early 1978, and the Conservative Party had been forced to prepare a full slate of candidates without having any idea how long they would have to wait; and, as it happened, Callaghan delayed until the last moment, in May 1979.

Once selected, Ann started to put down some roots in the constituency that she would now be visiting routinely once a week.

As Burnley would be her second home for the foreseeable future, she needed overnight accommodation, and with the help of the constituency stalwarts Enid and Maurice Tate, she found a small flat at 210 Todmorden Road. This placed her squarely in Burnley's political ghetto, within hailing distance of the Tates down the road at 260 Todmorden Road, and two other Conservative councillors and two Labour councillors as well.

Weekly visits to the constituency now started to dominate Ann's life. She would leave work early on a Friday to be at the constituency by the evening, and because she did not want to put her elderly Methuselah through the gruelling ride to Lancashire every week, she sometimes left it with her constituency colleague Linda Crossley, who would make sure it was there to meet her at the rail station when she arrived. These weekend trips forced Ann to move out of the delightful Ottershaw. Commuting to her work at the University of London in Malet Street, was irritating enough; but the extra journey to Burnley each week was one commute too far. She gave up Moat Court and moved into a flat in Barnsbury Road, Islington, owned by the Tory MP Mark Wolfson, which she shared with a girl who was an outstanding gardener. When Ann returned after a long and hard weekend in Burnley, she would sit out on a balcony at the back of the flat which was festooned with flowers and shrubs and replenish her resources. It was a necessary respite from Burnley's unremitting grime. Ann stayed around the greener suburbs of north London for a number of years before herself joining the ranks of the property-owning classes.

The regularity of her weekend visits to the constituency she was nursing greatly impressed the local party activists. The local Young Conservative group were her greatest fans, and she also cemented her position at the Lancashire Federation of Conservative Clubs. This put her in touch with men who would later rise to prominence in Conservative government circles, including David Waddington, a former Home Secretary who now sits in the House of Lords, and the one-time local Member of Parliament, David Trippier. That was the civilized part of the weekly visit. The tougher part was the regular

Saturday evening visits to the local Conservative working men's clubs or 'halls'. She would visit them on sufferance rather than with enthusiasm, more to encourage financial contributions to a local party that was severely strapped for cash than to make a political message; for the appetite of those attending the clubs was less for politics than for drink.

Burnley had seven such halls at the time, and they were pretty unsalubrious places. In fact, the name 'Conservative Club' disguised the fact that they were largely drinking dens for working men looking for a night out, a drink, a smoke and a game of pool. The cynic might say that their political awareness went no further than responding to the call of 'Number Ten' in Bingo – a fixture of the clubs' routine – with the shout, 'Maggie's Den'. Even that was premature at this time. The sight of the diminutive candidate finding her way through the tables in the smoke-filled room would always unleash a titter, and the more jovial of the clubs would have its pianist strike up the tune Widdecombe Fair, while the visitor tried to smile, and look as if she was an ordinary girl relaxed and among friends. The presence of women was not greatly encouraged in these institutions in general, and there was a golden rule that no woman should go near the pool table. The men had been well worked up by a local comedian by the time ten-thirty arrived, Ann's cue to step on to the stage to give a pep talk to the troops. The usually bold politician could be forgiven for climbing those steps slightly gingerly, waiting for some local wit to say something to raise a laugh; but her audiences were usually respectful, if largely uncomprehending. As the election loomed, Ann would be accompanied by candidates for the local elections – which were being held on the same day as the general election – and some of the members would confuse the candidates and the elections in which they were standing.

Linda Crossley recalls the visits, on which she sometimes accompanied the young candidate: 'It took an awful lot of courage for her to go in on a Saturday night, to a working men's club . . . and let's be quite honest, they weren't *all* Conservatives.' Widdecombe herself admits those visits were a trial, albeit an essential one: 'I was very relieved when I went to Devonport to find there was only one working men's club and even more relieved when I went to Maidstone and found there was none.'

Ann did not shy away from pressing the flesh with local employees who would have little truck with the Conservative cause. On one memorable occasion she went down to Hapton colliery, early in the morning, as Crossley recalls: 'She went down with the workers, wearing her helmet, her kneepads, her overalls. She put her kneepads on the wrong way round, but in general the miners were fascinated.' The kneepads were in fact irrelevant, recalls the prospective candidate, as she was required to crawl along on her front, hauling herself along not on her knees but on her elbows. When she got to the bottom she found miners chipping at the seam with axes (this was pre-mechanization). The memory gave her a shudder. In fact, the mine was in the neighbouring constituency represented by David Waddington, but, says Crossley, 'a lot of the people she had met actually worked there, and that is why she went – to find out first-hand how they lived and worked.' Ann also made regular visits to the local Pendelfin factory to canvass support. Here they made decorative animals; in due course she collected quite a number, and a china rabbit still adorns her sitting-room mantelpiece.

There was no disguising the distinctively southern Widdecombe twang, and it aroused some comments. Enid Tate remembers: 'Unfortunately a few people remarked about her voice. Ann's voice is quite distinctive, and a lot of people said it didn't fit in exactly with Burnley. But I've been able to point out to these narrow-minded folk what we would have missed if we hadn't had her as our candidate!'

As soon as James Callaghan announced that the general election would be on 3 May 1979, Widdecombe's action plan for Burnley was put into effect. It began with the publication of her manifesto for the constituency.

The sitting MP and Widdecombe's rival for the Burnley seat could not have been a clearer product of the Buggins' Turn school of Old Labour politics. Born in the Rhondda Valley, Dan Jones grew up in the Welsh mines, going down the pits aged fourteen, but he had since worked in the aircraft industry and made trade union connections. Jones had held the seat continuously since 1959 by dint of its solid Labour majority. By 1979, his seventh election campaign, he was into his seventies, dependent on sticks to walk around, and far from a fighting force. This was reflected in his performance in Parliament as well as in the constituency. As part of her preparation for the campaign, Ann Widdecombe did a search of *Hansard* for Jones's contributions in the last year and found just two. This enabled her to dub him the 'mouse in the house', bringing a wry smile to her supporters' faces.

Widdecombe played on the doubtful suitability of someone of Jones's advanced age seeking re-election with a barely disguised gibe in the letters column of the local paper. 'Reference Mr Dan Jones's letter (*Express Mail*, April 12th). I do not wish to comment on the personal position of Mr Jones and his age, as this is a matter for his own conscience and the electors of Burnley. But may I, through your columns, ask Mr Jones what his position is with regard to the policy of early retirement now favoured by some unions, and what is his position with regard to compulsory retirement at 65 in occupations other than his own?'

Widdecombe sought to provoke the taciturn Jones into a number of newspaper arguments and face-to-face debates, but he refused all approaches. The contrast between the elderly Jones and the thirty-one year old Widdecombe could not have been sharper. While she looked for every opportunity to reach the general public both directly and through the media, he stayed with his own people, occasionally being photographed among men of his own age.

The unremitting Conservative candidate drove her colleagues in the local party hard. The constituency was under-resourced in cash and staff, the offices run down, the facilities squalid. For example, the machinery available to pump out the slogans from Widdecombe's car – the redoubtable Methuselah – as it went round the constituency clad in posters was no more than a simple tape-recorder; leaflets were run off from a Gestetner copying machine in the dismal constituency office. So there was a strong sense of self-sufficiency, which suited

Ann's temperament admirably. Team spirit was at the heart of this
make-do campaign, and Widdecombe had Enid Tate drawing up the
posters and blowing up balloons. The length of Ann's surname posed
a problem for Tate, and Ann recalled that Enid once said to her,
' " You'd better marry somebody with a short name." And I said,
"Well, I can keep my own name as well." ' The slogan adorning all
publicity was 'I am an Ann's man', because of its catchy sound, its
stress on the personality and the appearance of the words.

Another member of the team was Linda Crossley and she
remembered an occasion when 'We were careering around in the car,
which was all covered in posters. And it was full of balloons, but Ann
could not stand blowing them up. Somebody else had to blow them
up – maybe it was just an excuse to get others to do this work. We
had loads of balloons, so nobody could miss us coming! We used a
loud-hailer, too.'

On the political side, Widdecombe showed great capacity to pick
the emotive topics and drive them home in the media. Shortly before
the election campaign started, Airey Neave was assassinated by the IRA;
under a banner headline, 'Hang Terrorists Say The Tories', the local
newspaper, the *Burnley Evening Star*, noted on 3 April 1979 that the
Burnley Tory election campaign would include a call for the re-introduction of hanging as a punishment for terrorism. The article read:

> Miss Widdecombe said her law and order campaign has not been
> influenced by the murder on Friday of Mr Airey Neave, the Shadow
> Spokesman on Northern Ireland. Ann Widdecombe says, 'I would
> not want Mr Neave's murder to be used as a plank in the party
> campaign. Many people have died as a result of terrorism. I think
> people were concerned about law and order before Mr Neave's
> murder, although it has had the effect of shocking people.' The
> Conservative Party is pledged to holding a Commons debate on the
> death penalty and if the vote was in favour, would then introduce a
> Government Bill.

Widdecombe's message on law and order would not have come as a
surprise to constituents or party members who followed her. She had

used the platform of the 1978 Conservative party conference to call for the hanging of terrorists, murderers of police and prison officers, and armed robbers, and her amendment to a party motion was seconded by Burnley Conservative Association's chairman Councillor Maurice Tate. Now she reiterated her demand for the return of the death penalty in her election address, delivered a week after the Airey Neave murder. The death penalty, she urged, should be restored for terrorism, murder committed during armed robbery, and the murder of police and prison officers. She also dwelt more generally on crime and law and order; the address stated, 'Two thirds of the increase in crime since the war has taken place during Labour governments. The victim no longer feels he gets a fair deal and most people feel that the system has started to put the criminal first.' The call for a fair deal for victims would continue to be a Widdecombe war cry for more than two decades.

Immigration and 'benefit scrounging' were two other targets of the election address. It demanded that the number of immigrants allowed into the United Kingdom be cut, and it called for policies for 'alleviating the concentration of immigrants in some areas', although it did not go into detail about how this might be done. Immigration was of particular concern to Burnley at that time, as its Stoneyholme district had a dense Pakistani population. This provoked local constituents into coming to the new parliamentary candidate to express concern that their children were attending schools where 80 per cent of the children in some classes were not native English speakers. Widdecombe recalled, 'It was not the fact that they were immigrants that they objected to, it was the fact that they did not speak English and so it slowed down all the classes.' In fact immigration issues overwhelmed the campaign for Widdecombe, who notes how attitudes to immigration changed in the subsequent twenty years.

Crime also featured in the campaign, and the election address called for magistrates' powers in dealing with young offenders to be revised and made more effective. 'Sentences ought to deter as well as reform,' she said. On social security, her expressed view was that 'The system of benefits needs restructuring so that those in real need benefit but those who scrounge are unable to do so. At the moment the disabled suffer from a hotch potch of benefits which need rationalization.' Education was another concern, bringing forth the demand that performance be checked by national   examinations at junior and senior schools: 'Efficiency in education is more important than experiment. Slack education hurts the deprived child most.' Here Widdecombe harked back to the debates in Oxford, during which she had impressed not only her student audiences but also visiting distinguished MPs like Richard Crossman and Shirley Williams with her call for an emphasis on educational excellence, rather than equality as represented by the comprehensive system.

Conservative campaigns at Burnley were typically low-key and defeatist, but Ann injected razzmatazz into the fight by bringing in numbers of dignitaries who had a national prominence for walkabouts and meetings. These included Shadow Chancellor of the Exchequer Geoffrey Howe; Winston Churchill, grandson of the great man; and Geoffrey Pattie, who visited Burnley's Lucas factory. Richard Luce, the shadow spokesman for foreign affairs and a subsequent minister in the first Thatcher administration, also came to the constituency as an expression of personal gratitude to Ann Widdecombe. She had recently published a document, at Luce's behest but under the auspices of the Bow Group, which examined what had happened to the supply of hearing aids to the deaf since the government had taken over the supply of NHS aids. The document concluded that the move had hit the private dispensers of specialist aids, and that, since these were sometimes unavailable on the NHS, waiting lists might be lengthened as a result.

According to the *Burnley Evening Star*, the Burnley general election campaign appeared to be 'coming to the boil' at the end of April. There was great enthusiasm and optimism in the Widdecombe camp, with Enid Tate reported as saying that the party was mounting one of its strongest ever campaigns to take the seat away from Labour domination.

'We have been getting ready for this one for two and a half years,' she said. 'We have the candidate to do it in Miss Ann Widdecombe and she will fight tooth and nail for the seat.' She said Tory canvassing revealed that increasing numbers of the electorate were worried about the future; their jobs, pensions and their security from vandalism and hooligans . . .

On 1 May the hype reached fever pitch when the same paper reported on its front page,

> The Tories believe they have done it. With the aid of some formidable 'artillery' – big name party personalities – they have thoroughly shaken up the constituency. Miss Ann Widdecombe – Burnley's diminutive 'Mrs Thatcher' – fighting the seat for the Conservatives, says, 'Without any gimmickry . . . our canvass is revealing a big swing in our favour. People are telling me on the doorsteps, how dissatisfied they are with the current set-up. Many of these people have voted Labour all their lives. If everyone who has told me that they intend to vote Conservative does so – then Dan Jones and his supporters are in for something of a shock. I think we can sweep Dan Jones away in this election.'

In fact, there was never any doubt about the outcome; this was just a piece of last-minute rallying of the troops. The Conservative group at the count played the usual trick of trying to worry the Labour people by asking for more boxes when they knew there were no more votes. But Widdecombe had appreciably improved the Conservative vote, both numerically and proportionally. Labour retained its solid vote of 20,172, but the Conservatives halved the Labour majority, from 12,000 in 1974, to 6,000 on this occasion. The result was sufficiently encouraging to allow Widdecombe to claim it as a great moral victory. 'I feel great satisfaction and Mr Jones must know that I will be breathing down his neck. The mood in Burnley will be reflected throughout the country and we will have a working majority and a great five years ahead.' The same sentiments were echoed in the *Burnley Evening Star*, which reported that Burnley had not seen the last of Miss Ann Widdecombe. 'I shall be around for some time yet, although it will be entirely up to the local party association who they choose for the next confrontation, when it comes. To me, Burnley is far from being a lost cause. This election has proved that it is not as solid Labour as some people would believe. It will, however, demand a lot of hard work and sustained effort to win. Having made the inroads, we should be able to go from strength to strength and I would ultimately hope to see a Tory victory in the town. The results show that when people have to choose between Socialism and a more reliable system, they will vote Conservative.'

Widdecombe's devotion to the constituency both before the campaign and during it had amazed the local officials, and in retrospect she wondered if her weekly visits may not have been excessive. 'If I was doing that sort of thing again, I would probably go up every three weeks and pack a lot in.' But even if her devotion was not fully repaid in hard votes, it certainly was in loyalty and the growth of the Widdecombe fan club. A number of Burnley people joined her entourage and continued to support her later election campaigns – even going so far as to join the Widdecombe whirlwind which blew through Plymouth Devonport next time around.

SEVEN

Disappointment in Devonport

S HORTLY after the unsuccessful Burnley campaign, Widdecombe
made a sale and a purchase that would have their impact on her
domestic life, if not her developing political career. The sale was
of Methuselah, her 1958 Morris Minor; having bought the car from
her godfather for £50, she now got £300 for it, as it had become a
'bit of a collector's item'. Methy, as she called it, had been the scene of
that first passionate kiss with Colin, as well as the reliable vehicle
which, festooned with balloons and stickers, had taken her round and
round Burnley, and she parted with it regretfully. In its place came a
Renault. The purchase was of a four-room flat in Woodlawn Road,
Fulham, which had the enormous attraction of a garden and two
resident cats. Ann had noticed the two cats and joked to the owner
that she expected they would be coming with the flat. The owner
spotted a cat-lover immediately and said that that could be arranged,
as she was going to Spain. They were called Blackie and Pie; Ann
renamed them Sooty and Sweep, and they immediately became part
of her life.

But the flat had some less attractive features which would plague
the would-be Member of Parliament for quite some time after she
bought it in 1981. The place was a 'wreck', and she had taken it on
with the (slightly unlikely, in her case) objective of 'doing it up',
accepting that there would be some problems and expense involved.
In the event, the problems ran a lot deeper than either she or her
surveyor had thought. She recalls: 'The kitchen was archaic – it came

out of the last century. The bathroom came out of somewhere in the middle of this century. It was an old wreck, really, which was within my price range for that reason.' Ann's mother, Rita, and her friend Pat Potts were recruited to help with the decorating, and they dealt with some of the more evident cosmetic problems which had caused the walls to become discoloured. But the problems were not all so easily solved. When she saw a bookcase 'tipping a bit', Ann pulled away the carpet and saw that rot had eaten away at the floorboards. A specialist company then warned her that it could have spread throughout the house, and a wall had to be removed at great expense. It was a 'terribly worrying time' and Ann wanted to be shot of the flat, but had rather predictable difficulty in selling it. When the fourth offer was withdrawn, she decided she had to get rid of the flat as soon as she could, and buy another house later on.

Time-wasting domestic obstacles of this kind were the last thing she needed as she hunted for a constituency which would accept her as their candidate for the next election. Having done her time fighting the hopeless seat of Burnley, she now had her sights set on a seat which was at worst marginal, and at best safe. A number presented themselves. The selection of parliamentary candidates for the 1983 election was telescoped as a result of delayed boundary changes, and this forced Ann, along with the many other would-be candidates, to race up and down the country at high speed to make the selection meetings. She recalled moments of high farce, as rival candidates connived to make their timetables easier by swapping appearances at selection meetings. Among the speeches she made in the course of this marathon selection exercise, one was to the constituency party at Plymouth Devonport, and it seemed to her to be well received. So she was understandably shocked to be told she had made only the reserve list, not the final list. When she phoned up the area agent to ask why, she was told, 'Oh well, they thought you'd look funny on television with your crooked teeth.'

But that was not the end of the story. Those selected for the final list dropped out one by one, and Ann was back in contention. There was then another 'beauty parade' which resulted in a tie between her and another hopeful, Tony Patterson. This would require yet another presentation. The drama of the selection was such that the television programme *Newsnight* wanted to cover it, and the media-hungry candidates were happy to accept the invitation, if only to make an impression that might stand them in good stead in their next application, if this failed. In fact, Ann trounced Patterson this time around, and on 7 April 1983 her nomination was secured.

Devonport had a high-profile sitting member in Dr David Owen, who was fighting his first election as head of the Social Democratic Party, which had broken away from Labour two years earlier. The seat was technically a marginal, as Owen's majority over the Conservatives in 1979 had been only 1,000; but boundary changes since then, and Owen's massive national prominence, were special features in 1983 that would cause the Conservatives particular problems.

The Tory campaign began on a cool late April morning, two weeks before the election date was announced, when Ann drove her newly appointed agent Keith Griffith to the austere side of Devon's Hay Tor to plan the Devonport election. This isolated spot was a place, she judged, where thoughts and ideas would flow freely and creatively. Griffiths had only recently been brought into the constituency, so this was his chance to get to know Widdecombe. He found her bracing style congenial, and the professional partnership became a firm personal friendship as well. This surprised the him, as he calls himself a 'chauvinist' not used to working with women as equals; but Widdecombe was different. 'It was exhilarating! It certainly fired the ideas. Ann and I were able to bounce ideas off one another and start a strategy for the campaign. Even at that stage of her political career, she had a very, very clear understanding of where her campaign should go and how it should be structured.' Early on, the two set their minds to boosting the local organization, which lagged behind that of the other two main parties. They had a lot of boning up to do themselves, for the territory was unfamiliar to both of them, as Ann recalls: 'We spent the whole of the campaign with maps under the dashboards trying to pretend that we weren't really looking up

where things were and that we knew. And there were some hilarious
moments in it; we had Cranley Onslow, the then Conservative
minister, down to speak at a school; we had located the school on the
map, but the school had moved. So when we got there – it was no
longer there. It was things like that – it was quite hysterical.'

While her thinking about tactics impressed the agent with its
clarity, on political ground he found a person whose ideas carried
more shades of grey. 'This was a mature politician – right of centre in
matters of economy, matters of law and order, some matters of that
ilk. But she was left of centre in those areas of social concern. She was
what one could describe as a traditional Conservative – a pragmatic
politician with principles.' Widdecombe herself indicated to *The
Times* during the campaign that she could not be easily categorized as
a Thatcherite, hard right on all things. In a soundbite that contained a
touch of irony, she said she was 'dry with some damp patches'. But
not all found this convincing, and one commentator described her,
less flatteringly, as 'a pale carbon copy of Mrs Thatcher'.

The high-profile Owen was the focus of Widdecombe's
campaign. Griffiths: 'We never actually allowed our local people to
think that they couldn't beat David Owen. We dismissed Priestley
[Ann's old student colleague, Julian Priestley] and the Labour party in
the first few days, and then David Owen was the target.' Owen's
capacity to pull a personal vote for the new party and shake
traditional Labour and Tory allegiances worried the Conservatives;
but Widdecombe prophesied breezily early in the campaign that
'Our vote will hold up, his vote will split.' The Tories would try to
play the two rival parties off against one another, so if one was seen to
be lagging, they would support it, and attack the other, hoping in this
way to keep either from racing ahead.

The campaign had some highly personal undertones, of which
the most interesting for the Conservatives was the almost tangible
hostility between Owen and Priestley. Before jumping ship to the
SDP Owen had been Priestley's political mentor, especially on
European matters where they were of like Europhile mind, and the
Labour man could not forgive the Doctor his treachery. For his part,

Owen could not stand Priestley. Ann discovered this unexpectedly when the three candidates were lined up to go on to a platform for a three-cornered debate. The ever eager young Priestley jumped on to the platform first and sat down at the end of the line-up of chairs. Owen gestured to Ann to go next, but Ann thought this was a piece of male patronage, and understandably objected, gesturing to Owen to go instead. Then he begged her to go, whispering that it was simply that he could not stand Priestley or face sitting next to him. Sour relations between her opponents were a quite different matter, and Ann was eager to help out. Subsequent photographs of the three Devonport candidates show Widdecombe sitting between the other two.

The campaign's dominant theme would be defence, and the Tories selected as their slogan 'Defend Devonport'. Memories of the victorious Falklands campaign were still very fresh – indeed, the local Roborough Airport had been the base for Harriers used in the campaign – and they banked on that playing into their hands. Defence also had a particularly practical resonance for this constituency, as its naval dockyards were an important employer whose future would look uncertain if Labour's softer defence policies were implemented. Widdecombe's credentials for talking about defence were enhanced by her having recently written *A Layman's Guide to Defence*. This pamphlet had been published under the banner of Women and Families for Defence, a campaigning organization set up just a year earlier by Lady Olga Maitland to counter the promotional impact of the CND-based Women of Greenham Common. Ann was a founding vice president of Women and Families for Defence and a much valued supporter of Maitland. Her statement to the *Western Evening Herald* on 30 May showed some considerable understanding of the subject: 'The Conservative Party is committed to maintaining an effective nuclear deterrent and to keeping most of Britain's conventional forces. We believe that this is the only way to keep peace in Europe. The experiences of the last 38 years (since the end of the Second World War) prove this.' Britain was right to negotiate with the Soviet Union for arms reductions on all sides, but unilateral disarmament was 'too dangerous'. 'This is the danger we would face under a Labour government,' she added, urging people not to 'leave Britain undefended'.

This uncompromising stance had strong local appeal. A weaker line on defence, which Widdecombe held out as the threat posed by Labour, would result in the closing of local dockyards, with great loss of employment. While Priestley was the obvious target for the attack, and Widdecombe did not shrink from holding him to account for the doveish noises coming out of Labour headquarters, she also sought to tar Owen with the Labour brush. Griffiths: 'David Owen wasn't that far from the Labour Party even then, and it had essentially abandoned the defence of Britain. In the context of Devonport, a city steeped in naval defence, it was obviously a key factor irrespective of the Falklands.'

Early morning visits to the local dockyards hammered home the defence theme. There she could exploit her family involvement in the navy, as she was regularly met by officers who had known her father either when he was head of victualling for the service, or during the two years when he had been stationed in Plymouth. Not all the people greeting her were so well-disposed, though, and onlookers recalled some of the stauncher Labour supporters giving her 'a bit of verbal hassle'. They were promptly told by fellow dockers who respected the candidate's efforts to 'back off' – though Ann herself was never averse to locking horns with her opponents. For all her combativeness and enthusiasm, these visits in the cold were inevitably uncomfortable, and may have been responsible for a bad dose of flu from which she suffered at the time. This was kept under control during the campaign, but afterwards was diagnosed as pneumonia. Griffiths recalled one morning at the Albert Gate docks when her voice had gone and her frustration was palpable. On another occasion, when she was campaigning in the centre of Plymouth, party worker Mike Gibson came to the rescue of the invalid and spoon-fed her cough mixture.

An issue calculated to rouse the grass roots of the Conservative Party quite as much as defence was crime, with the now routine

Widdecombe demand for the re-introduction of the death penalty. She told a public meeting how she would determine when the penalty was appropriate. 'I think one would have to restrict it to murders of police and prison officers, acts of terrorism, and any murder at all committed in the course of armed or violent robbery.' While there was a strong case for the restoration of capital punishment for all premeditated murders, she said, this could raise problems of definition. The categories she suggested were clear and unambiguous. 'I think it was right that we tried doing without it. We did not know whether it was a deterrent or not.'

Her ability to inform herself on local issues was also evident when she stood firm about retaining Plymouth's four grammar schools, while converting secondary moderns into comprehensives. 'A school attracts by its record and what it actually achieves,' she said. But she supported maintaining grammar schools: 'For working-class children especially, the only chance most of them have of getting on is through education.'

Later in the campaign she resumed the attack on the SDP, claiming that socialism pervaded the new party just as much as Labour: 'In as much as you can extract policies from the SDP, and believe me it's difficult, they are socialist policies,' she said. The SDP had made clear that it saw tax relief on mortgages as 'one of the greatest sources of social inequality' and would reduce it. Effectively, 'their policies would end the legal right for tenants to buy council houses . . .'

Owen's high-profile presence acted as a magnet for the press, who came to the constituency in droves. To balance the attention they gave to Owen, the press were obliged to give Widdecombe some coverage, and she and Griffiths set out with enthusiasm to make her as accessible as possible to the media. Griffiths: 'We had a candidate who could think on her feet and give the press, when they arrived, notably the local radio and television, the sort of response and coverage and statements they wanted. These forced David Owen and Priestley to respond in kind.' Griffiths enjoyed finding her the airtime; she relished the interest, and gave considerable thought to her statements and comments. Nevertheless, the amount of media interest caught the Conservatives somewhat on the hop, and Griffiths admitted they were 'flying by the seat of their pants'. 'It was like flying a plane with two engines with one engine cutting out every now and again. You woke up in the morning with a planned campaign. We had press availability time every morning, not a press conference, and it was up to the press to use it.'

The hyped-up local press also responded rather better than had the Burnley media to Widdecombe's canvassing carnival tricks. The battered old Maxi she had decked out with stickers was not the usual Tory fare, and the music crackling out from a hastily rigged-up sound system intrigued the *Western Evening Herald*.

> Devonport voters are reportedly enjoying the less-than-staid spectacle of Miss Ann Widdecombe delivering her loud-hailered campaign speeches to the merry accompaniment of Liberty Bell, the Monty Python theme music. The tuneful Tory battle-bus, a be-stickered old Maxi, was first spotted by a delighted Labour supporter who dubbed it, somewhat predictably, Ann Widdecombe's Flying Circus. 'It seems to be an appropriate theme – circus music for their circus,' he told Election Diary uncharitably.
>
> A quick call to Miss Widdecombe's jovial agent, Keith Griffiths, confirmed the story of Labour's gloating voter. 'It's a nice piece of music, Liberty Bell,' said Mr Griffiths, adding that Ann talks over the music. 'The Tory Party stands for freedom and liberty and we have a young lady candidate. It seems appropriate.' So there! Both parties are agreed on that, though presumably for different reasons. What will Miss Widdecombe do next? Perhaps she will go walkabout with John Cleese – the Minister for Silly Walks . . .

The Maxi was not Ann's but her parents', and she had borrowed it for the campaign. One evening, having loaded it up with posters to take over to Devonport, she found when she came to leave for the constituency that it would not start. In dire distress she called Keith Griffiths, who despite its now being late at night, leapt into his car and came over to pick her and the posters up. But, as the two approached Devonport, his car also spluttered to a halt, to wry press amusement. He commented to the paper that a foreign body had got into his works, not unlike the Social Democratic Party!

The razzmatazz caused by visits from some leading Tories was a mixed blessing for Widdecombe: sometimes icing on the cake, sometimes requiring her to rescue them from less than helpful comments. For example, when Ted Heath came to glad-hand constituents, he cast doubt on the prevailing monetarist philosophy, saying in a speech that 'monetarism was dead'. Ann was forced to make clear she was 'basically a Thatcherite'. Indeed, Widdecombe made a virtue of her (slightly lukewarm) support for the Prime Minister, often starting her doorstep patter: 'I think Maggie's done well, don't you?' One of Heath's aides also caused an upset by telling the press that Owen was such a formidable political figure that it would be a 'great shame' if she beat him. Widdecombe was predictably furious with the former Tory leader, with whose policies she had little truck at the best of times; but his pulling power was undeniable, and was proven when an onlooker who had just shaken Heath's hand handed Griffiths a holdall containing £500 in notes. The Devonport candidate was clearly seen as a loyal supporter of the Prime Minister, and when Margaret Thatcher herself made a flying visit to Wadebridge in North Cornwall, Ann was there to greet her and be photographed in a typically well-judged publicity operation.

Sir Geoffrey Howe, another supporter from Burnley, and now Chancellor, came to Plymouth and paraded on the historically famous Plymouth Hoe, with Ann and the Conservative sitting members from the two neighbouring constituencies, Janet Fookes and the late Alan Clark, in attendance. Cabinet ministers visiting Plymouth are required, for tradition's sake, to recall Sir Francis Drake by rolling a ball on the green. Howe commented, to the wry amusement of those around, that he had 'dropped his balls'. Ann was *not* amused, but no doubt kept her counsel. This suppressed disapproval of his sense of humour may have explained why Howe gained the impression that the young candidate was 'demure and shy', while Clark and Fookes seemed to him 'more robust characters'. Howe was to change his opinion when, seven years later, he saw

Widdecombe stomping up and down the House of Commons, rallying her troops behind the pro-life clauses in the Human Fertilization and Embryology Bill.

Despite Owen's national prominence, the campaign was a cliffhanger. Griffiths says the SDP leader was even forced to admit publicly that he was worried about being beaten by Ann Widdecombe. This boosted the Conservative team, given that the handsome doctor had been voted the most popular politician in Britain. The Tory camp was also encouraged by a poll (undertaken jointly by the local polytechnic and television station) showing the Conservatives 10 per cent ahead of Owen – a lead that would rise later to an almighty 16 per cent. By the end of the campaign, Widdecombe's Tories were working at full stretch. Linda Crossley, her devoted supporter from Burnley days, came down to lend a hand and remembers: 'Three days before polling day, we worked all night, sitting at typewriters and getting the canvass returns done. We eventually did send Ann to bed, because there was not much else she could do. Anyway, she had a busy day ahead of her the following day.' Ann brought in her brother, Malcolm and his two sons, and her mother and father to boost the team.

The day before the election, Widdecombe remained buoyant, although by now the returns must have shown her struggling. She told a local paper, 'Really, sticking my neck out, I expect a majority of around 1,000. But I certainly cannot rule out a possible recount, and I am preparing for a long night.' The result was a long way from her hopes. She transformed the Conservatives' performance, scoring almost 16,000 votes; but Owen far exceeded most expectations, netting 20,843. Priestley fell into a low third place, with fewer than 10,000. The local paper was aghast, saying that Owen's feat was no less than a 'Houdini act'; Ann said he had 'come from nowhere'. She later gallantly repeated her view that she genuinely respected his tough view on defence, and to that extent felt his place in the House of Commons was deserved; but there was no disguising her bitter disappointment. On top of that, Ann could no longer look for succour in her religion. Her earlier faith had started to desert her.

EIGHT

'God is a Great Ball of Light'

'God is a great ball of light. The Bible talks a lot of the outer darkness. The nearer you get to God the more blinding light there is. And the further away you get from God and Heaven the deeper the dark. I am always mocked if I am asked to explain it in picture images because I see a Christian Heaven – people with gowns and harps, hallelujahs and all that – my picture of Hell is complete with devils with tridents and burning lakes and darkness.'

That was Ann Widdecombe's view of God in the year 2000. The flaming ball that sears her consciousness is the product of a lifelong process of reflection and belief that goes back before she can remember. 'I was brought up believing in Jesus. I never questioned the existence of God and the utter truth of Christianity until I was much older, never ever.'

The journey between her early and later visions of God embraces doubt and many shades of belief. Ann's early God was a severe guardian. 'I wouldn't have said in those days, "Thou God seest me," but that is the background behind much of the teaching I had. Whatever you did, God saw. He knew what you were doing. He knew what you were thinking. There was an appeal to a Higher Being. And there was certainly an undeniable concept of Temptation. If you were nasty to another child, if you were spiteful – that was a Temptation. And if no grown-up found out about it – God knew.'

Ann began saying her prayers at bedtime from the age of three or four, supervised at first by her grandmother and later by her mother: a nightly ritual that was carried out until Ann and her parents went to live in Singapore. They started to acquire some meaning after she read a book called *If Jesus Came to my House*. 'The story had a little chap who used to say, "If Jesus came to my house he would share all his toys" . . . and ends up with Jesus inviting you into His house, the church.'

This awareness of an indescribable Higher Being grew out of Ann's family heritage and evangelical upbringing. She was brought up in a practising Protestant household, but the Widdecombe family boasted an impressive variety of religious backgrounds: her Anglican father had a brother who was a Church of England vicar, while her mother was a Baptist born to a Baptist mother and Roman Catholic father. Rita and Murray were married in an Anglican church and baptized both Ann and her brother, Malcolm, as Anglicans. Malcolm, ten years older than Ann, became a Church of England canon of the evangelical and Pentecostal persuasion, and was to be a significant influence on her religious development.

Ann studied the Bible from an early age. At first, she read just a few verses at a time, and not 'great chapters', but the knowledge accumulated. 'If you keep doing that and you're being taught Scripture and you're being taken regularly through the major parts of the Bible, you very quickly get them. I was extremely familiar with the Bible.'

The daily ritual of prayers and Bible readings prepared her for regular Sunday attendance at church with her parents. She sometimes went twice, once in the morning and once in the afternoon. She also went to Sunday school with the local children. 'All my life until I went away to boarding school, I went to church and Sunday school, unless I was ill. When I was about eleven, these Sunday services were no longer compulsory and I had the choice. I can remember one Sunday when there was something on television I wanted to watch, I said to my mother, "No, I'm not going with you today, I'm going to watch television." She very wisely said, "All right, if you prefer doing that." And, of course, I felt as guilty as anything – I had been given the choice, it was left to me. My parents didn't put pressure on me, they went off to church, but I was left feeling guilty. I never did it again.'

When Ann returned from Singapore and was reunited with her brother, her religious development attained an evangelical element. Malcolm, now aged eighteen, was deeply committed to the evangelical movement and sought to interest his sister in it. He remembers his young sister clearly making her personal religious commitment at a service to which he took her – though Ann herself recalls the occasion a little differently. 'Malcolm took me to an evangelical service in Tunbridge Wells. The practice is that at the end of a mission service you are invited to come forward to commit yourself to Christ. Now, I can't actually remember going up, but I do remember very specifically being asked if I was going to ask the Lord Jesus into my heart. And I said, "Yes."

'I was surrounded by strangers that expect you to say, "Yes, please," and "No, thank you," so when you're asked a question beginning with *nonne* rather than *num* (the Latin words for questions which either expect the answers 'yes' or 'no' respectively) then you're going to say, "Yes"! And although for a long time after that event I would have said, "This is the moment of my commitment," I now take a different view. But for Malcolm, as an evangelical, that was the moment at which I committed myself to Christ.'

The only knowledge Ann had of Roman Catholicism before she went to the convent school was the little that her mother passed on to the child, gained from Rita's own father. 'My first experience of Roman Catholicism was during two terms at the prep school in the lead-up to going to La Sainte Union de Sacré Coeur Convent in Bath. I was ten, and I remember asking my mother, "What are Catholics?" and she replied, "They worship the Virgin Mary." That was my mother's definition of Catholicism. It was all I knew of what to expect of Catholicism. It was completely different from anything that I had known and, of course, I was being taught at home that it was wrong.'

At the preparatory school Ann learnt quickly that the religious practice and knowledge she had acquired as a Protestant were different from the practice and teaching of Catholicism: 'I remember being very surprised by it all, being aware that at home I was taught that certain things were wrong. You didn't pray to saints, which [at the Convent] we spent all our time doing. Certain things were believed to be superstitious. You shouldn't have idols – 'statues' as they called them at school – and I didn't know what the rosary was. We were also taught doctrine. In my very first experience of this, the nuns talked of this funny thing called "extra munction". It was some time before I realized this was "extreme unction", the last rites. I hadn't a clue. To me it was Chinese.

'I became aware, only very gradually, that Christianity was actually split right down the middle. It was something that later was to have a massive impact on my life.'

In the senior school, as a boarder, Ann experienced two changes to her religious learning. First, the doctrine was replaced by Scripture as an O-level subject; and secondly, non-Catholic and Catholic students were segregated for religious instruction. 'The nuns thought of the non-Catholics as "heretics" back then. The Catholic group were being steeped in doctrine for something they called the Bishop's Exam and our learning was the sort of Scripture that I had known all my life. I did extremely well – always came first – because I knew the Bible, and enjoyed that. But the practice was still something completely different. We prayed every morning to the Guardian Angel, to the Virgin Mary, all the angels and saints, sang hymns about great St Joseph, spouse of Mary, "In our death shades be thou nigh," all that sort of stuff.'

Segregation of Catholics and non-Catholics included having to attend separate churches on Sundays. Non-Catholic students at the Convent were obliged to take part in the Catholic service of mass, but they were excluded from taking communion and from confession, while Roman Catholics were forbidden from attending churches of other Christian denominations. 'In those days Catholics could not go into non-Catholic churches without getting a dispensation. Meanwhile, as non-Catholics we had to take part in the Catholic mass, although not the communion, obviously. At 6.30 a.m., three days a week, I got up and went to mass, and again at 7.30 a.m. on a Sunday. And we said the Angelus, a list of prayers, every midday and had to take part in the rosary every Saturday night. I just kept losing my rosary beads quite deliberately – down the back of the piano and in all sorts of places. We also had to participate in the Benediction every Friday morning.

'As boarders, we prayed in the morning when we got up. The nun would walk in saying, "Great St Joseph," and we had to say, "Pray for us." And if you didn't, because you were still asleep, she would stand at the end of your bed saying, in her strong Irish accent, "Great St Joseph," until someone responded in the required way. In the evening you also prayed. You prayed twice at meals, before and after the meal, including a prayer for the "faithful departed". The whole thing, from morn until night, was based around Catholicism, its constant prayer and practice.'

Ann's upbringing had led her to see Catholicism as an alien creed, and its ritual as dubious, but as she learnt more about it, and met more of its practitioners, she became increasingly impatient, and upset, with the barriers that Catholics erected against Anglicans, and vice versa. 'What I did absorb, albeit I think almost subconsciously, was that our creed was the same, our Bible was the same, our Lord's Prayer was the same, albeit ours contained the line "For thine is the Kingdom" . . . There was a great deal that was the same. Because I set my face against it, I never sat down and translated the Latin mass – it was all in Latin in those days. But had I done so I would have recognized the extreme closeness to that of our communion service.

'But underneath it all, I did develop an impatience with the war between the two churches. One nun I can remember at school one day, asked in the course of religious instruction – I was regarded as having knowledge of these things for some reason – "Does your church believe in The Holy Ghost?" And I thought, "I just don't believe it; you've got here a teacher of religious instruction who doesn't actually realize that the fundamental beliefs of both Churches are exactly the same."

'On another occasion I heard an evangelical preacher say that the Catholics believe that Mary was divine. They don't. I would hear such falsities, and total lacks in understanding, on both sides of that big wall that was undeniably there pre-Vatican Two. I think that did have an effect on me. Because I used to get quite stroppy about it. "There's more that unites us than divides us." That realization was growing.'

Ann transformed that realization into a short story, called *The Huguenot*. Here roles and religious observance overlap, and barriers between Protestants and Catholics are far less substantial than they at first appear to be. In the story, a Huguenot on the run from the Catholics prays for protection in a Protestant household. Helen Williams, Ann's Convent friend, recalled the story: 'The Catholics search the house in which he takes refuge, and he is not found. As he departs, the young woman of the house drops something into his pocket, then holds back his hand so that he cannot know what it is. When he gets out into the light of the moon, the Huguenot finds a rosary – so, in fact, a Catholic had saved him! I'm not sure what this story says about Ann's religious allegiances, although it could mirror something about the two religions being played out in Ann's own life.'

The story provides early evidence not only of Ann's religious awareness, but also of her facility for exploring contradictory circum-stances and roles. When Helen heard Ann recounting the story, she was struck by its open-mindedness. 'It surprised me that she understood where we were coming from. There wasn't in her what I found in some evangelicals, who don't really think things through, but end up with a prejudice.'

Once Ann entered the sixth form, the school regulations permitted students to leave the Convent grounds on Sundays and go out on their own after their midday meal. This was the opportunity Ann had been waiting for: 'This allowed me the freedom to attend the Bath Abbey afternoon service. More than ever, I became very entrenched in what I had grown up to believe, because persecution frequently enhanced devotion. And so I became fixed in my belief. What I believed in and did not believe in was straightforward: I believed the creed and from a Protestant angle; I did not believe in invocation of the saints; and I did not believe in anything of Catholicism that I found superstitious.

'I believed in a God – a Supreme Being of infinite goodness – who was very close and had an ear available. For me, there were two great forces, which I still believe: good and evil struggling against each other, both in a global sense and in individual psyches. God is good, and the Devil is bad. I believed that; so did every Catholic in the school.'

In her final year at the Convent, the American evangelist Billy Graham and his religious 'crusades' started to inspire Ann Widdecombe: 'We talked about him a lot at school and we were very excited by his crusade to Britain. I knew he was on at Earl's Court and I was determined to go.' Ann was at home at that time and, for the first time, she travelled to London on her own, and in the evening. 'Because all my companions were Catholics, I had to go on my own. He was fantastic! And I was hugely moved, although I can no longer remember the content.'

That last year of school and relative religious freedom ultimately rewarded Ann's struggle to remain true to her beloved Church of England. Having lived through seven years of a strict and ritualistically religious convent life, Ann Widdecombe was confirmed an Anglican in Bath Abbey. She invited her headmistress and her Latin mistress to celebrate that occasion. 'We had a big discussion about it, so that it was not inconceivable that they might have come to an occasion like that. I think if I'd been conscious enough to identify it at the time, the church had already started moving while I was there, and that I actually lived through a period when the churches had begun to consider talking to each other.' But, although Ann's mistresses acknowledged her religious commitment to non-Catholicism with a cake, both declined to attend her confirmation into her Protestant faith.

In 1966, when Ann went up to the University of Birmingham to study for her first degree, one of the first things she did was to join the University Evangelical Christian Union and participate in its Saturday evening meetings. She lived in at Mason Hall and for three

years participated in its morning prayer and weekly Bible study
groups; sometimes these meetings were held in Ann's room. 'My
worship was concentrated on St Stephen's Church, which is where
the evangelicals went, and with the Birmingham University
Evangelical Christian Union (BUECU). In the whole of my time at
Birmingham I had nothing to do with Catholicism. It didn't cross my
path.'

The Pentecostal movement began to grow while Ann was at
Birmingham, and she became involved – as did her brother Malcolm,
at the church to which he was attached in Bristol. 'The whole
business of speaking in tongues and making prophecies started to
happen and the movement took hold. There were fierce debates
among evangelicals in Mason Hall as to whether this phenomenon
was of God or not. There was a strong Pentecostal group that
believed it absolutely was and other groups that believed it was
wrong. We still managed to function as an evangelical group for three
years.'

She also had another chance to see the American evangelicals in
action – and this time to assist in the missionary activity. 'There was a
Billy Graham mission during this time relayed on screen in
Birmingham, and I went along. I used to take part in counselling
those people who came forward to commit to Christ. We would give
out leaflets and spread the word, although I was never one of those
who stood on a soapbox and yelled.'

When Ann left Birmingham for Oxford University, she was still
an enthusiastic evangelical: 'I never remember thinking, "This doesn't
feel right." I was an evangelical right up to the last moment.' But by
the time she got to Oxford some three months later, the fervour of
her upbringing had lost its hold, and the period of her loss of faith
had begun. This coincided with a period of general transition, when
many of her previous assumptions were challenged. Ann's devotion to
work at the Convent and in Birmingham meant she had exposed
herself to little of the surrounding social and other trends. But her life
at Oxford was quite different: here she deliberately relaxed, did less
academic work and set about absorbing the best of university life. Her

exposure to Oxford students who were unbelievers or at best lapsed Christians led her to question her own beliefs. Her changing personal circumstances, and in particular her romance with Colin Maltby, a lapsed Christian who called himself a 'theist', was another contributory factor.

'I started to do things I hadn't done before. I joined the Oxford University Christian Union, I didn't join the Bible group. I don't think that was an accident. I accepted a card and put it on my mantelpiece so that I knew about meetings, but I was consciously looking for time to breathe and to cogitate and review – I think. I still wanted breathing space. I don't believe in great psychological analysis, but somewhere something was saying, "I just want to stand back from this a bit." '

Malcolm saw this process at Oxford in a quite different and more severe light. 'Much to her dismay she found a lot of the Christians at Oxford were "a load of wets". She began a period of agnosticism. It's one of our family jokes that she came to stay with me at our old vicarage at the time. I had a meeting to go to, and Meryl (my wife) had a meeting to go to. Ann offered to look after the children and said, "I could read them their bedtime story and their Bible story and say prayers." And I said, "Yes, you could start your prayer off with 'God, who mayest be there . . .' " '

Although Ann continued to be involved in Christian activities in the first year at Oxford – she assisted with a mission in her college and hosted a resident missionary and some students – her absolute commitment was not so great. University politics and debating were taking up more time, and her enthusiasm for religious matters absorbed her less. She recalled: 'I still went to church, I still prayed, I still read the Bible, although probably not every day.' She also took part in a debate on a motion which read: 'If you want to smell fresh air, don't go to church' at Oxford University's Edmund Burke Society. 'I very strongly took the side of the Church, and Almighty God.'

Widdecombe called this period the start of 'a gradual erosion' of her commitment to Christianity and her relationship with God. But she still held back from full-blooded atheism. 'I was never prepared to say there is no God – I think that is a supreme arrogance, I don't know how anybody can prove that. But I was not prepared, at that stage, even to say, "I do not know whether God exists." When I did come to agnosticism, I also never said that God might not exist. Rather, I took the pure agnostic position that "Man can have no knowledge of anything beyond material phenomena." '

In spite of her ensuing loss of belief in Christianity, she appeared to retain a belief in good being divine, and the devil as the force of temptation. Her pursuit of the good was unshakeable, even while she engaged in a struggle with her religious belief. So she eschewed 'the humanist line' – as avidly if it were some wishy-washy form of socialism – even as her faith wavered.

Malcolm, who was by this stage an ordained priest of the evangelical persuasion, with his own parish of Holy Trinity in St Philips, Bristol, did not disguise his disapproval of this trend in his sister's spiritual life. Ann: 'My family always thought it was a terrible thing that I had been influenced by Oxford. I don't think so at all. I just needed the space as a matter of reflection and I took the opportunity of those three years, initially probably without even realizing it, to take stock. I did not become an agnostic at Oxford, but I did cease to be an evangelical.'

The period of loss of faith was as painful as it was inevitable, and she likened it to the break-up of a marriage. 'There are very few people who have actually been through that who could say to you, "One moment happened and then I divorced." I mean, if you suddenly meet with a great betrayal that's probably true. But if a relationship is deteriorating, there are very few people who could say, "Yeah, that was the moment – nothing before and nothing after." '

Over the next six or seven years, Ann went through a period of doubt and uncertainty. She oscillated almost daily between 'being a Christian' and 'not being certain' of her faith. 'Within the periods of becoming agnostic and then again becoming a Christian, there would have been days when I said, "Of course I'm a Christian," and the next day, "I don't think so," and the next day, "Of course I'm a Christian."

It's like saying, "Of course I'm still going to be married," and "Actually, I don't think I am."

'Human beings do not sit down and rationalize their lives and wake up one morning and say, "I have now rationalized this." You don't act like that; you get to things by degrees. I've got to most of my convictions by degrees.

'I never held to the belief that we have all the solutions within us and all we have to do is to become better people to sort out the whole wide world – tosh! But I would have taken the line that said, "Yes, there is good and evil but it doesn't follow that they're God and the devil." Those forces do exist but we create them and other things such as illness and disease – we create those forces. Beyond material phenomena we have no knowledge. That was my position absolutely. And I went to church only as invited.'

These doubts and loss of conviction were undoubtedly partly the result of a private need to stand back from her assumptions and inheritance. But events in the wider Anglican Church were also a contributory factor. At the time when Ann was looking for spiritual leadership, she saw a church which was mired in its own doubts about some fundamental Christian tenets. She could not understand how the church could make a bishop of Hugh Montefiore, who had just claimed that Jesus could have been a homosexual. Much later she despaired when Bishop David Jenkins questioned fundamental tenets such as the resurrection and the virgin birth. The absence of leadership was as transparent as it was crippling.

'I took considerable interest in what the church was doing. I watched the Bishop of Durham with horror. I used to get personally affronted when the General Synod came up with stupid decisions, as though I was still an active member of the church. Even at the point where I had no time for it, when the Anglican Church was doing or saying things I did not approve of, I was quite affronted.'

There was as much mystery and imprecision about Ann's return to Christianity as there was about her leaving it. Of one thing she was sure. The re-finding of her faith was slow and painful. 'Coming out of my wanderings in the spiritual wilderness was painful. More painful, because I didn't notice the "going out", which was gradual. Coming back to my faith was quicker, and it was painful, because I didn't admire the church that I was coming back to, I had started to despise the Anglican Church, that's the truth of it – all those endless compromises; I had also started to admire Rome. But at that time I could not face Rome because of the doctrinal reservations I had, the superstition I still saw in much of Roman practice. My roots were Anglican but I didn't admire what I saw. It was that, that was painful. And as I've said many times, it would have saved an awful lot of hoo-ha if I'd come back to the Roman Catholic Church.'

An interest in Roman Catholicism was triggered when she saw her old Convent school chum, Helen Williams, taking final vows to become a Catholic nun. Ann was impressed by the changes that had taken place in Roman Catholic Church practice since her schooldays. 'There appeared a huge turnaround in ritual within the church between my leaving the Convent and now, a period of about five or more years.

'That service for Helen could have been an evangelical Anglican service. They were playing guitars, it was all in English, not in Latin, and the priest had his face to the people. I went through Bath Convent with the priest with his back to the congregation for the whole of the service. It was a shock. I couldn't believe these types of rituals had turned around.'

Slowly but surely, Ann's faith returned. 'I am unable to explain why my faith returned to me. But it did. It came by degrees, it was gradual. There was no flash in the night, no one event. There were moments when I found myself reading the Bible, almost to my own surprise. It came gradually and I didn't resist it. It was neither an emotional nor an intellectual occasion. It was an entirely spiritual thing. When I came back, that was it. I became convinced.'

Ann found herself vacillating over important issues such as the existence of an afterlife for quite some time. 'I remember that I was not convinced by the existence of a personal afterlife. I can remember that. When I came into Parliament at thirty-nine and a half. But I was vaguely practising again – vaguely.'

NINE

A New Member, a New Crusade

ANN Widdecombe does not recall the moment when the returning office at Maidstone announced her victory. But she remembers the champagne corks popping at the count, and then at the campaign headquarters until the early hours. It was 1987, and Ann had been elected to the safe seat of Maidstone in Kent with a vote of 29,100 and a strong majority of 10,364. Hyperbole and big statements were not her style, but she was excited beyond words when she addressed the waiting supporters. 'I knew that, barring huge catastrophes, I had a seat for ever, so long as I looked after it properly. It was a very big moment. But I didn't go in for anything Churchillian at the speech. It was "Thank God for that. It's done and dusted, but isn't it wonderful." '

Ann was 'thirty-nine and a half' at the time, and for thirty of those years she had been looking forward to this moment. The dream had endured through the dark days of the Convent, when she had argued for the Conservative side with her friend Helen Williams. At Birmingham, as she had listened to Churchill's speeches on record, she had filled her mind with images of the House of Commons. She had touched the cloth of successful parliamentarians at Oxford, and had so impressed Richard Crossman that he predicted she would be the first Conservative female chief whip. Then, such a prospect had seemed almost impossibly remote; but in those heady days, she must have thought anything could be possible.

She put her two abortive election attempts down to experience.

Burnley in 1979 had been unwinnable, and she had not been too
disappointed at the result. The outcome of the Plymouth Devonport
election in 1983 was less clear-cut, and some regret lingered; but that,
along with every other failure and disappointment, could at last be
put behind her. Now she was determined to put her very individual
mark on the hallowed place she was about to enter.

When the selection panel at Maidstone interviewed her they
hoped she had the potential to be another Margaret Thatcher. The
local party were still smarting from their failure to select the real
thing back in 1959. They felt they now would look doubly silly if
they rejected the able, vocal and passionate woman in front of them,
and she went on to greatness. So the constituency followed their gut
instincts, and Ann Widdecombe was given a seat which, barring
catastrophe, would bring her comfortably into Westminster when
Margaret Thatcher decided to call an election.

But Widdecombe's relationship with the local party was not the
easiest at the beginning of the eighteen-month run-up to the 1987
election. Some prominent members griped that the candidate did not
have a house in the constituency. Ann did not want to cause any
upset and rented a small cottage in the village of Staplehurst, but it
was an expense and inconvenience she found hard to bear, as her
London living arrangements were far from simple. After the fourth
attempt to sell Fulham and buy elsewhere fell through, she took the
first offer for Fulham, and bided her time to make a purchase. Ann
put her cats into a cattery and her furniture into store, and went back
to her parents' house, while she looked for somewhere. In the end,
she found a safe and secure property near the House of Commons, in
the Kennington area of central London, just across the Thames from
Westminster. Fortuitously, the four-room flat she bought in April
1986 from the Duchy of Cornwall was also well situated for the drive
out to the Kent constituency.

Ann took advantage of Maidstone's accessibility from Kennington
to nurse the constituency diligently, to the point where she was able
to silence critics who said she was an absentee candidate by showing
them she had attended 200 events there in a single year. The press

were less easily placated. Local papers were bored with the Conservatives and preferred the Liberal candidate, a charismatic barrister called Christopher Sutton-Maddocks. A flurry of polls at the end of the campaign pointing to a surprise Liberal victory sent a shiver through Conservative ranks, and Ann found herself having to chivvy her troops in a way unthinkable at her two previous elections. A natural caution deterred her from giving notice to her employers at London University until the election process was complete, and she had a new 'job' to go to. As soon as she won, of course, giving notice would be the first thing she did.

Caution turned to euphoria at the general election on 11 June 1987, when Ann Widdecombe won her seat with a greatly increased majority. So eager was she to 'feel the green leather under her posterior' (as she would put it to supporters) that she and a fellow Kent MP, Jacques Arnold, visited the House of Commons before Parliament had resumed after the election and sat on the benches. In those initial halcyon weeks she asked Virginia Bottomley, by this stage an experienced parliamentarian, to guide her round the byzantine corridors, restaurants, ladies' loos and obscure customs of the House of Commons. Not too long afterwards, she would meet Bottomley in less harmonious circumstances.

When Ann arrived at Westminster for the first working day, she found herself sharing an office with Gillian Shephard, who had had a successful career in local government before moving with ease into a safe constituency in Norfolk. The contrast between her career and Widdecombe's would soon be evident as Shephard raced up the ranks. In fact the two women already knew each other slightly. They had met shortly before the 1987 election, at a meeting for candidates at Number Ten hosted by Margaret Thatcher. Passing by each other in the 'splendid' ladies' loo (as Shephard recalls), they started talking about themselves and their hopes and fears for a parliamentary career. Shephard remembers Ann saying, ' "I have wanted to do this since I was nine years old." It was very precise, it wasn't "since I was a child", it was "since I was nine". I thought, "This is a serious woman." ' Shephard was surprised how casually Ann referred to her previous

work at the University of London; it was in stark contrast to
Shephard's own professional self-confidence, which was to ensure her
quick rise to Cabinet level.

MPs' facilities in the House of Commons at the time were
extremely cramped, and sharing offices could mean sharing desks,
tables and chairs. So Shephard got a very strong and quick sense of
Ann's working style, and could not fail to observe that it was both
very enthusiastic and 'very disorganized'. 'There was a lot going on at
once. But she was very positive, very enthusiastic.' The room reverberated with Ann's haranguing of hospital administrators to find beds
for her constituents, recalls Shephard – aware, perhaps, of the contrast
with her own more cerebral style.

Widdecombe had to plan her maiden speech, an event most MPs
dread and seek to put behind them as quickly as possible. But, with a
sang-froid that Parliament would grow to admire in the new woman
member, Widdecombe delayed hers until she could speak on the
subject which concerned her and her colleagues at Women and
Families for Defence, namely the importance of Trident missiles. This
issue would not come up until the discussion of defence budgets, in
October; but Widdecombe decided it was worth the wait. When the
time came and she delivered her speech, she was congratulated
afterwards by David Owen, a former Labour defence minister, and by
her father, who had come up to London to watch his daughter in
action. As a former Admiralty official, he would also have appreciated
the subject and the tone of the speech. The only hitch came with
vociferous interruptions from two Scottish members – who later
apologized, saying that the speech was 'so good they had not realized
it was a maiden speech'.

By the time Ann had made her maiden speech she was already
busying herself with a subject much closer to her heart, and one
which would occupy her for the next three years. This was abortion.
The subject presented itself when David Alton, a Liberal MP who
had won third place in the members' ballot and thus the chance to
introduce a private member's bill, announced that his measure would
deal with the period during which it was permitted to have an

abortion, aiming to restrict it to the earliest weeks of pregnancy. Here was an issue to which she could devote her energies and emotion wholeheartedly; it would enable her to stake her claim to a moral high ground, and, most importantly, it would give her the vehicle that the new backbencher needs to gain prominence in the House and so win the attention of senior members of the party. Arguably the campaign would become almost too successful, and lead to Widdecombe being identified as a troublemaker whom the government could not trust to hold a big post – but that stage was some way off.

Abhorrence of abortion had been a fundamental tenet of Widdecombe's beliefs since her teens. The Anglican in the Catholic school had absorbed that element of the foreign teaching even as she had rebelled against Catholic practice. Widdecombe's view, based on her reverence for innocent life, was straightforward: 'I just grow more and more appalled. The conscience of the nation is deadened. We can't see those babies, therefore we throw away life as an unnecessary inconvenience.' The emotional repugnance at abortion became translated into a political conviction. She, along with her friends in the 'moral lobby', saw abortion getting easier, and they put that down to the march of permissive liberalism that was undermining society's old values, especially that of an individual's responsibility for his or her actions. Widdecombe had her crusade at last; and she wrote to Alton pledging her wholehearted support, and asking how she could help.

But Alton, a Catholic of Irish immigrant extraction, and the youngest member of the House of Commons when he was elected in 1979, had had enough cranks harassing him over the years, and the last thing he wanted was another embarrassingly over-enthusiastic devotee who might damage his cause. So he did not give her the response she hoped for, but replied in formal terms, suggesting that she contact Sir Bernard Braine, the Conservative Father of the House and the leading Tory supporter of his abortion measure. Widdecombe did as she was bid, but in due course made contact with Alton again. This time the two formed an alliance, of both a professional and personal kind, that was to endure. Indeed, Ann Widdecombe would later become the godmother to one of Alton's children.

Alton had staked his claim to a place in the history of abortion law as early as 1980, when he had proposed a limit to the first twenty-four weeks of pregnancy. This represented a significant tightening of the 1967 Abortion Act – sponsored, ironically, by Alton's then boss, David Steel MP – which had set the limit at twenty-eight weeks. Since then efforts had been made to bring the cut-off point down to twenty weeks. Enoch Powell, an early hero of Widdecombe's, had participated in the process, introducing the Unborn Children (Protection) Bill 1985, which sought to prevent the production of embryos for pure scientific research. Alton's proposed change on his return to the fray in 1988, a deadline of eighteen weeks, was a major jump, based on the view that advancing medical science would assist premature foetuses to survive from ever earlier ages. Widdecombe: 'We said the future is coming down, you've got to provide for the future as well as for the present.'

Bernard Braine laid all Alton's doubts about his new and fervent supporter to rest. He saw Widdecombe's value as both a passionate believer in the Alton proposal and as a woman who was prepared to be vocal in support of it, and suggested to the Speaker that he might call her for the second reading debate. He did so, and her contribution in turn impressed Alton, who invited her to be a 'teller', or counter of the votes for her side of the argument. This was Widdecombe's initiation into parliamentary procedure. 'I hadn't a clue what telling involved. Anyway I did it. I was actually reading out the results, because he wanted a woman's voice reading the results.' In the teeth of the opposition of all four party leaders, the bill passed the second reading, winning 296 votes – the largest number of votes for any Private Member's Bill since the Second World War, boasted Alton.

Media interest in the abortion issue was intense, and the 'pro-life' lobby faced great demand for public comment. Ann Widdecombe's value as a woman on their side was quickly recognized by the campaign, and in time she became not merely its chief whip and coordinator but also a spokeswoman with a steady flow of rhetoric and quotes. She was the fourth member of a group of Tory MPs at the hub of the anti-abortion campaign; the other three were David Amess, Ken Hargreaves and Bernard Braine. However, being the anti-abortion expert for the media also brought its problems, as Widdecombe started to be seen by other MPs, and by ministers, as a 'single issue politician' – a threat to her promotion prospects, and a label of which she would later struggle to rid herself.

The group were bound together by much more than the abortion issue. All were hostile to what they saw as the rash of permissive social policy measures passed in the 1960s, and subsequent efforts at social and scientific engineering. So they opposed medical experimentation with embryos and human body parts. They demurred on extending rights to homosexuals, abhorred easy divorce and supported the re-introduction of capital punishment. Amess explained, 'We think that life is sacrosanct, life should be preserved at the conceivable stage. You say   everything you can to preserve life. We believed that restoring capital punishment would save lives. We believe having that overall threat there, it would stop not everyone, but then not everyone's mad who commits murder, but it would stop some people murdering. That's our belief.'

The majority of sympathizers with the campaign, particularly on abortion, came from the Conservative back benches, but there were a number of frontbench supporters too, including like John Patten and Chris Patten, John Gummer and Tristan Garel-Jones (though a number of years later, Garel-Jones revised his opinion on abortion, taking a more liberal view). Ranged against this group of moral campaigners was a government that was more interested in making its mark with economic measures than with ethical ones. Abortion was certainly not on their list of priorities, as Mrs Thatcher and Kenneth Clarke (the Secretary of State for Health) told Widdecombe directly. Virginia Bottomley, the health minister, felt that the group was anti-rationalist and high-handed. 'I felt some of them [the pro-lifers] were fairly obsessed. I found their strong religious convictions slightly difficult. I'm an Anglican. But I've also spent many years working in the inner city and know just how difficult people's lives can be. My interpretation of the Christian perspective was more forgiving and tolerant. You should not deprive women of the opportunity of exercising their judgement.'

The progress of Alton's bill was marked by internecine warfare in the House of Commons, which again raised Widdecombe's profile, but made her no friends. Tory was pitched against Tory while the Labour and Liberal parties were almost universally opposed to the measure – with the notable exception, of course, of Alton himself. Widdecombe recalls: 'A whole host of tactics were then brewed up, in which people tried to delay us getting in to committee, we tried to pre-empt other bills getting through in time. A huge tactical battle went on.' After her second reading speech which impressed Alton and the anti-abortionists, Widdecombe joined the standing committee of MPs that would examine the bill. By now Alton knew he had a stalwart supporter. 'I was quite pleased to see Ann's name there, because I then realized that she could handle herself, and that she would be a doughty ally.'

The presence of a woman would also counter the claim that his side was misogynistic; and Widdecombe would be used to present the case to the growing band of protesting women in the House and the country. Alton: 'It was good that this was not just seen as a collection of misogynists, who were somehow hostile to women's rights, or something of that kind. There were some very formidable women who supported my bill, and Ann was chief among them.' Widdecombe leapt at the opportunity to round on the women's movement, and its champions like Germaine Greer, and to voice her belief that women should make their own way, without positive discrimination or special privileges, just as she had.

While the women's movement believed women should have the right to choose to have an abortion or not, Widdecombe believed that abortion was absolutely wrong, and made no secret of her private belief that there were no circumstances in which an abortion could be justified, except perhaps in the most extreme case possible, when giving birth would result in the mother's death. But the abortion debate produced issues that tested Widdecombe's straightforward view. The bill's treatment of the disabled foetus was particularly complex, and quickly put the anti-abortionists on to the defensive. Widdecombe was reluctant to accept disablement as grounds for abortion, but was persuaded that, if a pragmatic approach enabled them to win a tightening of the time limit in the law, a concession could be justified. Widdecombe argued for the compromise on grounds of statistics and probabilities: 'We felt that to make an exemption for the handicapped would be to rat on our most basic principles – a handicapped child has as much right to life as anybody else. But we found when we examined the statistics that after the eighteenth week, only 8 per cent were actually aborted for handicap. The other 92 per cent were for completely different reasons. I was one of those who said, "If you had a shipwreck and there were a hundred people on board and you could only pull off ninety-two, you wouldn't just stand back and let the whole ship go down because you couldn't save the other eight – you'd pull off your ninety-two." So I said, "If we're going to lose this bill unless we make this concession – we had better make it." So we made it, and we exempted the handicapped.'

The group accepted handicap as grounds for late abortion, but still arrogated to themselves the right to oppose publicly the principle of abortion under any circumstances. This sowed confusion in the ranks of potential supporters who either could not believe that the concession had been made, or else found it hypocritical. The decision to give out two different messages was later seen by Widdecombe as a mistake: 'It was something of a tactical error. It was actually quite hard getting the message over to people that we had made that exemption. A lot of people had made their votes dependent on it. It was clear that there were people who weren't going to vote for us unless we made the exemption for the handicapped.'

One of those who took a sceptical view of the pro-lifers' zeal was Margaret Thatcher herself; when the Conservative Pro-Life lobby met her en masse, they found her preoccupied with the difficult issue of abortion of the handicapped foetus. It was later said that she favoured reduction of the limit to twenty-four weeks, on the grounds that that was the earliest point at which a foetus could be viable outside the womb.

As the bill went through the committee stage, its proposers, backed by the Society for the Preservation of the Unborn Child (SPUC) and other pressure groups, triggered an intense debate throughout the country. Extreme feelings were aroused when opponents of abortion used highly disturbing visual images, such as photographs of aborted or dying foetuses (which continue to adorn Widdecombe's office to the present day) to show the horror of abortion. Penny Kemp, Green candidate for the Maidstone constituency in the 1987 general election, remembered how Ann Widdecombe stirred up an audience with photographs of a dying foetus, and then used the issue to diminish her opponent. When Kemp sought to argue both against abortion and in favour of euthanasia (another issue on which Widdecombe has strong hostile feelings, and a theme of her novel *The Clematis Tree*), she riposted, with a particularly black put-down: 'See, not only does she want to murder your babies, she wants to murder your grannies as well.'

The double-act of Widdecombe and Alton met every sort of hostility, but they had their lines prepared to deal with it. They made abortion the issue of the moment, and became linked as hate figures in a way neither could have expected. Alton recalls the *esprit de corps* that grew between them: 'When people are literally haranguing you and barracking you, and showering obscenities, it tends to unite those who are standing together. Otherwise we might not have had a great deal in common.'

Hecklers at a public meeting at Goldsmiths College in London targeted Widdecombe with particularly virulent abuse. When one woman shouted that she had had an abortion and it hadn't done her any harm, Widdecombe replied, 'Are you sure about that?' This retort, said Alton, had 'quite a devastating effect. It was not a personally nasty remark, but it forced this young woman to ask a question of herself. Why was she in this state, if it had had no effect on her?' The audience were not pacified, and the two speakers had to be rescued from the hall under a police escort.

Alton spoke with appreciation of his fellow campaigner's spirit. 'She was not a yuppy politician who was only good at giving a soundbite, or at a TV photocall or interview. She could stand up and make mincemeat of anyone who took her on.' Alton himself addressed an audience at Malcolm Widdecombe's church in Bristol, where the church was surrounded by protesters and he was stoned. Ann Widdecombe wrote in 1990, 'There have been very difficult moments during my stand on abortion in which I have been spat at, punched, kicked, had missiles thrown at me and been howled down, but I have never been put off standing up for what I believe in. That was an understatement, in fact. Ann Widdecombe relished nothing more than the opportunity to rout a foe – especially one from the women's movement!

While the issue reverberated round the country, the bill in the House of Commons was in difficulty. Unless a bill passes the stages of the legislative process in a single parliamentary session, it has to be dropped, and time was running out for Alton's bill. Only the government could save it, and this government showed no such inclination. Indeed, many were actively opposed to the bill and all its works. They saw its proponents as fundamentalists and its purpose as illiberal, and one leading government member was prepared to describe Widdecombe herself as 'nutty'. Alton: 'We approached Margaret Thatcher's government to give time for my bill, but they refused. Ann and I agreed that we could not leave the issue there. We wanted it either to be given the chance to be defeated on a free and fair vote in the House; or to proceed. We campaigned for that vigorously.' In due course parliamentary procedure ensured the bill was talked out.

But the moral crusade had to go on; the fighters for the purity of their consciences would not be vanquished. In Widdecombe's words, 'It was war!' In the autumn of 1988, Widdecombe took over the baton from Alton. She had come only seventh (out of twenty) in the private members' ballot that year and might easily have decided there was no chance of her bill proceeding. But Widdecombe found a way to use parliamentary tactics to promote her bill on abortion (which mirrored Alton's in calling for the reduction of the deadline from twenty-eight weeks to eighteen), even if it meant disrupting others. These have since been recognized as highly innovative, and Widdecombe was not reticent in appreciating the difficulty they caused: 'We had some particularly clever tactics. During that year I got whatever reputation I enjoy for having grasped parliamentary procedures.'

The parliamentary tactics she employed showed just how avidly this new woman on the parliamentary block had studied the arcane procedures of the House of Commons. Fellow members recalled her pestering and harassing the party whips for the latest development or twist in the timetable of the day, to ensure that she was up to the minute and on top of things. Amess: 'I can recall her getting involved in quite detailed conversations, you wouldn't say arguments, but all sorts of negotiations with government ministers like Ken Clarke and Norman Fowler.' Widdecombe described her blocking mechanism: 'I said, "Okay, we're seventh, we're not going to be able to get anywhere. So the first thing we have to do is to block off all the days that would be reserved for other bills for their second readings." Five of us presented pro-life bills and we blocked off five report stage days with a bill right at the top of every report stage day. So that when we got to that report stage day, any other bill which was coming in wasn't going to get looked at.

'The second thing we did was to set up a method of objecting to every single bill that came up on a Friday for second reading. The bills that aren't debated are taken forthwith, and if you shout "Object", they don't get a reading. So we divided it up, and the Conservative members of the pro-life group objected to the bills that came from the other side. And David Alton and crew objected to the bills that came through our side.'

The system worked efficiently, until a bill came along on a subject in which Tory backbenchers were really interested. This was press privacy, and it was promoted by John Browne, a Tory who had suffered at the hands of the press after failing to declare business interests. His Protection of Privacy Bill was popular among Conservatives, many of whom had no special love for the media at this time, so they were furious when the diehard pro-lifers showed no compunction about sacrificing Browne's bill at whatever cost to their own. Widdecombe: 'I went into the lobby to vote for his bill, and suddenly realized that we were getting very close to the number required for the Browne bill to go forward, which was a hundred. That would actually mean he could get a division and take his bill on to the next stage. We were up to about ninety-eight, so I left the lobby.

'This caused the most fantastic uproar. The supporters of his bill were understandably very bitter; they said they were going to withdraw support from our bill, and the most tremendous row ensued. It all calmed down in the end.' In fact Widdecombe and Alton were forced to drop their opposition to 'a backroom deal' to save Browne's bill, as one newspaper reported.

The guerrilla warfare continued the following year. When Widdecombe came top in the ballot for private members' motions, debated on Friday mornings, she found she had a means to take the abortion bill forward. In effect, she gave the business managers an ultimatum, threatening that there would be no end to the debate on this bill, until the House voted in favour of Widdecombe's bill having another reading. This flew in the face of the customary 2.30 p.m. cut-off time for bills of this kind, and could wreck Commons business. Widdecombe revelled in the shock it gave the government. 'There was uproar, of course, because if we got that we would have got our second reading. There was uproar, we had a majority and people knew we had a majority.'

Government business managers responded to this dirty tactic – used only once before when Enoch Powell had wanted to push through his own abortion measure in 1985 – with their own tactic. The announcement of a by-election is the only device which has priority over a private member's motion on a Friday morning. So, early one Friday morning in January 1989, when Widdecombe's motion was scheduled, the government arranged for Dennis Skinner to introduce the writ for the Richmond by-election – won, incidentally, by William Hague, the future leader of the Conservative Party. To talk out Widdecombe's motion Skinner filibustered for three hours on the vagaries of the Yorkshire weather. Even Widdecombe was impressed. 'It was a very clever piece of work, and he therefore busted our motion out completely.' There was some fall-out to Widdecombe's tactics on this occasion, as the Procedure Committee subsequently outlawed both the by-election device and the timeless business motion.

The anti-abortionists then picked on Skinner to punish him, and wrecked an adjournment debate he had called. These debates are held late at night, last no more than half an hour, and usually involve nothing more than a member putting his case and a minister replying. This occasion was very different. Skinner was not allowed to open his mouth before the wreckers got to work. Widdecombe described the disruptive process with gusto: 'So I said, "Right, we'll wreck that debate, doesn't matter what it's about, people wreck our business, so we'll show them, we'll wreck theirs." We amassed loads of people, mainly pro-lifers but also others who just wanted to see the fun.' The House was packed for the occasion.

First the pro-lifers raised points of order, until the Deputy Speaker stopped this tactic. Then they called: 'I spy strangers' – a device to exclude 'undesirable' individuals from the public gallery. On this occasion the only members of the public in the House were two researchers who had been posted by the pro-lifers to the gallery, normally empty at this time of night. The device required a time-consuming division, and, ironically, in order to ensure that a division took place, the pro-lifers supplied tellers for both sides.

The wrecking tactics went on as long as necessary to halt Skinner in his tracks. Widdecombe was a key player. 'They couldn't close down the division while we stayed in the lobby, so I just sat on the bench. Eventually I got up to walk out because I thought the fifteen minutes was up. When you come out, you have to say "All out" which means that everybody's out. And I didn't say it, and one of the whips said to me, "Are all out?" I said, "Oh, I'll just go and check". I knew damn well there was nobody in. It was absolute playtime but it made a point: We were serious, we were at war.'

The devious tactics caused havoc in the government, and upset some of its leading members. Tristan Garel-Jones, deputy chief whip at the time, noted much later: 'Given that the harridans were on the march on both sides of the fence, I found the harridans on the anti-abortion side – the Wintertons, Ann and all that lot – were on balance a more tiresome lot than Harriet Harman and Jo Richardson.' A damaging backlash was now building up in Parliament, and one paper reported the views of the government: 'Pigheadedness by cross-party backbench coalitions is preventing Parliament from doing its job . . . Those who abuse the Private Members' Bill procedure on both sides of the House should seek to behave more like legislators, less like crabby schoolchildren.' Exhortations to behave better aside, government patience was running out, and in late 1989 Garel-Jones gave the first sign of capitulation when he told Widdecombe: 'We know we've got to get this sorted otherwise we're going to have an abortion bill every year. The whole system's becoming infected by it. We must deal with this thing so that you can come to a vote.'

The government concession was to introduce abortion provisions into the Human Embryology and Fertilization bill, a piece of legislation following on from the Warnock Report on the use of foetal tissue in scientific and medical research. The bill called for a reduction in the cut-off date for abortion from twenty-eight weeks to twenty-four. This was not enough for the pro-lifers, who stuck to their target figure of eighteen weeks. The battle to seek the reduction produced (in Widdecombe's words) 'the most complex series of scenarios that had ever happened'.

The first skirmish was over the composition of the MPs' committee that would examine the bill. When the Leader of the House, Geoffrey Howe, appeared to renege on his promise to allow the committee's composition to reflect earlier votes in the Commons on abortion rather than the composition of the House, the pro-lifers (with just two seats) went on the attack. Widdecombe: 'We went potty. We had to run an unofficial opposition to combat the combined force of the "pro-choicers". It was a hopeless business. We felt that faith had been broken. It created quite a bad atmosphere.' Suspicions of government dirty tricks were fuelled by a civil servant, who told them under conditions of anonymity that he was 'worried about what was happening. He was very unhappy at the way the Department of Health were trying to manipulate the bill.'

To sting the government, the pro-lifers delayed government efforts to move the bill out of committee and back on to the floor of the House. They also demanded a meeting with their *bête noire,* Virginia Bottomley, the Minister of Health, whom they saw as a primary obstacle to their campaign. Widdecombe: 'We had one hell of a meeting. We took about quarter of an hour just to get the government to admit one point that we had maintained solidly throughout was true, which they were not admitting. Finally and eventually they admitted it.' The few friends Widdecombe still had left among her political masters quickly disowned her.

The eventual debate and subsequent voting on the abortion cut-off periods were predictably fraught. As she marshalled her troops, harried the government and chivvied the business managers, Widdecombe was in her element. Geoffrey Howe recalls: 'Ann was leading, as chief whip for the pro-life lobby. I remember her walking up and down the middle of the floor of the chamber during the complicated voting procedures and shouting out commands to her troops, like a sergeant major.' Bottomley, with a feminine eye for detail, saw Ann Widdecombe running around the floor of the House with a broken heel on one shoe. 'It was to do with tension – I had never seen someone going around the House of Commons with their heel fallen off.'

The tension arose largely from the technical complication of the unique voting procedures devised for the bill. Few parliamentarians on either side understood them (Widdecombe did, of course) and the pro-lifers produced a guide to explain them. Voting took place in several rounds, with MPs given the opportunity in each round to state their preference for a higher or a lower limit on the permitted term for abortion. The first choice was between twenty-eight weeks – the existing deadline and the most generous option available – and eighteen, the pro-lifers' target and the most restrictive proposal on the table. This was followed by a vote between twenty-six weeks and twenty, and between twenty-four and twenty-two. At this point, the pro-life lobby lost the vote, and although they claimed a majority of the House supported their preference for twenty-two, the House in fact voted for twenty-four weeks. The government's preferred outcome had triumphed, producing a massive disappointment for the pro-lifers.

The twenty-four-week cut-off date was not the only source of dismay to Widdecombe and her pro-life friends. They were also furious at the bill's extension of the permitted period for abortion for handicapped foetuses, from twenty-eight weeks right up to birth.

Widdecombe and her supporters blamed a technical error in the voting instructions, and said that Bottomley knew the mistake had been made but failed to tell them. The latent hostility between the two women came to the surface. 'Virginia had a copy of my whip two days beforehand, subsequently said that she had seen it, had spotted the error, but had thought she shouldn't interfere. And certainly at no point did she advise us on our procedures at all. She was actually very hostile throughout the whole proceedings.'

But Bottomley blamed Ann: 'Ann had got the wrong end of the stick about the amendments. I made sure that she was told this, because I felt it was part of the process of ensuring that the thing was done properly. I had been shown her briefing when she visited me at the Department of Health. I made clear that she should have this misunderstanding corrected. My legal advisers had shown me this, and I said that "It is important that her people are aware of this error in their interpretation," where others would have said, "I'm not on either side of this anyway, so go ahead." I didn't agree with the line she was taking but I wanted her to know.' It does seem rather odd that if Bottomley had indeed given this warning, which would fatally damage the pro-life case, Widdecombe would have simply ignored it.

Another blow was the loss, by the Speaker's casting vote, of a clause to require a child's handicap to be stated on the abortion form.

'The entire evening was ghastly,' recalled Widdecombe. Alton was a little more sanguine, saying: 'It was not as much as we had wanted, but we got something.' Widdecombe later wrote: 'We were not happy with the result. We had always known there was the risk we would have to put up with twenty-four weeks, but none of us was prepared when the House voted for abortion up to birth for disability or danger to the mother's health. That is totally unacceptable but there is no point us trying again in this parliament. We now have to educate the general public.'

The exhaustion and nervous tension of the occasion affected Widdecombe deeply. It was reported that she was distraught and visibly upset as she left the House by taxi.

Alton and Widdecombe continued to campaign against other parts of the Human Embryology and Fertilization Bill, such as its clause allowing scientists to experiment on human embryos for up to fourteen days – a point on which Bottomley again opposed her. When Alton and Widdecombe spoke at venues like the Royal Albert Hall and the Manchester Free Trade Hall, the barracking was ferocious. Then, at a meeting at Bradford, Widdecombe directed her scorn at a new and significant target. This was the liberalizing tendency in the Church of England. Alton recalls: 'Something else was clearly stirring in Ann's heart. She mocked in her most amusing way the then Archbishop of York, John Hapgood. He had spoken in favour of the right to experiment. Given Ann's intellect, it was going to become increasingly difficult for her as a committed Anglican, to remain in the Church of England.' The ground was clearly being prepared for her departure from the established church three years later, and her subsequent conversion to Catholicism.

While the government squirmed under the assault of the pro-lifers, the Conservative grass roots lapped it up. Friends and supporters flocked to Widdecombe's banner, and when she addressed a fringe meeting of the Conservatives' party conference in Blackpool in 1990, some two thousand people gave her a standing ovation. Her manner of speaking, with its evangelical tone, off-the-cuff delivery and walkabout style, gave a foretaste of the rousing 1998 conference speech which again brought the Conservative party to its feet. The signs of the rousing orator were there, even in these early days, and she was puzzled that she had not received the call from the party to give her a platform more often. 'After that, I told quite a lot of people, "If this is something I can do, the party really should use me much more." '

Yet the Thatcher government ensured that Widdecombe would go no further while she was the highly visible champion of the anti-abortion awkward squad. Amess explained: 'I suspect that initially some colleagues dismissed her as being a bit of a crank, eccentric and all of that, but it was impossible really to ignore her obvious talent.' Mrs Thatcher may well have shared this view. Frank Field, who served on the Social Security Select Committee with Ann Widdecombe and was impressed by her competence, once mentioned her in favourable terms to the Prime Minister. But Mrs Thatcher replied only that Ann's voting record was very high. This was indeed the case, as Widdecombe held the best voting record in the 1987/8 parliamentary year, with 98.4 per cent attendance, and was second the following year; but it was a mixed compliment, suggesting that Widdecombe had little else to contribute other than her votes.

Abortion was not the only target on which she riled the government. In February 1990 she led the first successful attack on the government of the day when she sought to force the social security system to pay the full cost of putting old people into private nursing homes. Ann was responding to the financial plight of a ninety-three-year-old constituent, Florence Smith, who had recently moved into a private nursing home only to discover that she could not afford to pay the difference between the charge levied by the home and the social security pay-out. To Ann's horror, Florence was at risk of having to go into an acute hospital bed. Some thirty-two other Tories followed Widdecombe into the Labour lobby and the government took a heavy blow. Gillian Shephard, Widdecombe's old room-mate, who had long since been promoted into the government and was above the backbench fray, regarded Ann's rebellion on this subject as 'simply magnificent', and could not understand the government's failure to recognize her talents. But many more staid male members were much less amused.

Reshuffles came and went, and each time Widdecombe became more frustrated at seeing her name excluded from the lists. By 1990, the more able members of the 1987 intake had made it on to the first rung of the ministerial ladder, but Widdecombe had signally failed to make any progress. She took her own soundings. 'I thought, "There is something very wrong here." And I talked to certain people and they said, "Well, you're seen as a single issue politician." ' Garel-Jones pinpointed other areas: 'It remains still true that it's slightly more difficult to get noticed if you're a woman, than if you're a man. The whips' office was aware of her as a campaigner on embryos and abortion. Whips are instinctively (as I am myself) wary of anyone who is a rabid campaigner. I think the combination of being a serious campaigner and a woman held her back.'

In due course Gillian Shephard, whose own progression had been meteoric by any standards, took up Ann's case and approached Tim Renton, the Chief Whip. 'Why are you wasting this excellent person?' she asked. Renton sniffed at the question's impertinence: 'If you think the Conservative Party is about the career development of colleagues, you're wrong.' Shephard was not impressed: 'I thought, "Stuff off." ' In fact, shortly afterwards, Widdecombe was appointed parliamentary private secretary to Tristan Garel-Jones, minister of state at the Foreign Office, an apparently friendly anti-abortionist who (at that time at least) would not have taken issue with her views on the subject. The appointment was greeted with some scepticism, remembers the Conservative MP Phillip Oppenheim. 'It was considered, in certain quarters, as an odd promotion. There was a feeling that she was being kicked upstairs because she was marginally awkward and this would shut her up.'

Garel-Jones greeted his new junior with affection, tempered with some wariness. 'Even though I regarded her as slightly enthusiastic and therefore not exactly my cup of tea, I did realize very early on that she had many good points. These are, first, that she tells the truth and second, that she is immensely loyal. I was prepared to overlook her commitment to issues, because I just thought that those two qualities were pretty good.'

The promotion caused Widdecombe to reassess her earlier political life. She saw that her days of rebellion and trouble-making were over, as she would now be required to follow the instructions of her government masters. She warned constituents, through the local press, that she would no longer be able to speak out or vote against the government and that she would have to hold her tongue. 'My "rent-a-quote days" are over,' she quipped. 'I'm classified as a member of the government in terms of collective responsibility, so I am not allowed to vote against them. I'd have to resign if I did.' Whether anyone believed her or not, the very fact that the word 'resign' had already entered her vocabulary just at the moment when she had put her foot on the ladder of advancement may be said to indicate a politician who was less interested in conforming to the rules of the political club than in the rightness of her belief, and the propriety of practice.

Widdecombe would not have to work for Garel-Jones for very long. Shortly after her appointment to his department, the convulsion began that turned Mrs Thatcher out of office. At first, Widdecombe could not believe what she was seeing aired in the media and discussed feverishly in Commons tea rooms. The possibility that the party would oust a sitting Prime Minister seemed to her 'outrageous', and she did not waver from the prime ministerial camp while Thatcher remained in contention. She went to the lengths of refusing to dine at the same table as Edwina Currie and Emma Nicholson, two Heseltine supporters. 'I said the rest of the world would think we were quite mad, and this is somebody who has turned the country round, and we're chucking her out while she's still PM.' Widdecombe saw that the Prime Minister had allowed herself to become 'isolated and withdrawn from the rest of the party and out of touch, and all of that', but she did not think that this was sufficient grounds to ditch her, given her achievements.

When Widdecombe and a group of her right-wing colleagues – including David Amess, Michael Brown and David Davis – realized the gravity of Thatcher's position, they assembled in a small room at the Commons to talk about the possibilities for action. There followed a 'panicky discussion' about tactics that might avert the otherwise inevitable coup. 'I just could not believe that we were talking at that late stage about things that should have been done weeks earlier.' The upshot of the meeting was that Michael Brown went to Number Ten Downing Street to appeal to the Prime Minister to stay.

At seven o'clock the next morning, Widdecombe received a call from Garel-Jones telling her that the Prime Minister would resign that day, and that 'We are going to run both Major and Hurd.' Widdecombe was dubious of the merit of having two names on the ticket, and she asked Garel-Jones, 'Why are we running both Major and Hurd?'

'He said: "If people don't want Heseltine, they've got to have somewhere to go." He would be supporting Hurd.

'He asked: "What do you want to do?"

'I said I would be supporting Douglas.'

Garel-Jones realized the choice was 'not obvious for someone of Widdecombe's right-wing conviction', but thought she was following his guidance. In fact, Widdecombe's thinking was more subtle. 'I would not vote for Heseltine because he had brought Thatcher down. I had a hard choice between Major and Hurd, but at the time, as I remember, we were about to engage in the Gulf War. I thought, you've got to have somebody who has been a major player on the world stage, which Hurd had been, and indeed at that time was. He seemed the safer bet. John was forty-seven at the time and very young.'

She joined a team of Hurd supporters that included her old pro-life colleague John Patten, and battle was joined. The Widdecombe contribution was typically vigorous. 'I went into Douglas's room in the House every single day of the week, and we spent all day ringing people up and all this sort of stuff. It was huge fun. It was immense fun.' It was also doomed. The team knew from an early stage that Major's campaign was picking up steam, while Hurd's was stationary, and were prepared for the outcome. There was also widespread relief that Heseltine had lost because, in Widdecombe's words, 'Things were still too raw.' Garel-Jones recalled, 'She threw herself, heart and soul, into the campaign and of all the people involved in the campaigning, was the most devastated by the result.'

Hurd's failure to make headway against John Major saddened Widdecombe, and she was concerned about the implications for her embryonic career in government. Garel-Jones reassured her that her enthusiasm had been drawn to the attention of Hurd and he in turn would mention it to John Major, who had won the ballot and become Conservative leader and Prime Minister. Major's triumph was critical to the ministerial career on which Ann Widdecombe now embarked in earnest.

TEN

Major's Minister

THE arrival of John Major at Number Ten Downing Street would open a door to government for Ann Widdecombe that was barely ajar when Mrs Thatcher departed. A furore over the absence of women from Major's new Cabinet had preceded her appointment as Parliamentary Under Secretary of State at the Department of Social Security, but when Major called her to tell her of the new job, he went out of his way to stress that she was not a token woman put there to bulk up the government numbers. Widdecombe privately suspected more of the male chauvinism that she had encountered throughout her career, but 'wasn't too worried. My line was, "I don't care what the reason is. Here's my chance." '

Congratulations at her entry into the ranks of the government flowed from many quarters, including some political enemies. But, to her disappointment, none came from Margaret Thatcher, whom Ann Widdecombe had loyally fought to keep in power. This looked to Widdecombe like 'detachment' rather than 'rudeness'. The new junior minister assumed that Mrs Thatcher had so little to do with the lower ranks of the government that she probably did not know who Ann was. Such 'detachment' did Mrs Thatcher no service, and very probably hastened her fall. John Major, on the other hand, went well out of his way to be chummy in the lobby, and that hastened his unexpected rise to the top of the government.

Widdecombe quickly found the taste of power at least as satisfying as the adrenalin and indignation that flowed through her in the course of her backbench activity. The only regret she expressed much later, when consigned to the ranks of the opposition, was that she had been 'one shuffle short of the Cabinet'. In fact, Ann Widdecombe had occasionally told colleagues she had wanted to enter the then exclusively male preserve of the whips' office, but the Conservatives were not ready to admit so feisty an operator.

John Major and Ann Widdecombe were not total strangers when he made the call. Some years earlier, they had had a chance meeting at a kebab restaurant in Kennington, close to the flats that both occupied at the time. The restaurant's simple circumstances fitted the two unpretentious Tories who would not have cared for the swankier watering holes of Westminster or the West End favoured by haughtier colleagues. Ann was sitting at a table in the restaurant, dressed in clothes suitable only for gardening, when John Major, then Financial Secretary to the Treasury, dropped in for a quick meal. She was reading a thriller by Douglas Hurd at the time and Widdecombe recalled that he told her the ending. Major later denied that he would ever have been so tactless. In the course of the evening, the two politicians found they shared an interest in animals, when the restaurant owner produced his dog and they both cooed over it. Major's respect for Widdecombe grew over the years, and when he had the opportunity to acknowledge it, he eagerly did so. 'I thought she was an original, I thought she was intelligent. I thought she didn't trim, and I thought she was brave, and I thought she had all the ingredients to make a senior minister.' Widdecombe's straight speaking and firm opinions continued to impress Major, especially in contrast with the behaviour of many of his duplicitous colleagues. 'There are too many identikit politicians, she emphatically wasn't identikit. Ann has convictions that don't always fit nicely into party policy. But she's not a troublemaker, she's not a rent-a-quote, she doesn't set out to be difficult, she is by instinct immensely loyal. She'll come and say "I don't like this" without fear of whoever you are. It's people like that you need to have in government, not the people who say "Yes sir, no sir", "This is absolutely right," even when it's complete drivel.'

Major had himself held the position of Parliamentary Under Secretary of State at the DHSS (as it then was) five years earlier and knew what it entailed. 'The social security job is one of the hardest worked, if not the hardest worked junior jobs there is in government. The paperwork is enormous. And the number of people who understand social security is but a handful in the House. To have a good grounding in social security puts you in a very strong position in your later political career.' Major saw this large and important ministry as a suitable nursery for the junior minister. It was a place where she could learn to deal with issues and measures affecting ordinary people who had hit upon hard times. Widdecombe would initially report to Tony Newton, the experienced if low-key Secretary of State, and the two struck up a good working relationship. She described her initial brief as a 'hotch potch of jobs' including housing benefit and income support.

While Ann Widdecombe was examining the means of support that the state provided for those in economic difficulty, a financial crisis was building up in her own life, with potentially devastating effect. She was the owner of two houses by this time, a cottage she had bought in the constituency in 1988 and her Kennington flat which she had bought in 1986. But she had showed as little financial sophistication in buying them as she had shown in her early property dealings. The cottage was acquired at the top of the market, and although she could afford the mortgages when she bought them, as the deep and long recession of the early 1990s began to bite, she was hit very quickly. The bank ratcheted up the pressure to meet payments and she got a taste of the woes that many of those on the receiving end of her legislation were suffering. 'It was very hairy at the time. I had never come from the background of having vast quantities of money. And I'd been through that awful property disaster in Fulham, so I'd been set back anyway. It all became too much, and like an awful lot of people, the bank started off sympathetic but didn't stay sympathetic.'

The problems for an MP facing bankruptcy were even worse than for someone with a conventional job, as a bankrupt cannot sit in

Parliament. So both her livelihood and her career were at stake when on 3 March 1991 a Sunday paper exposed her financial plight, and said that the HFC bank had been granted a judgment summons for £5,389.71 against her as early as May 1990. In fact Widdecombe discovered the bankruptcy had not been properly served, as she had not been given due notice. 'It was an extremely hairy time, I'm pretty sure that in today's climate I would have had to resign. I didn't then; the climate was different then. Parliament was much more generous towards people in trouble.' In the end she was able to pay everything off and is now well supported by a book advance and a generous parliamentary salary. But the trauma of that period stayed with her. She recalls: 'I was walking along the road the other day and I heard a girl say to somebody else, "It's payday next Thursday," and I thought, crikey, I haven't thought "It's payday next Thursday" for years. But there was a time when I was utterly conscious where every penny was coming from.'

The cost of living on the breadline was, ironically, the first subject after abortion to give her a high public profile. A survey published in June 1991 by the National Children's Homes charity had shown that a quarter of those receiving benefit were incapable of buying even the most basic food. The report cast the plight of the poor in a particularly unfortunate light, but when the BBC *Today* programme asked her to defend the scale of the benefit, Widdecombe argued that the glass was half full, not half empty, that the report was good news, not bad. 'If in fact three-quarters of all of those surveyed said they usually do have enough money to buy food, what is the crucial difference between those who are successfully feeding themselves and their children, and those who are not? It does not seem to be the level of state support.'

So if the poor were to blame for not feeding themselves properly, what could they do to improve the situation? Widdecombe answered that they should not buy food in expensive places, like supermarkets. 'I said, quite reasonably, "I'm not surprised, if you go supermarket shopping you don't always get the least expensive things and perhaps they should consider buying fresh foods, and looking at other ways of doing it." ' Uproar ensued, with the government minister on a salary of £42,272 appearing to preach to those on the very lowest subsistence levels how they should spend their money. She recalled that it was 'distorted as "Widdecombe blames the poor for their own poverty,". "Eat up your greens," all that sort of stuff'.

Widdecombe was out on her own as religious, governmental and Conservative colleagues all came down on her. The Methodist Church said it was an indictment of society for one child in ten to go hungry, while Michael Meacher, Labour's social security spokesman at the time, said, 'Ann Widdecombe combined Lady Porter's sensibility with Edwina Currie's finesse.' Further research into Ann's eating habits revealed that she liked traditional cooking, and ate beef 'despite mad cow disease'. She told one paper about her experience of life in Singapore as a young girl, when the family had a chef 'who used to come up with the most wonderful food'. There was some suggestion at the time that Ann Widdecombe did not even buy her own food. That would certainly be disputed by regular shoppers at Sainsburys at Nine Elms who can testify to the fact that Ann buys her own food and provisions.

At this point the first sign appeared of the personal abuse that would be heaped on her later in her ministerial career. The *Daily Mirror* depicted her as a heartless nanny who patronized the poor and as an eccentric who was out of touch with ordinary people. The abuse was very specifically related to her gender, and similarities with that heaped on Mrs Thatcher, especially in her early years as party leader, were marked. On this occasion, the *Mirror's* top headline on the affair ran: 'Tory Spinster Is A Recipe For Disaster'. Its second headline, in big letters, ran: 'What A Fathead'. Then it bullet-pointed the following:

- Minister tells poor families what to eat
- She has only herself and a pet cat to feed
- She scoffs takeaways and too many potatoes

These minor skirmishes had long since faded from the public consciousness when John Major called a general election in April

1992. At the Department of Social Security, where Widdecombe had served for just sixteen months, there was so little confidence of another Conservative term that Ann took her pot plants home from the office and had a farewell drink with her officials. The party's defeat of Neil Kinnock's Labour party, with a majority of twenty-one, was as welcome a surprise to her as it was to the rest of the party. 'We came in again with a lot of euphoria. There was a lot of talk about Labour being unelectable, and we swept the local elections, later. It was a very, very happy time.' There was also some good news for Widdecombe herself, as she was confirmed in her job at Social Security. Tony Newton was moved out of the department, and Peter Lilley moved in as Secretary of State. He was a noted right-winger, and Widdecombe looked forward to the next five years.

But the broader picture at Westminster was much less happy. There, the fault-lines on Europe already showing at the end of the previous parliament were now threatening to break up the Conservative Party. Rebellions were routinely staged, as if the party still enjoyed the luxury of a large majority, rather than maintaining control by a tenuous hold that could give way at any time. The precarious situation brought to the fore Widdecombe's survival instinct, and she had no patience with the rebels who threatened it. 'We had lost the habit of discipline. The whole of that parliament, we were prisoners of the rebels.' Widdecombe was regarded as a Major loyalist, regularly given the names of rebels to bring into line. Their logic exasperated the doughty Conservative. 'They were prepared to bring us to ruin, at the risk of bringing in a pro-European party. Looking back, I now wish to God we had lost. Then Labour would have had to deal with the ERM.'

Widdecombe watched as the party's split on Europe demoralized John Major. She recalled wishing him a happy New Year in early 1993, to which he replied, ' "Well, it couldn't be worse than last year." And I said, "Come on, we won the general election last year." And he said, "Yes, one good day in the whole year." That was how much the thing had changed between winning in '92 and the January in '93. It had all changed.'

Major appreciated her loyalty: 'She was supportive in public and she was supportive in private. Even though, very possibly, she didn't agree with every aspect of my policy she was rigorously loyal, and harshly dismissive of people who were trying to undermine the government's policy. I think her view was, if you disagree with the government's policy to such an extent that you seek to undermine it, then you ought not to be in government. She's in government – she will support the policy.'

While the press hounded the government on its two weakest topics, Europe and the recession which had continued to ravage the economy, Widdecombe returned to the technical topics she had left behind in the previous parliament, which concerned pensions, pensions and more pensions – indeed, she was now called 'pensions minister'. She greatly enjoyed the topic's density and the fact that it was self-contained. The transition to a new boss was also seamless. Newton had impressed Widdecombe with his knowledge of the subject – 'he knew as much as the officials' – and he was a 'genuinely nice man', but Lilley was more intellectually adventurous, and was prepared to tackle topics from which Newton had shied away. He was also more cautious in dealing with the press than Newton, who had given Widdecombe a largely free rein to write her own press releases and speeches; Lilley wanted less publicity, and more control. 'He was incredibly cautious, particularly with press and media. I used to take the line that if the press and media ask me to do something then the presumption was I would do it, if there were good reasons not to then I didn't. We had a completely different approach towards the handling of press and media.'

The technical issue that first preoccupied Widdecombe in the new administration was the need to equalize the ages at which men and women could receive their state pensions. At the time men received their pension at age sixty-five, and women at sixty, but a legal judgment had obliged the private sector to equalize the ages of occupational pension schemes. Now the state had to follow suit with the age at which men and women could receive the state earnings related pension (SERPS) and the state pension. The problem for the department was not the principle of an equal age, but the practice of finding, and implementing, the unified age. The growing ageing population was 'bothering us like mad', she said, because it meant that the number of people working was static, or even falling (because the absolute size of the British population was shrinking), while the number of those ceasing to work and becoming eligible for a pension was growing. The department had been told that the ratio which applied at the time, of 3.4 workers to one pensioner, would change over the next twenty-five years to 2.4 workers to each pensioner. An enormous strain on the national insurance system was inevitable.

Four possible solutions to the debate over the age at which to equalize the pension were initially canvassed. The government could pick sixty, sixty-three or sixty-five; or they could give people the choice of any age between sixty and seventy – an option called 'the flexible decade'. Opinion on the optimum age was widely and actively canvassed in government and with the pensions industry, an operation which took Widdecombe into areas of expertise with which she was quite unfamiliar. The interest in complexity and nuance that she had previously shown in mastering the rules and procedures of the House of Commons in order to conduct her campaign on the abortion bill with maximum effectiveness was now brought to bear on pensions law, actuarial ratios and the like.

The outcome of her research was an initial preference for the 'flexible decade' solution, reflecting a desire to give individuals a choice instead of imposing a fixed age. But this could have had consequences she did not foresee, such as widespread retirement at the earliest possible age, sixty, which would be 'phenomenally expensive': estimates at the time put the annual cost of lowering the retirement age for men to sixty at £4 billion. So Widdecombe returned to square one, and assessed the other solutions.

While the Department of Social Security was now concentrating on ages sixty, sixty-three and sixty-five, the Treasury was pushing another age altogether: sixty-seven. This option had the merit of postponing the age at which the government had to pay out money, so it could be presented as cost-effective; it also kept people working longer, and so satisfied demographic concerns. But European and Scandinavian models also tended towards older ages, and some members of the government argued that it was 'outside the British experience, and thus stood out a mile'. The government eventually turned it down because it would attract political opposition from those who said it was 'the Tories trying to save money again'. So the 'sixty-seven option' went the way of all brave ideas.

The assault on sixty-three as the new retirement age was heaviest from those who saw it discriminating against women, who would be required to work three more years. Widdecombe had no patience with this argument: 'It would have been sold as "We were penalizing women in order to benefit men." It wouldn't have been that way at all, but that would have been the sell.' The more powerful argument against this age was based on financial grounds: men, who made up the larger part of the workforce, would work less and so contribute less.

Debate now narrowed to the two remaining possible ages: sixty or sixty-five. Widdecombe recalls: 'We were left with a very stark choice which I explained to them. Opinion in the department and among ministers was divided and everybody had their own preferred options.' But by this point, Widdecombe herself had settled on sixty-five, and she set about persuading the department to accept it. Peter Lilley, who was thought to prefer retirement at sixty, recalled Widdecombe being very 'robust' in the debate. 'She advised us not to beat about the bush, just get on and do it. Equalize men and women and prepare to do it to sixty-five.'

Widdecombe dealt with the inevitable unpopularity of such a view among women employees, who would obviously be required to work longer before being eligible for their pension, by putting off the date of the change for some fifteen years, so that it would not affect the current workforce. That approach, already adopted widely throughout Europe, was undoubtedly politically expedient. 'If you say to people "Sixty-five," they'll think "Eurgh!" But if you say it's not going to happen until 2010, immediately that is so far into the future people don't resist. It sold the thing politically, completely. And it got a long-term problem sorted out.'

There was another pensions problem which directly occupied the junior minister at this time: the Maxwell affair, provoked by the theft of a company's pension fund by the company's owner. Widdecombe was involved in dealing with Maxwell in three ways: first, in addressing the large implications of the episode for the pensions industry; second, in setting up the system for recouping Maxwell pension assets; and third, in mollifying Maxwell pensioners.

When the scandal broke, some members of the department and the government wanted to wash their hands of the fallout. As far as they were concerned, Maxwell was a problem for the Mirror Group and nobody else. But Widdecombe saw the political consequences in respect of both the pensions industry and the Maxwell pensioners, and dismissed that view. 'There were those who saw it and those who didn't and needed persuading,' she said.

The issue for the pensions industry was particularly acute because the Conservatives had placed enormous store in a private-sector alternative to the state pension; now Maxwell threatened to undermine confidence in this route. Widdecombe: 'The whole integrity of occupational pension funds suddenly came into question, because until then, people thought occupational pension funds were as safe as houses.' So one key task was reassuring the public that pension companies unconnected with Maxwell were not tarred with the Maxwell brush. As part of this exercise to prop up confidence in the industry, Widdecombe told the House of Commons in December 1991 that the government would limit to five per cent the amount the occupational pension fund can invest in the employer.

On a more immediate level, the government had to settle on the appropriate action to deal with the crisis. Senior officials of the department visited the Maxwell companies to assess the depth of the financial problems. Widdecombe again: 'If government was going to play any role at all we had to be convinced that the situation was not rescuable by the company concerned. We weren't going to intervene in anything otherwise.' The department did not want to sanction bad management. So a loan was provided to act as a buffer for pensioners who faced an immediate shortfall in their income, while the long-term process of finding lost funds was given to Lord Cuckney, a distinguished banker who had earlier been a civil servant. 'We told them: find the funds, find out where they've all gone and find out what remains. Secure what remains, and then decide what the payout to Maxwell pensioners would be from that.'

Government refusal to bail out the pensioners quickly and in full upset some Maxwell employees. Widdecombe's mantra, which she repeated over and over again to the large number of bitter Maxwell pensioners, was, 'It would be entirely premature at this stage to commit us for or against any form of action.' The media latched on to this as it seemed to confirm the earlier claim, following the 'let them eat beans' furore over the cost of food to the poor, that she was mean and heartless. So when the *Daily Mirror* engineered a confrontation between the minister and Ivy Needham, a sixty-six-year-old widow who was registered blind and had worked for a Maxwell company, they expected a row. Ivy was a particularly vocal pensioner who had made a particular appeal to the private-sector instincts of the government: 'We are not people who have gambled on the stock market or have been greedy. All we are guilty of is putting aside our money for a reasonable pension.'

But Ann likes to recall how the journalists lost face. 'Ivy used to come and see us. And she'd be a great sweetie in the meeting, and she'd go off and rant to the press on the doorstep outside. At one party conference, Maxwell pensioners had turned up and Sheree Dodd of the *Daily Mirror* thought, "Wouldn't it be good fun to get Ann and Ivy having a big run-in?" So they arranged for us to meet, cameras rolling and all the rest of it. And Ivy said: "Oh Ann!" and embraced me, and I said "Oh Ivy!" and embraced her. And this wasn't expected. Needless to say it was never shown.'

Widdecombe's fascination with the minutiae of pensions policy amazed many among her colleagues and the public alike, who found it at best obscure and at worst tedious. She enjoyed the role as an expert who could show off her knowledge, knowing that it fell largely on uneducated ears. 'I loved it. I loved every minute of the pensions ministry. I believe that I did a good job on it. Whereas I think I did a very neutral job on other benefits because they were just such an awful hotch potch. But when you're doing pensions, you've got something that is discrete, and there were some really big issues to get your teeth into.'

Those in the seats of power appeared not to be quite so impressed by Widdecombe's success as pensions minister as she was herself. When John Major reshuffled his government in May 1993, she expected her triumphs in pensions to be recognized with a promotion. Her case seemed all the stronger as the two other leading Conservative women, Virginia Bottomley and Gillian Shephard, had both been promoted to the Cabinet, while Edwina Currie had long since disappeared into backbench obscurity. There was a gap at the Minister of State level; surely her turn had come.

She recalls the occasion when John Major got on the phone: 'I thought they were bound to be looking for somebody and I was the only one floating round. I was very confident that I would be made a Minister of State. Everybody around me said it was going to happen. And I allowed myself to believe that it was. When the call came through from the PM, I picked up the phone and I saw all the lights go on on my phone (obviously all the staff were listening in on their extensions). And the PM said, "Blah, blah, blah, I'd like you to go to employment." And my heart sank. I said, "As a parliamentary under secretary?" And he said, "Yes."

'My private secretary told me there was a very long gap in which he thought I was about to say "No." And I said, "All right, thank you very much." Rather sort of unenthusiastically.'

'I slept on it, and I thought, "I've got this wrong. I shouldn't do this." I didn't want to do it. "I have no desire to go on if that's all they think of me." I said the next day (to either my private office or to one of my fellow ministers), I said, "Actually, I think I've done the wrong thing – I don't think I should be taking this job."

'The Permanent Secretary, Michael Partridge, came to see me, having heard about my reservations, and I said to him, "I think I've got this wrong," and "I don't want to do this job," and "I don't want to be a PUS at employment, I've been here two and a half years;

everybody else who was here with me has been promoted, is moving on, while I'm left behind." and "I think this means they don't think much of me," and "Why should I stay around just waiting for the chop? I just want to go now – I've got other things to do." That's the way I put it.

'He actually talked me out of it. He said, "I've seen lots of ministers sitting where you are now saying they're very disappointed with their rate of progress, and they're not going to take the job and they're going to pull out." And he said, "I've talked every one of them round, and none of them so far has regretted it." So he said, "I think you should take it, and do it."

'Anyway, I ummed and aahed a bit, but in the end I decided I would take it.'

The lack of promotion was all the more surprising as Major said he had gained a most favourable impression of Widdecombe at Social Security. 'I thought she was a very competent minister, and whenever I saw her, if I asked her a question she knew the answer. I didn't see her floored at the dispatch box. She was pretty clear-thinking, it's a very difficult job that Social Security job, and I thought she did it pretty well.'

Shortly before the Prime Minister gave Widdecombe the news she would find so disappointing, he had spoken to the man who would be her new boss at the Department of Employment. David Hunt was a lawyer by trade, but had a long record in government and in the Conservative Party. As Major went through the members of Hunt's new ministerial team, he pinpointed one member who would need particular attention and mentoring. Ann Widdecombe, he said, 'is not everyone's cup of tea'. But the Prime Minister told Hunt that she had 'tremendous potential to be a really forceful member of the government. It may be something of a controversial choice, but it is someone I have every confidence in, and I'm particularly anxious for you to be her minister. I want you to work closely with her.' Hunt later said he was 'already aware of her formidable reputation for being very effective in debate, a very good constituency MP and also someone who wasn't afraid to voice her views'.

He very quickly discovered how forceful Widdecombe could be when he suggested to her that she might become minister for women, in succession to Gillian Shephard, the former Secretary of State for Employment, who had gone to the Department of Agriculture. Hunt suspected her feelings on the matter, and summoned up all his tact and diplomacy (a not insignificant amount, given his legal background). 'I asked her whether or not she might like the responsibility for women; "This is something I might mention to the Prime Minister," I said. In the meantime I had been made aware of her very strong views.' The request was being made, he insisted, not because she was a woman, but because he thought she would be very assertive in favour of women's rights on the appropriate Cabinet committee.

That cut no ice with Widdecombe. 'She developed the argument that there shouldn't be a minister for women as it showed a male paternalist attitude. She made it clear what her views were. Of course she would do what she was told to do, but her heart would not be in it. I hastily moved on to another subject. And then for two years I was minister for women.'

Widdecombe recalls events slightly differently. 'I said I believed it was a load of old baloney, and that I didn't want to do it. But traditionally it was a job that went with that department.' Major was sympathetic to her lack of interest in the job. 'Ann wasn't keen. And I sympathize with her because being a woman it would look as though she was minister for women because she was a woman — it would have looked a bit like tokenism. There was no dispute with us about it. She is a serious politician, she is not the sort of politician you want to put in what people sometimes disparagingly call women's jobs.'

Ann's outspoken style amused rather than infuriated Hunt, who had long tired of the efforts of junior ministers to grovel their way to promotion. But the department's whip, Irvine Patnick, had more trouble with it. Patnick, a blunt Yorkshireman, had opposed Widdecombe in the abortion debates of the 1980s and there was no love lost between them. So when he sought to act as a whip in the department and ensure that Widdecombe toed the line, he found her unduly sensitive, and prone to 'fly off the handle'. On one occasion, he warned her about her duty to inform the local MP when she planned to visit that MP's constituency. This provoked the minister, said Patnick, and 'She flew into a tirade against me. I took this to be the sign of a guilty conscience.'

Hunt recalls: 'I rather enjoyed the relationship that Ann had with Irvine, because Irvine would put his finger up to mention something at a meeting and Ann would bite it off. She was very forceful and determined that her ideas would win through and Irvine is a much more cautious individual. There came a time after she had bitten off most of his fingers, and there were no other pieces of his anatomy to bite, that the force of her personality just completely dominated.'

The frustration she exhibited with colleagues was reflected in her dissatisfaction with the work and purpose of the department. Much of her work involved uncongenial meetings with groups of organized workers, women and various socially and politically correct bodies. Fine-tuning equal opportunities legislation was of little interest to this highly ideological minister, who was most concerned to burnish her 'right-wing' credentials. The department also lacked large projects where she could get stuck in. The best that could be said for its mission, when Widdecombe joined in 1993, was that it had to pick up the pieces of a recession which had brought unemployment up to a record three million, and steer the jobless back to work in line with the economic upturn that had begun. The declining importance of these tasks was recognized two years later when the Department of Employment was merged with the Department of Education.

Ann Widdecombe may have found much of the department's work lacking in substance, but in accord with her restless – some would say workaholic – temperament, she found a crusade which she felt had meaning and importance, and then applied herself to it wholeheartedly. This was the removal of discrimination against older employees, who were being weeded out as companies sought to bring in young workers, especially for jobs in high technology. Widdecombe: 'People who had been put out of work in their fifties were finding it massively difficult to get back into work. One of my

Newborn Ann with her mother and brother Malcolm, 1947.

Ann with Anda Panda and Meng the houseboy in Singapore.

Seven-year-old Ann in Singapore.

Boating with her father.

Ann, aged
twenty-three, at
Oxford.

Ann with boyfriend Colin
Maltby after graduating from
Oxford, 1972.

The Burnley by-election, 1980:
Methuselah the Morris Minor
pressed into action, and Ann in
campaigning mode at Hapton
Colliery.

Ann is received into the Catholic Church, 21 April 1993.

Ann meets Mother Teresa.

Ann's audience with Pope John Paul II, January 1996.

Acknowledging her ovation at the
1998 Conservative Party Conference. (© *Press Association, 1998*)

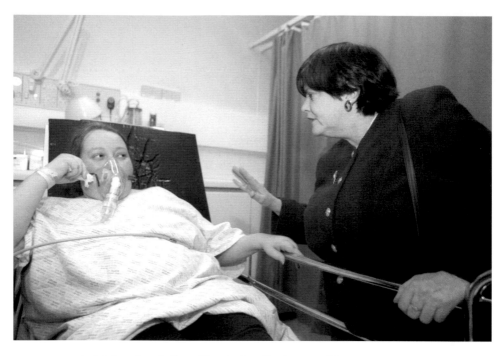

At University College Hospital as Shadow Health Secretary, 1998.
(© *Times Newspapers Ltd, 1998*)

Ann in her House of Commons office.

The Shadow Home Secretary with William Hague at the 1999 Party Conference.
(© *Times Newspapers Ltd, 1999*)

The author of *The Clematis Tree*. (© *copyright Times Newspapers Ltd, 2000*)

jobs was to argue with companies about their policies. We've got to persuade employers that what they should be doing is valuing older workers, recruiting older workers. I said that not even the state pension age should act as a bar – as long as people want to work, let them, because that's the way the future lies.'

If Ann sought any proof of older people's ability to work long past retirement age, she needed to look no further than her father, a key influence on her professional life from an early age. Murray continued to be a workaholic long after he left the Admiralty. His analysis of the failings of the Oxford Union steward back in 1972 was only the first of many assignments in his 'third age'. Murray, like his daughter, found work much more fun than relaxation, and retained his crisp analytical powers until he was well into his eighties. So, as far as Ann was concerned, the idea, put around by some, that old people could not adapt to new conditions and technology was 'complete hogwash'. Employers' discrimination against older workers was self-defeating, she would assert. They were usually more mature and reliable than the young, and whereas young people were likely to take a company's training and move on to another job, older workers were likely to stay longer as finding new jobs would be harder – an argument possibly undermined by the success of her scheme. She also insisted that older people could learn about computing and pointed out the example of staff at the Benefits Agency, which fell under the Social Security umbrella, where computerization had been success-fully introduced by many older people who lacked any previous computer experience. 'So I knew that older people could be taught the new technology.'

Widdecombe also argued that the strategy made sense in demographic terms. The falling ratio between workers and pensioners was producing a pensions time bomb; but if people could be persuaded to work until they were older, they would postpone claiming their pension until later and put off the point at which they became a burden on the state system.

The campaign in favour of older employees, launched in July 1993, was not universally appreciated. Employers were not used to being preached at by a Conservative government. They argued that international pressures dictated their need for youthful employees, while Widdecombe's monetarist colleagues saw her social and moral arguments as interventionist or 'nannying'. The party's remaining hard-line economists, MPs Alan Duncan and Phillip Oppenheim, continued to argue that economic policies should be driven by the market and not government or other external influences; but this form of economic thinking was on the wane under Major, and Widdecombe was allowed to pioneer a more directive approach.

Promotional rather than legislative effort drove the scheme forward, and Widdecombe showed herself an energetic campaigner both with companies and with employees. In December 1993 she launched a drive to find the country's oldest male and female full-time employees. This was dubbed 'Getting On' and was successful beyond the minister's dreams. Instead of the handful of seventy-year-olds she had expected, a host of over-eighties presented themselves. The winners, announced in February 1994, were a woman of ninety-two who had sold motor accessories for thirty years, and a man of ninety-four who worked in a motorcycle shop; both received MBEs. Said Ann, 'If somebody of ninety-three can still be giving satisfactory work – what is the problem with somebody of fifty-three?'

If the 'Getting On' campaign was driven by Widdecombe's moral, humane impulse, her enthusiasm for the Jobseekers' Allowance, introduced in early 1995, was powered by a toughness that would be seen as 'very hard and Tory'. Widdecombe: 'The attitude of people on the dole was that they would say they were looking for work, but they were not required to show proof of it. There was no real detection for fraud; there was no real insistence that they had to do certain things like show they were taking steps – and show what those steps were. I believed very strongly that we should start to link money to a job search, rather than just money for being out of work. And that was what the Jobseekers' Allowance effectively set out to do.' The measure did not merely seek to reduce abuse of unemployment benefit by the unemployed; it also targeted part-time students who were without work, and collecting benefit.

Widdecombe was forced to defend this second element against the charge that it discouraged those seeking to acquire new work skills.

Widdecombe had impressed Hunt by her ability to grasp the detail of a complex issue, as well as by the reputation for combativeness she gained from leading some 'winding-up' debates which had backbenchers waving their order papers in appreciation. He said later: 'She was very demanding as a minister but at least one knew where she stood. The civil servants also knew that when they put up these interminable files in ministerial boxes late at night, they would always get the work done because she was enormously industrious; one of the most hardworking people I have ever come across in politics. One of the reasons why I got on particularly well with Ann Widdecombe was that she had done most of the work for me. And every Secretary of State dreams of having a junior minister who will do all of the hard work then take a back seat.'

But while she was going down well with her immediate boss, she had no way of knowing how her work had played with Major – who was about to announce another reshuffle. The omens for a promotion were good, but the outcome was not certain. 'I thought, "Surely, surely, they can't refuse me this time." But I had also reached a resolution, which was, if they didn't promote me in the next shuffle – that was it, I just wasn't going to hang around. As far as I was concerned I had given it another year beyond what I thought was sensible. Anyway, it turned out okay. They made me a Minister of State – but they kept me in the same damned department!'

In her new role, Widdecombe would work for the first time to Michael Portillo, the bright young thing who had made the Cabinet aged thirty-nine as Chief Secretary to the Treasury, and was now given the moribund Department of Employment to look after. But the task of shaking some life into it defeated even Portillo, and when he quit, the department as a separate entity was buried.

Portillo promoted into the department Phillip Oppenheim, a fellow spirit on the monetarist right of the Party. The conjunction of Oppenheim with Widdecombe, as his new immediate boss, was often amusing and occasionally inflammatory. Problems started shortly after the reshuffle, when Widdecombe summoned the ministerial team together to apportion responsibility for the legislation in prospect. The meeting, led by Widdecombe with a light hand, had gone well, and all but one measure had been apportioned. Then the subject of the Disability Discrimination Bill, which guaranteed disabled people rights in the workplace, came up. This measure had had an unfortunate history. An earlier bill dealing with much the same issue had been resisted by the Conservative government at great political cost to the then minister Nicholas Scott. But now the government had taken the bill on, and a minister needed to be found to pilot it through the House of Commons. No one wanted it.

Widdecombe assessed the workload of her colleagues and asked Oppenheim to take it on. Oppenheim, 'disgruntled at being in this second-rate department' (as he saw it), flatly refused, saying he thought the measure was 'regulationist': 'We didn't have anything against disabled people, but we were lumping the burden on employers and it could be very expensive. Ann Widdecombe did not want this portfolio either, and it came down to me and her.'

Oppenheim went to Portillo, the Secretary of State, for support and argued the case for Ann to take responsibility for the bill. He told Portillo: 'Widdecombe was touchie-feelie, she's a woman, she can carry this bill through, I am not the kind of guy you want doing a bill like this. I am a hard-faced Tory. He bought this self-serving piece of sophistry. She was livid, she never quite forgave me for that.'

Widdecombe took the bill successfully through the Commons, to Oppenheim's little-disguised pleasure. The bill was jointly sponsored with the Department of Social Security, where the responsible minister was William Hague, and, according to Hague, the two developed considerable mutual respect. Hague remembers many joint negotiations over employment provisions in the Disability Discrimination Bill. 'I often got my way with her, but only by getting other people to side with me so that I could get a majority against her. I wouldn't get my way by a successful negotiation on my own.'

The internal discussions in the department between Oppenheim and Widdecombe were much trickier. In fact, the spat between the highly diligent minister and her smug, disillusioned junior grumbled on until Widdecombe wrote to Portillo to stir Oppenheim into action. She regarded Oppenheim as 'bone idle', and some six months into her term, after a scan through the number of outside ministerial visits made by her team, which showed Oppenheim almost completely inactive, she could not restrain her irritation. Oppenheim remembers: 'She marched into the private office, through the outside office, bosoms aquivering, and plonked herself squarely down and said, "You are not pulling your weight, Phillip." She was bothered and pissed off that she was taking the disablement bill through. I confronted her, I was pretty annoyed, I don't normally lose my temper. She had great delusions of grandeur.

'What riled me was that this was a woman with a phenomenally safe seat who did not have to worry about her weekends in the constituency that much. I had one of the most marginal Tory seats, a mining seat, a very tough seat. I had to go up to my constituency every weekend in the run-up to the election. To be lectured by someone with a very safe seat about not pulling my weight really pissed me off.

'I said, "People don't want to see junior or middle ranking ministers round the country, they don't know who you are, you ruin their day, you should be in Westminster or in your department." In any event, I thought there was a Civil Service agenda here. Our Permanent Secretary had an agenda, get the ministers out of the department. I felt she had fallen into a Civil Service trap.

'I dropped her a note which I copied to Portillo and had a chat with him. He took my side, although he was not against her on a personal level. Widdecombe relented, I think she realized she had overstepped the mark. It was "nanny Widders". I think she felt I was a bit of a butterfly, a bit of a dilettante, enjoying myself. I don't think she realized the amount of grind I put in.'

The bad feeling between Oppenheim and Widdecombe never quite dissipated, and surfaced on occasion in unintentionally comic interludes, including one over bad language. Oppenheim: 'One thing the old girl hated was any swearing in ministerial meetings. We were quite a robust bunch, and a bit of language was used now and again. Widdecombe hated this and on one famous occasion, shaking with rage, she virtually slapped my wrist. She said, "You will not swear in ministerial meetings when I'm there!" It was splendid.'

This departmental fracas and Portillo's aloofness, if not downright evasiveness, left Widdecombe worried about the Secretary of State's opinion of what and how well she was doing – and that would be critical to her promotion chances, as the Prime Minister would consult him before giving her a new job in a reshuffle. So she went to her friend David Amess, her loyal colleague, in the abortion debates, and asked him to have a quiet exploratory chat with Portillo. Amess was well placed to do this, having been Portillo's Parliamentary Private Secretary and remaining on good terms with him. Amess reported back to Widdecombe that Portillo had no problems with her, although there was no concealing the personality mismatch. Amess: 'I think she quite likes her political bosses to be very warm, embracing people. That's why she liked John Major and Tony Newton. She responds better to that than distant, cold people. She's a much warmer person than you would imagine. She really couldn't hit it off with people like the two Michaels in the way she did with the others, because their styles are so different.'

In any event, Ann's diligence told at last, when she was promoted to Minister of State in the department of state she had always coveted, the Home Office, in the reshuffle of July 1995. Two years earlier, Edwina Currie had turned the job down partly because she couldn't stand the thought of working with Ken Clarke, but mainly because she had no interest in going round prisons. For Widdecombe that was the very positive attraction; so when John Major invited her, her response was especially warm. 'It was the first reshuffle in which I was really pleased by the thing I had been given. I had always wanted to go to the Home Office, the fact is I admired Michael Howard, and I loved the Home Office.' Ann Widdecombe would not change her mind on the Home Office. As to her assessment of Michael Howard, that would be a quite different matter. But the political world was not the only place where Ann was attracting attention. Her religious life and journey to Rome had also been widely covered over the last two years.

ELEVEN

Crossing the Tiber with Father Michael

WHEN Ann Widdecombe was received into the Catholic Church on 21 April 1993, she became, in the words of David Alton, her friend and supporter, 'a much happier person, much more at ease having taken the decision'. A six-year-long period of despair at the state of the Church of England was now ended, and she could enter the second period of her life assured that she was in a church whose leadership she trusted, and in whose faith she shared.

But this private transformation took place in the full glare of public attention. When she knelt down before her priest and said, 'I believe and profess all that the holy Catholic Church believes, teaches and proclaims to be revealed by God, and I give obedience to Pope John Paul II, and all of his successors,' a multitude of press cameras flashed and whirred, and the pictures of the government minister dressed in pale blue and wearing a white hat, kneeling, head bowed and eyes closed, appeared on television screens round the world that night. A ceremony which the church would normally expect to take place in conditions of privacy had been opened up to the national and international public. The devout Anglican Frank Field attended the second part of the ceremony at the House of Commons and likened the public show to theatre rather than solemn religion. 'She is like a great star of the soap opera and cultivates that tradition very effectively.'

The degree of press interest surprised Widdecombe, but she experienced none of Field's reservations about its propriety. She had, after all, attended public and highly demonstrative professions of faith as early as the age of eight, and had been moved by the preachings of Billy Graham in the 1960s and 1970s. Religion, in her book, should be very public and expressive, and she could see no reason why her own ceremony of conversion should not be exposed to a wide audience. Her religious conviction was equally uninhibited. She later said, 'I am looking for a church which calls a sin a sin and has done with it.' Catholicism gave her that.

The first ceremony at which Ann professed her Catholic faith, and which the cameras attended in profusion, took place at 7.30 a.m. in the crypt of Westminster Cathedral. The early time would allow her to be at her desk for office opening hours, as she was in the middle of complex pensions legislation. The second ceremony in which she took a leading role occurred later that day, in the crypt of the House of Commons, where she attended her first mass as a Catholic. The cameras were not allowed at this one, but large numbers of her 'extended family' from both Houses of Parliament piled in, so that, in its own way, that service was as public as the first.

Parliament had played a very considerable part in Ann's voyage over the Tiber (as reception into the Roman Catholic Church is often called), and the location of this service, and her invitation to many members of Commons and Lords to be present, reflected that debt. The journey to Rome had begun the moment she had arrived at the House of Commons in 1987. Although she had stayed an Anglican in accord with her family tradition, after her return to faith she had struck up friendships with religious parliamentarians, primarily Roman Catholics, who supported David Alton's private member's bill on abortion. Anglicans had taken little interest in her campaign, and her alienation from the faith of her fathers dated from this point.

Alton was her first close Catholic friend in the House of Commons. But two other Catholics, David Amess and Ken Hargreaves, quickly entered her circle, and the group would meet most weeks in the Pugin Room in the House of Commons, to discuss religious issues. The topic that preoccupied the group was the failing appeal of the Church of England and the possibility that this would lead to a growing interest among parliamentarians in the Roman Church. That was Widdecombe's position exactly. She abhorred the proposal to permit the ordination of women priests in the Church of England and, as it appeared to gain widespread acceptance, her general unease at the church's vacillating leadership turned to uncompromising hostility. She condemned the proposal in the language of the Catholic firebrand. 'It undermined the apostolic authority of the Church. It was theologically impossible for women to perform the specific role of the sacramental priesthood because they were not chosen by Christ to be part of His apostolic succession.' Later, in 1993, she told the House of Commons: 'If a woman represents Christ as victim and priest at the Holy Communion, there may just as well be a man who represents the Virgin Mary in a nativity play.' Her view echoed that of the Vatican, which said that 'If the role of Christ were not taken by a man, it would be difficult to see in the minister the image of Christ.'

The decision to put the issue of women's ordination to the vote of the General Synod of the Church of England prompted Ann to attack the church in many newspaper letters and articles. She also told the Bishop of Maidstone, David Smith (later Bishop of Bradford), that a vote in favour would prompt her immediate resignation from the Church of England. Ann's brother Malcolm recalled her fury: 'If the Church of England ordained women then that was it, she was gone. As far as she was concerned, it was nothing theological, it was more a "cave in" to the feminist movement and equal rights.'

On 11 November 1992 the Synod voted by the required two-thirds majority (plus two votes) to ordain women – and Ann Widdecombe fulfilled her promise to leave the Anglican Church. The first person she told was Chris Moncrieff of the Press Association, and her decision became a matter of immediate public interest. She recalls: 'He told me, the Church of England has just decided to ordain women. I looked at my watch – he said it had happened seventeen minutes ago – and I said: "Well, seventeen minutes ago I ceased to be a member of the Church of England." ' She then relayed her decision to her bishop (by this time Gavin Reid); he wanted her to delay a couple of days, but she told him the decision was irrevocable.

The seeds of press curiosity had been sown, but Widdecombe had not expected such a harvest. 'I was not the personality I am now. I was not a member of the Synod, as John Gummer was. So I did not expect the enormous amount of interest that suddenly erupted around me. All the media began to ring up, and it all came to me. I did a whole series of interviews that night. Specifically, I did one on the *Nine O'Clock News*. From that moment I got cast in a role as one of the leaders of this anti-movement. I had quite a hairy time over the next few days as the press started to run stuff on how Anglicans were leaving in droves. Well, we did eventually, but it was by no means obvious at that stage.'

The decision to leave the Church of England was clear-cut and unavoidable, and one Widdecombe had contemplated for a long time. But she was undecided about her plans to move to another church. While she was still in a state of some uncertainty, Alton introduced her to Father Michael Seed, a priest from Westminster Cathedral who was Cardinal Hume's colleague and ambassador on ecumenical affairs, and someone with a breadth of experience in the Christian church. His journey from low church Baptist to Roman Catholic had not been too dissimilar to Ann's spiritual odyssey, and the two established an easy relationship. Seed also met regularly with the group of four MPs in the convivial surroundings of the Pugin Room bar at the House of Commons. He regarded them as 'a pack'. They met in the Pugin Room or a dining room; we would find them somewhere. They might be in Ann's office having whisky. In fact, I used to say to Ann, when she had a difficult theological problem, "Whisky will help you." '

Meetings between Ann and Father Michael were intense and frequent following her departure from the Church of England. Political journalists seeking a quote on a topical issue were surprised to discover they were interrupting the minister in the middle of a meeting with the priest. But Seed had a lot of work to do. Widdecombe was extremely well versed in Christian theology and the Bible, and wanted detailed explanations of the teachings and doctrine of Catholicism before there was any question of her accepting them. Unlike most converts, she was not worried about the Catholic belief that the Pope is infallible – indeed, she approved of the idea of unchanging and divinely sanctioned leadership – but she wanted explanations about such matters as the sacrificial nature of the mass, purgatory and prayers for the dead.

In the course of one discussion with Seed, she was seen tapping the table with a fork, in an apparent demonstration of passion. But Ann interpreted it differently. 'I was talking about purgatory, and I was demonstrating things on the table with a fork. I said: If you have got a perfect sacrifice, you cannot then say that it is perfect, but that there are other things just as good. I was just demonstrating with the aid of a fork – just as you might say, here is Hyde Park, there is Leicester Square. That's all I was doing!'

The issue was one on which sharp implements might seem to be appropriate. Widdecombe's philosophy of salvation prescribes a very severe admissions policy for entry into heaven. Individuals cannot win admittance for what they have done on earth, however much they may merit it or have suffered for it. Rather, they enter heaven through their acceptance of the 'all-perfect and sufficient' sacrifice on Calvary. 'You have free choice, as to whether you accept the Christ sacrifice or not. But your entrance to heaven depends on your acceptance of this sacrifice on Calvary.' Those who do not accept the perfection of that sacrifice, either because they are not Christians at all, or because they are Christians of a different theology, require special divine intervention. 'Those without the law should be judged without the law. That is down to the wisdom of God. It does not bother me.'

This process of exploring Catholic teaching had to take place discreetly. There had been great public interest in Widdecombe's departure from the Church of England, and speculation that she might choose Rome was rife; but she wanted time to make the decision, and she did not want it forced on her by a press leak. She maintained: 'I did not say at any stage that I was going to Rome. I quite genuinely did not know then.' So she ensured that Seed's visits to her offices, either in the Department of Social Security or in the House of Commons, took place in great secrecy. 'I was very, very careful. I went to the Cathedral very, very faithfully every Sunday. In my last days in the Anglican Church, I divided myself between St Margaret's, wherever I happened to be in the constituency, and Westminster Cathedral. So I went on Sunday mornings, but never stayed behind afterwards, or did anything to give rise to speculation. Eventually, the queries ceased.'

Her decision to leave the Church of England also prompted many Anglicans to seek her advice. 'We had a lot of clergy wanting to go to Rome, but not knowing on what possible terms. Did they have to do the whole course of priesthood again, or could they have a very truncated version? Would it vary according to the individual? They got different messages from different dioceses. I cannot describe to you the chaos!

'I was quite misleadingly cast in the role of leader. As a result people contacted me, asking me what to do. Obviously I was not in a position to say what they should do. So I asked to see the Cardinal. I could tell that there was a lot of distress all around, and I wanted to discuss, not me, but Anglicans wanting to cross to Rome.'

But in due course Ann brought up her own dilemmas with Cardinal Hume. Ann said later that in the course of fifteen minutes Hume succeeded in resolving all the problems she had raised with Father Michael. The contents of the meeting would forever remain private, she said later; but she told Seed that Cardinal Hume had dealt with her very specific concerns by giving her 'a smudge mark' to blur the edges of each of the issues where she had difficulty with Catholic teaching. Seed recalled: 'She called me up and said, "That's it, all cleared up." And I said, "What are you talking about?" "I saw the cardinal and he's given me a smudge mark." When I saw Cardinal Hume I teased him about it. I said, "You're meant to be teaching the faith, not taking it away." But in fact, the point is very serious. The church is a mystery and there are too many things in it to always perceive all of them clearly.' 'Smudge Mark' would later be a nickname she used when communicating with Michael Seed, who became a good friend. Ann introduced a number of other MPs, among them John Gummer and George Gardiner, to Michael Seed and in due course they followed her across to Rome.

Hume had a profound impact on Ann Widdecombe following this first meeting. She discovered in him a man of profound humility and honesty who was to continue to influence and move her while she prepared to embrace Catholicism, and long after.

Ann was now set publicly to announce her membership of the Roman Catholic Church, and she told her brother and parents of the decision. Her brother, Malcolm was quite happy with her choice. 'I admired what she was doing and the stand which she was taking.' Then she told the media, and the earlier publicity was redoubled. Ann was cast as the leader of the multitudes then said to be packing their bags for Rome, and there was great curiosity about her motives and beliefs. The publicity that had surrounded her departure from the Church of England led many to assume she had made a political decision. Ann denied it. 'All the media were interested in was the fact that I had been "an Anglican from birth", that my brother was a canon in the Church of England, that I had been a prominent Christian throughout the abortion debate (which I had been) – and that I happened to be a woman as well. I knew that they wanted to build the story up as a movement of "Anglican deserters". But the big revelation was to be that I had not been an Anglican for numbers of years, and had not had a continuous period in the Anglican Church.' This point deserves emphasis. Some time before the ordination of women, Widdecombe had inwardly left the Anglican Church and started to identify herself in personal and religious terms with Rome. So her acceptance into the Roman Church was more like the end of a long journey than a quick-fire response to the Church of England's latest decision. While the ordination of women was the last straw, when the moment came to accept Rome, she was adamant she had been persuaded to cross over by love of the Catholic Church, and not because she was angry with the Anglicans. 'I did not walk out of the C of E to Rome. I said quite publicly at the time: "I don't know where I am going. I want an Apostolic church. Because I want a church that does not compromise, that does not waver with every fad and fashion, I probably am looking at Rome, but I have some pretty major doctrinal reservations." '

Some sections of the media sought to explain the move as the last journey of a high church Anglo-Catholic, who had always had one foot in Rome. Even well-informed Catholics like the MP Michael Ancram had assumed she was an Anglo-Catholic. But they were wrong. The fact that Widdecombe was not an Anglo-Catholic but in fact a committed evangelical who held 'no-nonsense, scripturally based views' made the decision to cross to Rome the more extraordinary and, for some, the braver.

Widdecombe's departure, together with the wider talk of rifts in the Church of England, stimulated apocalyptic prophecies of the church's decline. 'Some said I should have stayed in the Church of England and fought; some said "Good riddance" to people like me; and a lot of them said, "Come join our church" – Greek Orthodox, the lot.' Widdecombe was quite happy to confirm that she thought the Church of England was in terminal decline and unsalvageable. She was also ready to point the finger at the Archbishop of Canterbury. An open letter to him published by *The Guardian* on 26 January 1993 read: 'I was at Canterbury for your enthronement and thought the Church was entering a period of spiritual renewal. Instead it was entering terminal decline. This is not the place to rehearse again the theological arguments for and against the ordination of priestesses. It is the effect of the Synod vote we must look at now – a vote which resulted in no small measure from the lead you gave.'

Once the decision was made, the practicalities of reception into the Catholic Church had to be completed. On a religious level, Widdecombe had to find a confirmation name. Michael Seed advocated the name with which she was baptized, namely Ann. That would have been simple, and St Anne was, after all, the mother of

Mary, the mother of Jesus. But Ann Widdecombe insisted on taking the difficult route: her religious hero was Hugh Latimer, and she wanted to carry his name. Latimer had been Bishop of Worcester during the reign of Henry VIII and had been martyred by the Catholic Queen Mary. A man who believed in upright living rather than high theology, he was best known for his last words at the stake: "Be of good cheer, Master Ridley, and play the man, for we shall this day light such a candle in England as I trust by God's grace shall never be put out." But this choice posed a problem for Seed, as Latimer was a Protestant martyr whom the Catholics had burnt at the stake, and therefore a little out of bounds. Widdecombe insisted on the name, both because of her affection for the historical story and for the message it conveyed about her own conversion. She said she was 'a huge admirer of Latimer. I felt very strongly that although I was leaving the Anglican Church, and in some dudgeon, what I wasn't leaving behind was that part Anglicanism had played in my spiritual development. It was huge. All my believing life, up until that moment, I had been an Anglican. I was determined to acknowledge it.'

Seed tried to accommodate Widdecombe's need. 'I said, she can't have the name; we burned him at the stake. We wisely found another Hugh – St Hugh of Lincoln. I said, "You can also have it in memory of the martyr Bishop Latimer." We had a great debate, a little bit of a fight over that.' Seed said he later came to see the wisdom of her choice. 'I understood the ecumenical significance of what she was saying. It was shocking to my logic, then I realized my logic was quite strict and that what she was saying was much more profound.'

Seed also agreed to allow Ann another variation on standard Catholic practice. She wanted to follow the traditional line recited at the reception service, namely, 'I believe and profess all that the holy Catholic Church believes, teaches and proclaims to be revealed by God' with the additional sentence 'I give obedience to Pope John Paul II, and the successors to St Peter'. This request met with no argument. Seed: 'As far as I was concerned, as long as she said the original sentence as it stood, I don't mind what she says. One's loyalty to the Pope is included in the original sentence, but she wanted to spell it out. She is very, very precise. It was a bit of extra!' In fact Ann had always taken particular interest in the linkage the Pope provided to Peter, the first Pope, so the addition was particularly important for her.

Once the name and the change to the statement had been agreed, Ann met up with Seed to discuss the venue and the date. It was decided that the ceremony of 'reception' would be held at the crypt chapel of the House of Commons on 21 April, the date when the Catholics were holding their Easter mass. This would be close to her place of work and she hoped it would enable many of her colleagues and friends from her parliamentary 'family' to come and join her. But these arrangements would cause Widdecombe and her close Catholic friend David Alton very considerable embarrassment.

An article appeared in the *Sunday Telegraph* on the Sunday before the service which was headed 'Commons Crypto-Papists'. It portrayed the service as triumphalist and deliberately offensive to the Queen and the established church. It said that the decision to time it for 21 April, the Queen's official birthday, was a calculated affront to the monarchy, and this insult was compounded by one of the hymns included in the service. The decision to hold the service in the same building as the Queen's Parliament was interpreted as an affront to the Protestant hegemony established following the Reformation, even though Catholic masses had been held in the building for some time.

The article set off alarm bells down the road from the Commons, at Westminster Cathedral, where Cardinal Hume was greatly concerned. He had long had a good working relationship with parliamentarians and was concerned that the service might be construed (however wrongly) as some sort of affront. So, on the same day the article appeared, it was agreed to move the ceremony of reception from the House of Commons crypt to the crypt of Westminster Cathedral. However, part of Widdecombe's original intention would be retained, as she would still celebrate her first mass as a Catholic later in the day in front of her parliamentary friends and family at the Crypt Chapel of the House of Commons, the place originally chosen for the entire ceremony.

The change of venue dealt with one set of problems, but it created another. The House of Commons venue had certain strict rules about media involvement and it had a staff to police them. The same could not be said about conditions at Westminster Cathedral, where anyone could enter. So when Father Norman Brown, a blind priest at the Cathedral, brought down Ann's four friends and sponsors – the MPs Julian Brazier (who stood in for John Patten), David Amess and David Alton, and the former MP Ken Hargreaves – he did not know he was being followed by a fifty-strong press contingent.

Seed had been warned by Ann to expect a few reporters from her constituency and the Catholic press, but this was a quite different matter. Cathedral officials suspected that the crowd was less discomforting to Widdecombe than it was to them, and they linked it to Ann's appearance on *Newsnight* the previous evening, when she had talked about her conversion and the state of the Church of England and had given details of the service. They were not amused when they had to respond to questions from Cardinal Hume about the publicity given to the event.

Seed himself was very put out. 'It was meant to be a private service, but once they were in there was no way we could get them out.' He consulted Ann, who said they should be allowed to stay; so he summoned up all his considerable reserves of charm to deal with the media scrum. He arranged for them to line up behind Ann so that they were out of her gaze as she knelt at the chapel's altar. He then addressed the media. 'I said something like, "Gentlemen, you are here, now could I ask you to respect the integrity of this service and not to take any photos." ' The press accepted the constraint, and Seed recalled that the only photo they got was when she was anointed by the chrism and confirmed. 'They sat quietly for the first six, seven minutes. Afterwards, they all came to congratulate her – they became part of the service! But you had French television, Austrian television, the BBC. The lot!'

The press was well-behaved, but their coverage, and the impact of the publicity, were unfortunate. Seed said, 'It gave the impression that

Ann had been received into the media, not into the Catholic Church. That is total nonsense.'

Widdecombe herself later recalled her shock at the extent of the media interest. 'They kept very quiet, until the moment of reception itself, when suddenly 50 million bulbs exploded in the crypt. It was pitch black down there, so as the flashes exploded I closed my eyes. The next day the papers announced: "Ann Widdecombe with eyes closed in prayer" when, actually, it was because I was dazzled by flashes.'

That evening, Ann, dressed in pale blue, celebrated her first mass as a Catholic in front of a large invited congregation of parliamentarians. The service was led by Father Michael Seed. Ann's brother Malcolm attended, dressed in his formal robes, and he was accompanied by their mother. Ann and Seed had devised the service, which included the hymn 'Faith of our Fathers'. Those critics looking for a provocative message claimed this hymn advocated the conversion of the Church of England to Roman Catholicism. There was no mystery about the reason for the inclusion of the hymn 'Who can Sound the Depths of Sorrow' (sung as a solo by Ira Jessel, wife of the Conservative MP Toby Jessel): Ann linked it to her anti-abortion campaign. 'Many of those who were there had been part of my pro-life campaign. Also, my commitment to the pro-life cause was one strand of my coming to Rome.' While much criticism of the service was alarmist and ill-judged, some came from friends of Ann. Frank Field, for example, was upset that 'the priest rushed around throwing holy water over us, which I thought was a damn cheek. Then it went on too long and I was actually bored by it. But it was clearly a big day for her.'

Ann's happiness was very evident, and she said later she had not a moment's doubt that she had done the right thing, and the Catholic Church suited her. But some wondered if it would last. Converts typically experience a period of grieving for what they have given up, however willingly, and David Alton feared that, as a mainstream Anglican, she would miss the Book of Common Prayer with the King James text. Alton was also concerned that she should not divert her grief into attacks on the Anglican Church. He told her that he 'felt it was very important that she did not become bitter, or too antagonistic to the Archbishop of Canterbury or other people that she might have held responsible for what was going on in the Church of England. Life was too short to get involved in all of that.'

Ann did, nevertheless, continue to attack the Anglican Church in the years after her conversion – indeed, she made a powerful speech in the House of Commons debate on the ordination of women priests; but the attacks were balanced by the spiritual sustenance she acquired from a number of meetings with holy people in the Catholic Church. The most memorable of these was an audience with the Pope. This took place in the course of a visit to Rome on government business in January 1996. The honour was all the greater as she was received for twenty minutes, twice the usual length of audience allocated to most visiting dignitaries to the Vatican (barring prime ministers). She later told how she felt in the Pope's presence. 'I could quite easily have sat in silence for the entire allocated time and just absorbed that feeling of closeness to God, but the Pope was chatting away in very reasonable English.'

Ann's visit to Mother Teresa in Calcutta, in the course of a three-week trip to India, was another deeply spiritual moment. She also met Mother Teresa in London, and the two participated in a press conference at Westminster Hall. When Mother Teresa was asked about the seriousness of homelessness in London, she observed that Westminster Hall itself would make a useful night shelter for the homeless. Ann: 'I met three people in my life that remind me of Christ and the Apostles, the Pope, Mother Teresa and Cardinal Hume.'

The copious attention given by the media to Ann's conversion made her Parliament's most visible Catholic. This gave her a higher media profile, but she found it also brought burdens. In due course she would feel responsible for opinions expressed by the Catholic Church in Britain, and in the latter years of the Major government this became uncomfortable. She was particularly upset about an election document called *The Common Good* which was published by the Catholic Church in April 1997. One insider said Ann regarded it as 'the Catholic Church telling everybody to vote Labour'. 'She was fuming and said that it contained text straight out of the Labour Party's manifesto. There was great drama between Ann and the Cardinal's office. Only the Cardinal could really calm Ann down.'

The manner of Widdecombe's conversion to Catholicism had its detractors and its mockers. But those who knew her well said it enabled her to regain the spirituality she had known as a child and lost with age and the decline of the Anglican Church. The reaffirmation of her fundamental religious principles would give her greater personal security and confidence. These would be tested to the core in the next stage of her political journey.

TWELVE

The Hornets' Nest

WHEN Ann Widdecombe arrived at the Home Office in July 1995, she was stepping into a hornets' nest. At her first meeting, with Michael Forsyth, the outgoing prisons minister, she was warned that Michael Howard did not get on with his director general of prisons, Derek Lewis, and wanted him sacked. At her second meeting, with her Secretary of State, Michael Howard himself, she was pointedly asked for her opinion of Lewis. He told her he was unhappy about Lewis's performance at the Prison Service and had heard a rumour that he had been sacked from his previous job. Widdecombe later recalled: 'Within a couple of days I realized just what had been going on for some time.'

The atmosphere was particularly unpleasant because the department was awaiting a report on an escape that January from Parkhurst, the high security gaol, compiled by General Sir John Learmont, and the unanimous fear was that it would be highly critical.

The schism between Howard and Lewis was wrecking working relationships in the Prison Service. The bad atmosphere was very evident to Sir Stephen Tumim, the Chief Inspector of Prisons: 'When you heard Howard and Lewis together at meetings, neither of them seemed to be listening to the other at all. They were totally incompatible.' And yet, in terms of politics and working style, the two men had much in common. They were both tough operators, both described by colleagues as loners with little capacity to work in partnership. Lewis was a workaholic, effective, 'quite cold but superficially charming', said one former colleague. Howard was 'an awkward man, who did not get on well with people,' said Tumim. A senior civil servant who also saw them at close quarters thought the pair needed 'a violent row to get the hostility out of their systems'. That was not likely to happen while each saw the other as an obstacle to doing his job well. Both men wanted to be the chief, obeyed by others. Howard expected his civil servants to fall in line behind his decisions, and made no secret of his impatience with those who resisted him. He said: 'It's the minister's job to decide and set out his views, and it's the civil servant's job to put them into effect. I didn't expect happiness, jubilation or three cheers.' Lewis, for his part, saw Howard as just another interfering minister who should accept his briefings, and leave him alone. Bob Thomas, chief press officer for the Prison Service, recalled that Lewis 'didn't take any truck. If he had a different point of view he made it clear. It was his Prison Service, and he ran it the way he did. He wasn't like your normal civil servant who's been on low pay all his life and still has a mortgage.' Lewis was by this time a wealthy man, having had a successful management career in business before joining the Prison Service.

The two men had been at loggerheads since Howard was appointed to the department by John Major in 1993 to toughen up the government's stance on law and order. Lewis had been brought in eighteen months earlier by the liberal-minded Home Secretary Kenneth Clarke, but he had no political difference with Howard, although (like many Conservatives) he found Howard's rasping style of delivery 'Victorian'. His problem was simply that he would not be dictated to; so when the Home Secretary advised him to bring the army in to deal with a prison problem, he responded by telling the minister to leave it to him. Meetings between the two had got so tense that on one occasion, Lewis had stormed out in frustration. His relationships with other ministers were also choppy. Baroness Blatch, the Home Office minister in the Lords, asked him an 'innocent question about prisoners and drugs, to which he snapped back, "You can't do that." I thought, why can't you do it? He spent an awful lot

of time trying to tell us you can't move too fast in the Prison Service
... he said it was a volatile situation, if we're to avoid a Strangeways,
if we're to avoid prison riots.' However, Lady Blatch seemed to have
overcome her reservations at some point, as she later supported Ann
Widdecombe's defence of Lewis and made representations to the
Prime Minister on his behalf. Lewis's major rows took place with
Howard, and they concerned a couple of high-profile escapes which
were causing Howard huge political grief. When a group of IRA
men escaped from Whitemoor on 9 September 1994, Howard held
Lewis responsible and hauled him over the coals. The Prison Service,
with Lewis as its head, was subjected to a massive investigation.
Howard viewed the subsequent escape from Parkhurst and the
ensuing Learmont Report as a re-run of Whitemoor. Would this now
now help provide the evidence and condemnation Howard needed
to rid himself of his troublesome prisons manager?

Widdecombe was initially perplexed by the hostility between
Howard and Lewis. This was not government as she had seen it in the
course of her five-year-long ministerial experience. But she reserved
judgement for the first few weeks of her new job. In that time she
started to master her brief, which extended over much more than
prisons, including immigration; and she also began to go round the
country's prisons, a tour which exposed her to the problems the
prisons faced – bad industrial relations, low investment and poorly
qualified staff. She also saw how Lewis was bringing private-sector
values of efficiency and productivity to the poorly managed Prison
Service and how this was having beneficial effects: for example, escapes
had fallen by 80 per cent and the amount of productive work done by
prisoners had been increased. She saw Lewis as exactly the sort of
industrial manager who could put government policy into effect and
'turn upside down' the public sector. The task was enormous, and in
her view he needed encouragement, rather than discouragement.

Anxiety about Learmont's expected attack on the Prison Service
and fears about Lewis's future permeated the department from top to
bottom, and constantly emerged in its work. When Widdecombe
decided to put out a press release announcing that escapes that

quarter had fallen, Howard's office advised against it. They would be publishing the Learmont Report in a few weeks, said his political advisers, and 'We would look stupid if we have to say how well the Prison Service was performing.' Sure enough, when early drafts of Learmont started to circulate, the worst fears were justified. It condemned the management of the Prison Service and pointed a very direct finger of blame at Derek Lewis, while specifically excluding Michael Howard from blame. It was very bad news for Lewis.

Widdecombe received the report on 27 September 1995, in the course of the Home Office Strategy Conference held annually at the Civil Service Centre, Chevening. She read it overnight, and told Lewis the following morning that Howard would use the report to attack him, but she would go to Howard and argue his case. Lewis recalled: 'She thought it was a pretty superficial piece of work which was basically designed to reinforce some prejudices. It was based on hearsay, and it neglected to pay attention to our achievements in reducing the numbers of escapes and improving the quality and time prisoners spent on rehabilitative work.'

Patrick Rock, Howard's political adviser at the time, observed, 'Ann took a different view of Learmont to Michael. I imagine she wanted to rubbish the report.' The report was in fact attacked by almost the entire top brass of the Prison Service as circumstantial and poorly argued, and Learmont himself was considered by Lewis to be inept. But its forthright conclusions served Howard's purpose admirably – as Widdecombe discovered when Howard took her aside during a break in the Chevening conference. She had been discussing Learmont's report with Lewis, but Howard advised her against getting too close to Lewis. He said he foresaw the Learmont Report could have serious implications for Lewis' position. But Widdecombe was determined to support Lewis. At this stage, though, she thought that the best approach was through rational discussion within the department, rather than by creating external pressure on Howard. It gradually became clear that this was a tactical error on Widdecombe's part as it played into the hands of Howard's political advisers, Patrick

Rock and Rachel Whetstone, who wanted to keep their intentions towards Lewis quiet and so prevent a build-up of support for him

Rock appeared to Derek Lewis, in his book *Hidden Agendas*, as a 'political Rottweiler with views somewhat to the right of Attila the Hun... Rock could be guaranteed to express the refined prejudices of the hearty right-winger.' Widdecombe saw the roles of Whetstone and Rock as 'making Michael look tough. They didn't think about what would happen after that, who would run the Prison Service and so on. No, the important thing was to give them a scalp and they'll all be happy.'

Battle was now engaged between Widdecombe and Howard's Rottweilers, and the minister knew she would need to have all her forces mustered.

Widdecombe and Lewis had forged an alliance aimed at turning Howard round using reasoned argument and sound evidence. On a Sunday morning at the beginning of October, they sat themselves down in the Home Office to prepare Lewis's defence to the Learmont Report. Howard later said he did not 'think he knew that Widdecombe had helped Lewis prepare his defence document'. At the outset Widdecombe got impatient with Lewis as he seemed to be missing the politician's point of view. Howard had seen this himself, and viewed it as stubbornness, even insubordination. But Widdecombe saw it as a blind spot on Lewis's part – the result of inexperience rather than wilfulness – which could be rectified with coaching.

Lewis had to realize that his survival depended on his ability to tell the Home Secretary what he wanted to hear. Howard was a consummate politician and Lewis needed to help his political master defend the Learmont Report to the House of Commons. If Lewis gave one hint that he had not learnt the political lesson, she warned, if he gave Howard one opening, the canny lawyer and Queen's Counsel would prise it open, and Lewis would go out the door.

At first Lewis resisted. He voiced his deep suspicion of politicians' short-term thinking, and protested at Howard's interventions when he was supposed to keep his nose out of the department's daily affairs. He referred to the Woolf Report, which he still regarded as his working manual, even though its generally liberal outlook was the opposite of Howard's. Lord Justice (Harry) Woolf had produced a blueprint for the prison agency after the Strangeways riot of 1990, and this referred to a 'structured stand-off from ministers'. Lewis took this to mean that the head of the prisons agency was autonomous and not subject to ministers' diktats. Colleagues later advised Lewis that unless he changed his thinking on this and accepted that Howard's style was more interventionist, he would soon be writing his resignation note. Lewis had no intention of doing this in a hurry, and turned his mind to dealing with some of Learmont's proposals.

One of these was the recommendation that the high security prison Parkhurst should be downgraded to a lower security status, and a super secure prison, the so-called 'super mac', be built elsewhere. Lewis wanted to rule out the proposal straight away, as the Prison Service had spent a massive amount of money on making Parkhurst more secure since the breakout nine months ago, and it was strategically placed on an island. That answer might reflect his gut feeling, but it was not going to satisfy Michael Howard, whose prisons policy and even his career were at stake. At this point all he cared about was the risk of escape, because each escape damaged his political standing. If Parkhurst's security were not enhanced, and there was another escape from the prison, well, that would be dynamite. Lewis then suggested that a member of the Learmont team of investigators, who had so rubbished Parkhurst, should now go to the prison and see for themselves the work that had been done, under a new governor, to improve the security. Widdecombe later commented that Lewis 'adjusted to things very quickly'. Indeed, this broad recommendation was eventually put to Howard as part of Lewis's response.

For most of that Sunday, Lewis and Widdecombe dissected Learmont. They drew up a brief document, and on Monday passed it on to Richard Wilson, Howard's Permanent Secretary. Wilson, who went on to become Cabinet Secretary, was a thorough professional, who stuck to the rule that civil servants did not make policy, but implemented it. Now he was caught between two ministers who were split top to bottom. His task was made harder because he was also having to negotiate on the future of a fellow civil servant. Wilson supported Lewis, and reported favourably on Lewis's defence document, while suggesting that it needed to be more forward-looking.

Widdecombe tried to fix up a meeting with Howard to discuss Lewis's document. She told him that she wanted a full hour and she needed Wilson to be present. She called Howard's office every day, but each time Howard found a reason for putting it off. When he offered her a brief telephone call, she rejected it. She was finally granted her meeting with Howard and Richard Wilson shortly before the Home Secretary left for the party conference in Blackpool. In an impassioned defence of Lewis, she argued that his failure to see the political viewpoint was due simply to lack of training, not hostility, and she reminded Howard how other businessmen in government had needed time to accept the much greater emphasis on accountability in the public sector. If Lewis were given some guidance about political convention, the government would have an excellent administrator for the Prison Service. The proposal fell on deaf ears. It seemed Howard had his doubts whether Lewis was capable of doing the job, and gave the impression that he had been determined to dispose of him for a long time.

When Widdecombe left the room after this particularly tense meeting, Howard asked Wilson if Lewis should be given a chance to prove himself. Wilson advised him to give it a try. He also saw the way that Howard's mind was working, and advised that if Howard felt he needed to sack Lewis, natural justice determined that he should have a chance to defend himself.

Widdecombe and Lewis now embarked on hand-to-hand fighting with Howard and his team within the usually sedate confines of the Home Office and the Prison Service.

Howard followed Wilson's advice, calling Lewis in to a meeting on the Monday evening to discuss his defence against Learmont's charges. The meeting was brief and chilly. Howard was not satisfied with Lewis's explanation, and wanted further and better particulars by the end of the week. Lewis prepared a massive document, and wanted to bounce his ideas off Widdecombe. She was in Blackpool, and so he decided to come up to the conference to meet her. News of this meeting reached Howard, and he summoned Widdecombe. He asked her brusquely why Lewis was visiting Blackpool, and she replied that he was bringing up the Prison Service response to the Learmont Report. She also said she would not be surprised if Lewis discussed some points that Howard had raised about Lewis's own position. At this point Howard said that the visit was 'completely inappropriate'. There followed a 'difficult conversation' of unpleasant proportions when it became apparent how differently they viewed Lewis's prospects of remaining as director general of the Prison Service. Whereas the junior minister was now clearly rooting for Lewis, it appeared to Widdecombe that Howard was looking more determined than ever to make him pay the price for the prison escapes. But he was not prepared to show his hand, and every attempt Widdecombe made to persuade him to disclose his intentions towards Lewis failed.

Widdecombe would not be deflected from her intention to meet Lewis in Blackpool, but she acceded to Howard's demand that she should not participate further in Lewis's personal defence. She accordingly told him she could not allow him to show her his new reply. She would, however, let him talk to her about it.

Lewis had also sought the input of Richard Wilson into his second defence document. But whereas Wilson had looked at, and made some changes to, the earlier version, he did not assist with the revised document. Lewis: 'There was a marked change in demeanour; Howard discovered that Richard Wilson had given me some advice on the first defence document. And Richard Wilson was much more "hands off" when it came to the second one. I sent that over to him and I don't think I got any comments back from him on that.'

The meeting in Blackpool between Lewis and Widdecombe took place on Tuesday 10 October, and was one of the stranger events in Widdecombe's political career. The venue needed to be private because 'matters of state' would be discussed, so she booked the meeting room of the small hotel in which she was staying. It was not one of the town's plusher establishments, where Secretaries of State and grandees stayed, but an out-the-way place, little grander than a bed and breakfast. Here the two conspirators expected to be left in peace. So they were dumbstruck when they saw through the room's transparent glass walls Howard's two political advisers, the Rottweilers, Patrick Rock and Rachel Whetstone, enter the hotel's lobby. When they saw them snooping round the room and peering in suspiciously, they did their best to laugh. 'It was pure farce. To this day, I think, how can grown-up people be so daft,' says Ann. Lewis recalls: 'They were continually walking in and out and around this place observing what was going on. We could see them walking past. Ann wasn't fazed at all.' The 'guards', as Lewis termed them, did not upset the meeting, and Lewis absorbed Widdecombe's comments for incorporation into his amended response. Eventually, Lewis noted, 'The guards departed and I came back to London to make the changes.' Rock later explained his presence at the hotel as a mere coincidence.

Howard came back from Blackpool on the Friday, with Lewis's defence in his briefcase. His conference speech on the Thursday had been well received, and he felt on a high. Howard had smarted for some time from Major's decision not to make him Foreign Secretary the previous July, but had now put that resentment behind him. He would deal decisively with some of the unresolved problems in the department and start the new political year with a clean sheet.

Lewis did not hear from Howard on the Saturday, but having read an article in the *Daily Express* saying that his head was on the block, he feared the worst. The timing of the article made Lewis suspect a pre-emptive leak. He had an appointment with the Home Secretary in his diary for the Sunday morning, 15 October; Widdecombe would be present at the meeting. The omens for it were bad.

First, Widdecombe had a preliminary discussion with the Secretary of State. Howard told her that he had made his decision to ask Derek Lewis to resign and it was irreversible. Widdecombe warned Howard of the consequences of his action. She would later claim her view was prophetic. 'You'll get away with this tomorrow, when you make the statement, because it will surprise the opposition. On Tuesday, things will start going wrong, because Derek will start hitting back and there will be resignations because he has so much support behind him. By Wednesday, the tide will have turned, and people will say you should not have sacked him.' The consequences of sacking Lewis for his own career would also be ominous, she told him. Then she showed, perhaps with a touch of sophistry, how things might work out better for him if he kept Lewis. ' "If you don't sack him, all the heat will be on him, and people will say he should go. But if you do sack him, the heat will be on you because you will have made a scapegoat. By Thursday, your position will be untenable. You should not do it." That did not move him. Then I said, "How will you replace him?" By now I was very upset.'

During this exchange Lewis had been waiting in the lobby, oblivious to the row in progress inside the Home Secretary's huge office. When he was summoned to hear the news, the two fighting cocks pulled apart, and a false air of calm was restored. As Lewis stepped into the room, Widdecombe gave a pronounced shake of the head, clearly seen by Howard. It warned the director general that the game was up. A stony-faced Widdecombe listened as Howard plodded through the formalities: the Learmont Report presented him with a public confidence problem; he could either ignore the report and its clear-cut findings, or act on them in the way they clearly pointed. He chose the latter. He had therefore to call for Lewis's resignation.

Howard told Lewis that his positive view of the Prison Service did not tally with Learmont's dismal analysis. 'I have to decide which of the two I prefer and I prefer Learmont's.' Howard wanted Lewis to stay on until the end of the year to ensure a smooth transition to a successor. He would agree to say nothing derogatory in public about Lewis, and a package of compensation would be provided.

Lewis was prepared for Howard's statement, and was on 'autopilot and emotionally detached' when he delivered his reply. He disputed vehemently Howard's view that his account differed from

Learmont's. But before he could elaborate, Howard jumped in, and stopped him in his tracks and said there was no point in discussing it any further. He then asked Lewis to deliver his resignation withoin two hours.'

Lewis demanded more time, saying he needed to discuss the matter with his wife. Howard allowed him until five o'clock that afternoon to hand in his resignation.

Widdecombe went from the meeting with Howard to her own office down the corridor to ponder a dilemma whose consequences would haunt her for the rest of her political life. She was now so angry she considered her political future. She later said she was very close to tendering her own resignation.

What could have been going through her mind as she stared, head in hands, at her Home Office desk, and thought about cutting short a political career which had taken her so long to build and had been achieved by dint of her own efforts alone? Her conscience told her that a serious injustice had been committed, and out of loyalty to Lewis and 'disgust' – Widdecombe's word – at Howard's treatment of him, she ought to make a very public protest.

Her instincts told her to resign. But the *realpolitik* of such an action needed much more careful calculation. It would hurt further the deeply unpopular Conservative Party, to which she had given her life; and it would upset the party's beleaguered leader John Major, whom she held in deep regard.

Then she assessed the chances of her resignation winning Lewis back his job. This could only be achieved if Howard was forced to resign himself. This was a possibility, she conceded. Many friends told her that week that her resignation could bring down the whole pack of Howard's cards. But where would that leave her? There would of course be a burst of media interest, but after a few days this would subside, and she would have to return to the obscurity of the back benches and a future away from the limelight.

The conflicts between what was best for the government, what was best for Lewis and what was best for herself were traumatic. Widdecombe is someone who prefers certainty to vacillation, and clarity to doubt. Reaching a decision of this magnitude would demand much soul-searching.

The key player in any dispute of this scale was bound to be the Prime Minister, John Major, whom she liked, and who had given her her first and indeed every subsequent government job. He alone could tilt the tables. So, later that Sunday morning, Widdecombe wrote to him to outline her position on Lewis, and to indicate how seriously she was at odds with Michael Howard. Her letter said, 'Although I accept collective responsibility for all government decisions, I find it extremely difficult to accept what we are doing to the director general for prisons.' She dispatched the letter immediately to Number Ten Downing Street.

Major rang Widdecombe back that afternoon to hear her case, and measure the threat. This was one of very many clashes of personality and ideology that were being thrown at the embattled Prime Minister, and in terms of the issues involved, it was far from the most important. He was sympathetic on a personal level to Ann's evident distress – the avuncular role suited this least pretentious of premiers – but he was not prepared to give her what she wanted and take a judgement on the merits of the case. In his view, these were not clear-cut, but 'marginal', and the decision was Howard's, not his. Major recalls: 'She was extremely loyal to her civil servant whom she believed was being unfairly treated; Michael believed he wasn't being unfairly treated. They took a different view of the same set of circumstances – that happens sometimes in politics. I did hear her out, I also heard Michael out. I also studied the facts of the case.

'Michael was the Secretary of State. If Ann had been the Secretary of State, unless it was such a clear-cut case – and I didn't think it was in that case – I would have invariably supported the person responsible for running the department. Or at least, I would not have interfered with the policy of the person running the department. They have a responsibility to Parliament and to the Cabinet.'

Widdecombe was flabbergasted. 'Gaffer be crazy,' she quipped to Major. 'The boss is mad . . . We have had a smashing party conference, and the first thing we are going to do is have a political uproar.'

Major told her there was nothing he could do, as Howard had told him the matter was irretrievable. Widdecombe tried to argue that Howard could make an (admittedly unlikely) *volte-face* on his decision, particularly as Lewis 'had not resigned and will not resign'. She argued that Howard had brought in a new allegation against Lewis, namely that his view of the Prison Service did not tally with Learmont's, and at the very least Lewis needed a proper chance to defend himself.

Major recalls the conversation: 'I certainly tried to comfort her, and prevent her from taking such a cataclysmic view of her disagreement with Michael. I didn't want her to resign. I knew how she felt; I talked about it. I told her I thought she was getting it out of context, and that it would do her no good and it would do the party no good, it would do the government no good. It may well be that she didn't resign because she didn't want to cause any difficulty to me, and I think it is quite possible that was the case. But we certainly had discussions of that sort.' Widdecombe later insisted she did not threaten Major with resignation.

At the end of the conversation, Major asked her what she would do. She had the choice of resigning, doing nothing or saying she would have to think about it further. The first choice would have sent the Tories into a further tailspin. It would quite likely have unseated a Home Secretary, as well as consigning her to the back benches for the rest of the parliament. The impact of such a fracas on her career prospects could be highly detrimental.

To choose the last of the three would have put pressure on Major to reverse Howard's mind, as it contained an implied resignation threat. But Widdecombe was not willing, or perhaps able, to play these sorts of power games with a Prime Minister whom she considered a close friend. The cynicism required for negotiations of this kind was not compatible with her intrinsic honesty and straightforwardness.

The urge to bring her fury with Howard out in the open was powerful, but it had to be curbed if she was to do the best for the party and the Prime Minister. So she took the second choice: she did nothing. She told Major she would stay loyal to him, and he could rely on her to support the party. But the pain and sense of injustice, and the knowledge that she could do nothing about it, rankled. She discussed the matter at length and passionately with a number of fellow ministers, including Gillian Shephard, but did not breathe a word in public. As the months passed and as Howard secured his position, that pain and sense of fury were to grow stronger.

After the phone conversation with Major, Widdecombe telephoned Lewis. She told him she had put her party first and he understood. He also realized she was removing the last possibility of saving his job. Lewis swallowed his disappointment. 'She told me she had considered resigning but had decided not to do so. I remember thinking it would have changed the complexion of things, had she done so. Had she done so, there was actually a big chance that Howard would have changed his plan.'

Baroness Blatch recalled: 'She would have resigned; she would not have hesitated. But she was a good supporter of John Major, the Prime Minister, and she felt she could not give him another high-profile resignation with all the ramifications of that. Against all her instincts she didn't resign.'

Major was relieved that the matter had been concluded so quickly and apparently neatly. But the decision not to resign plagued Widdecombe, and it lay at the very heart of her decision in May 1997 to attack Howard. In her speech to the Commons on that occasion, she said, 'I nearly resigned, and now regret not doing so. I put that on record, I now regret not doing so.'

When that speech was delivered, the constraints of party and personal loyalty no longer applied. Widdecombe did not have a frontbench position, and the Conservative Party was at such a low ebb that she could not have added to the demoralization. But Widdecombe would also argue (admittedly with the benefit of hindsight) that the speech was the stronger and the barbs against Howard the sharper because she stayed in her job. 'Had I resigned, the statement [describing the whole Lewis affair] would have been nothing like the statement I eventually made, because I wouldn't have seen the internal papers, I wouldn't have known anything about the defence Michael was about to make. It wouldn't have been "something of the night", it would have been "this is an unjust decision". The rest came later.'

Major's comments were of no help to Widdecombe, but the fight with Howard would go on to the last ditch. If she was to turn him round, she needed to do so before the Monday afternoon, when he would make his Commons statement announcing Lewis's departure. But Widdecombe and Lewis were by this time clinging to straws. She told Lewis to follow up her talk with the Prime Minister by drawing up a brief refutation of Howard's latest allegations against him, which he should send that evening to the Prime Minister, with copies to Howard, Wilson and herself.

In the meantime, more forces rallied to Lewis's support. On the same Sunday morning Howard had a phone conversation with Sir Duncan Nichol, the former businessman who had been brought in to run the NHS organization and was now senior non-executive director of the Prison Service. Nichol, who had already written two letters to Richard Wilson supporting Lewis, drove home the view that Lewis had performed well in difficult circumstances, that the Learmont Report was generally unbalanced and in places 'inane', and that Lewis's dismissal would pose severe problems for the service in terms of recruiting more people from the private sector.

Nichol said, 'It was either conspiracy or cock-up. Why did he hand the fate of the top management of the Prison Service to a bunch of people like that? Generals like Learmont know about military administration, and not much else.' But even as he put his case, Nichol realized it was a lost cause. Howard had now been handed a damning report, giving him the opportunity to sack Lewis, something he had long wanted to do.

Nichol was not alone in his efforts. That Sunday evening, the board of the Prison Service demanded to see Howard to protest at his move. Howard had not wanted the meeting, but they were so angry that they had insisted on it. They told Howard they were concerned at the 'operational interference' Lewis had experienced into the affairs of an agency which was supposed to be operationally autonomous. It was made clear to Howard that there was unanimous support for Lewis at the top of the service.

The following morning, Monday 16 October, Lewis and Widdecombe were summoned once more to Howard's office. Once more they were shown into the enormous room occupied by the Home Secretary. The scene was bleak and austere. Howard was sitting in his usual place at the vast oval oak table. Lewis went to sit opposite him. The private secretary sat beside the two antagonists to note the discussion. Lewis recalled: 'He was sitting in splendid isolation in his seat. Ann Widdecombe and Richard Wilson were almost cowering at the other end of the table.' Howard could be in no doubt that he was alone in his decision; his colleagues would not participate in the discussion nor endorse its conclusion. One report likened the atmosphere to a courtroom presided over by a hanging judge.

Howard reiterated his position that the gravity of the Learmont Report required him to seek Lewis's resignation. Lewis was given five minutes or so to make his case before Howard became impatient. He repeated: 'Oh, there's no point in any of this, I've made up my mind.' It was a replay of the meeting the previous day, and pointed to the same outcome. But at this second meeting Howard put the boot in further with a new ferocity by saying that any defence of Lewis he could make to the House of Commons would be vacuous and incredible, given that Learmont had said that 'the Prison Service needs visible leadership.' It was clear that Howard was not prepared even to acknowledge the role Lewis had played in reducing the number of escapes, increasing productive work among prisoners and improving administration. Widdecombe recalls: 'Derek put up a fight against it. He was not short of fight.' Howard then demanded Lewis's resignation.

Lewis left the room, knowing that Howard had merely been going through the motions of listening to him. 'If you are seriously considering the right thing to do, you don't spend just fifteen minutes with the person concerned. This was process for process's sake.'

But Lewis had already spoken to Widdecombe about his intentions if Howard persisted with his plan. When Howard and

Widdecombe discussed the case after Lewis had left the room, she told Howard that Lewis would 'not go quietly'. Howard riposted (from that position of certainty that now governed his behaviour) that he thought 'wise counsel would prevail and Lewis would resign'.

Widdecombe went out to the waiting room and saw Derek Lewis sitting there. Their alliance against Howard had come to nothing. They had used every ounce of their energy to deflect a wilful Home Secretary by reasoned argument. Now they were exhausted and in confusion. Widdecombe was 'blinking back tears'. Lewis was taken aback. 'I was a bit touched, I appreciated that it was bizarre to be sitting in the Home Office having just been fired, effectively, with the prisons minister in the room in tears, and me not knowing quite what to say.'

Widdecombe then returned to her desk and dictated another letter. 'I wrote again to the Prime Minister, I thanked him for his support – his personal support, not necessarily support of my view, he wouldn't have given that to me – and then I said, "I can't justify what we're doing in any terms at all – ministerial, human, Christian, any terms you can mention. I can't justify this decision." That was it.'

When Lewis returned to his office it was in a state of mourning. Audrey Nelson, his press officer, recalls: 'It was like a death in the family. That's how all the Prison Service felt. There was a great sense of shock.' Richard Wilson, fully returned to his role as the Home Secretary's favourite civil servant, chased Lewis for his resignation the rest of the day, but Lewis persistently refused to give it and had to be formally dismissed at lunchtime before Howard made his statement to the House of Commons.

The Home Secretary told a stunned chamber that the Learmont Report was highly critical of the operational management of the service, not the political leadership, and as a result he announced that Derek Lewis had been dismissed. Howard had crossed the first hurdle in his move to get rid of Lewis. But when Widdecombe addressed a meeting of prison governors the following day she got a sense of the resentment that was brewing in the Prison Service itself. Protocol demanded that she defend (with the least possible enthusiasm)

Howard's stance to the governors. They knew nothing of her position in the Home Office machinations, and loudly booed her. Audrey Nelson: 'It was a difficult encounter, and I was glad to be able to bundle her out of there, because it was very tense.'

The real political pressure would be felt by Howard, who had insisted on the sacking and would now have to defend it to a growing number of critics. Opponents in the Prison Service surfaced in the next few days, with two non-executive directors resigning and many governors sending in letters of protest. The Labour Party also smelt blood and called a censure debate on the Thursday. Lewis naturally did his utmost to stir up the opposition, and the day after his departure went to the opposition home affairs spokesman Jack Straw to show him the material he was using to make his case against the Home Office for wrongful dismissal. Lewis's writ – a huge and compelling document – was issued the day before the debate and immediately swung the media behind him.

Howard was also building up his side of the argument for the forthcoming censure debate, and to this end he summoned Widdecombe. The Minister of State was expected to make the winding-up speech in the debate, and Howard wanted to know what she had in mind. Howard was extremely agitated and, arms waving with fury, declared that he was locked in 'mortal combat, mortal combat. It's mortal combat between me and Derek. I need your help.' The threat his dismissal of Lewis posed to his own position had now become crystal clear, and Howard wanted to know whether Widdecombe would make public her support for Lewis. But the minister said she would play a straight bat and, if asked her view on Lewis, merely brush it off by referring to Howard's previous statement. This had included some token appreciation of Lewis's efforts in the Prison Service. When Howard asked Widdecombe to outline the contents of her speech, to check that their public positions tallied, she told him that she had nothing to show him. Howard was shocked, thinking that Widdecombe planned to resign and would not make a speech. She allayed his fears with a chuckle, saying that she never wrote down her speeches.

Shortly after this encounter, Widdecombe received another summons from an increasingly agitated Home Secretary. She arrived at his office in the House of Commons to find Simon Burns, a whip, in Howard's office. Howard told Burns to repeat a piece of news he had just received from a journalist to the effect that Widdecombe dissented from the decision to sack Lewis. She retorted that it was 'sheer speculation'. That did not satisfy the Home Secretary, who insisted vehemently that, should the subject arise, Widdecombe should tell the House she gave the decision her full support. But Widdecombe did not give any ground, saying merely that she supported all government decisions.

The situation was extremely unpleasant. Widdecombe noted later that it was ironic that at the time when Howard was accused of being sparing with the truth over Lewis, Widdecombe felt that she was being pressured to go further than merely supporting the government line. 'He was in a really awful state,' she has said.

When Howard went into the House of Commons that Thursday afternoon, many close to the Tory party thought they were about to witness a ritual humiliation so complete that Howard would be forced to offer his resignation. Not only did he have a divided ministerial team, he had an argument which did not bear close scrutiny. Widdecombe: 'He went in there, and I thought he wouldn't get through this.' Even Howard's own supporters were on tenterhooks. Rock: 'If he had made a dreadful speech and flopped, to jeers from the Labour side, he might have had to go. It was high noon!'

The debate hinged on a claim made by Derek Lewis that Howard had persistently intervened in the management of the Prison Service. This was potentially highly damaging, because Howard had relied on the distinction between policy and operations in defending the decision to sack Lewis, and remain in office himself. Howard's response to the breakout from Parkhurst in January 1995 was the last straw for Lewis. On this occasion, the Home Secretary and Lewis had had a violent disagreement about how to handle the Parkhurst governor, John Marriott. Both agreed that Marriott should go, but Lewis wanted him pushed sideways into another job to allow due process to take place, while Howard tried to browbeat him into suspending the governor there and then. The two engaged in a head-to-head fight which became so ferocious that the meeting had to be briefly adjourned to allow tempers to cool. During the break, Howard consulted government lawyers to discover whether he had the power to over-rule Lewis. He was told that this was precluded by the autonomy attributed to an agency.

But in the censure debate Howard gave a quite different impression of that meeting. He claimed that, far from trying to force Lewis to suspend the governor, there had been a polite discussion in which he merely wondered whether suspension might be more appropriate. 'I agreed with Mr Lewis's analysis that Marriott could not stay as governor of Parkhurst. I asked, as I was perfectly entitled to, if it was right for him to be moved to other duties as distinct from being suspended from duty. Mr Lewis explained why he thought that that would not be appropriate, and reaffirmed his decision not to suspend Mr Marriott but to move him to another job elsewhere in the Prison Service'.

Lewis viewed this as a blatant distortion and gave the Labour opposition team papers to that effect.

Howard managed to wriggle out of Straw's charge by playing with words. He had not directed Lewis to sack Marriott, he had merely demanded that he suspend him. The fact that Marriott had not been sacked merely showed that the debate between the two was fair and open, Howard asserted.

The debate showed Straw's lack of familiarity with the subject. When he was asked if he himself would have dismissed Lewis, had he received so critical a report as that delivered by Learmont, he appeared flummoxed. Later it was mooted he had failed to hear the question amid the uproar because he suffered from tinnitus. Widdecombe's speech eighteen months later was, she would say, the speech Straw should have made that day in October, when Howard walked free.

Howard came out of the debate unscathed. Distraught and depressed just a few hours earlier, he now felt vindicated. It put him on a high. Rock recalls: 'It was a triumph. You only had to look at the press the next day. Also, Michael Howard had a groundswell of support in the constituencies and among MPs. They supported his line on law and order.' Baroness Blatch remembers: 'Michael produced that amazing *tour de force* when he went out into the chamber. Frankly, I didn't think he could survive the day. He was clearly going to be savaged. Everybody was screaming for his resignation. He made this absolutely cracking speech, and got the troops absolutely raising their papers, and he managed to reduce Jack Straw to a gibbering wreck.'

Howard and his ministerial 'team' (they were of course still at complete loggerheads) went from the Commons chamber to John Major's room in the House, where the Prime Minister was laying on drinks. 'Michael was on a high,' said Widdecombe. Ministers in that position would normally thank their team and look forward to the next triumph. But Howard was much too self-absorbed for this, and had no such generous thoughts in mind. In fact, he talked not about the success, but rather how he could continue his attack against Lewis. Widdecombe was so shocked she left the room. John Major saw her distress and, not used to seeing junior ministers depart without so much as a by your leave, asked Ann in a quiet voice if she was leaving to go to another meeting.

Widdecombe went straight to her office, but was shortly afterwards called back to see Major when the other members of the team had gone. She recalls: 'By now I was very upset. John Major put his hand on my knee, in his familiar way. He said, "What is all this about?" I said, "This is the most disgraceful episode I have ever been involved with. Now that Michael thinks he's won, he's going to be vindictive." ' Major sought to reassure her that he would try to put a stop to Howard's efforts. That weekend, Howard duly called Widdecombe at her home to reassure her that he now regarded the incident as closed and would not be vindictive. Widdecombe replied that she had just spoken to Derek and he thought the same. That was a red rag to Howard, who questioned the propriety of her talking to Lewis at all; but when Widdecombe shot back that Lewis was someone she trusted, the still jittery Home Secretary was silenced. The Prime Minister received updates of the state of play between Widdecombe and Howard from his friend and neighbour Baroness Blatch. The relationship between the two Home Office ministers had flowered only after Lewis's dismissal, when Widdecombe discovered that Blatch was also unhappy with Howard's treatment of the director general. Blatch's role as intermediary with Number Ten was to be discreet but important in subsequent events.

Both Lewis and Widdecombe were determined to prevent Howard escaping scot-free from the fiasco. Both knew he had treated Lewis unfairly, and both were determined to expose him publicly and explicitly. Lewis pushed his case for wrongful dismissal through the courts and eventually forced the Home Office to pay out £280,000 in compensation and contractual entitlements. Widdecombe herself harboured the pain and anger created by the Lewis affair for the next eighteen months. She then produced a momentous and passionate speech which would rectify a wrong, as she saw it, and show Michael Howard that justice would be exacted.

But there were other controversies much closer at hand, and these would preoccupy Ann Widdecombe for some time before the Howard issue raised its head again.

THIRTEEN

Shackling Rules, OK

A Channel Four film in early January 1996 showing a pregnant woman shackled to prison warders outside the maternity ward at the Whittington Hospital in north London sparked off a most virulent controversy that embraced the entire Major government. The prisoner, a thief called Annette Walker, told *The Guardian* newspaper of the conditions of the shackling. 'Two officers sat down next to me on the bed. I asked them to leave as I was in pain, embarrassed, crying, but they wouldn't.' It was later reported that Annette was kept in chains 'until she was about to give birth, when officers removed them but insisted they remained on the other side of the screen'. A prison officer joked to her that she might jump out of the fifth-floor window to escape. The material was inflammatory, although not borne out by the film.

When Ann Widdecombe watched the film she saw nothing to alarm her. This was the proper functioning of established Prison Service policy. 'I watched the film very carefully. I was perfectly happy for women to be secured between prison and hospital. I was perfectly happy with the procedure that you removed the restraints as soon as medical treatment started, that was, when labour started. I was perfectly happy with the policy. I have to say that I think the whole thing was blown out of all proportion.' Her problem was that very few people agreed with her. The emotions evoked by this story sent shock waves through the Home Office, the Prison Service and the caring professions, who were looking for an excuse to wreak revenge on a Conservative government that they felt had long since consigned them to irrelevance.

The seeds of Walker's story were sown during a controversy that had broken out before Widdecombe arrived at the Home Office. A pregnant woman who had earlier tried to escape (while four and half months pregnant) had been kept in chains while giving birth. This was contrary to prison practice and the Home Office had apologized. But that incident set the tone and much of the media message for the later one: the heavy symbolic overtones of women giving birth in chains suggested a medieval and barbaric practice. This was far from the situation that prevailed at Holloway, as Ann Widdecombe would constantly tell the ranks of assorted soft liberals and bureaucrats, in words of one syllable, who began to abuse her when the television documentary was shown. But by then she had been cast as the new icon of hard-hearted Toryism: the media bandwagon was rolling, and it would not be rolled back for two years, when she herself was to punish Michael Howard, the actual architect of much of the new disciplinarianism introduced in the 1990s.

Those on the inside knew that the abuse thrown at Widdecombe as a result of the 'shackling episode' (as it came to be known) was gratuitous. Even her opponents accept that this prisons minister was not only more conscientious than any other had been for a very long time, but in certain respects more liberal than many. Her insistence on the expansion of education and 'purposeful activity' was in tune with progressive penal thinking. This was based more in a Protestant work ethic than in any desire to be kind to prisoners, but it was interpreted by the professionals in the service as forward-looking. Sir Richard Tilt, who followed Derek Lewis as director general of the Prison Service, noted with approval: 'The people at the top of the Prison Service broadly speaking do the job because they are interested in improving conditions and helping prisoners in planning constructive training and education and work schemes. So they will always respond better to a minister who is more liberal, less right-wing. And I think Ann was very much more liberal in her approach to prisons than either Michael Forsyth or Michael Howard.'

The alacrity with which Widdecombe was dubbed heartless and cold when the shackling episode burst into the press that January perplexed both the Prison Service and Widdecombe herself. But as the episode unfolded the Prison Service was substantially at fault, because, like the government, it was caught completely off guard, and quickly caused its minister severe embarrassment. This was particularly galling to Widdecombe, who had made enthusiasm and conscientiousness her hallmark at the Home Office. The prisons part of her portfolio, which also included immigration and firearms policy, was far and away the most absorbing. To understand the job, she felt she had to do a tour of the service, and soon after her appointment she began to visit prisons.

Her initial guide round the prisons was Lewis, on whose departure the job was taken by the acting director general, Richard Tilt. Tilt recalled that Widdecombe was unmoved by the prisoners' catcalls that regularly greeted visiting officials and politicians. In fact, the minister appeared to relish her form of 'prison visiting', and sometimes toured as many as four in a day. By the end of her term as Prisons' Minister, Ann Widdecombe had visited all 135 prisons in england and Wales. Tilt was dubious whether the visits served much point: but the energy was undeniable, even if the purpose was less so.

Prison visiting of the ministerial kind is undertaken not merely to keep staff on their toes, but also to boost morale, and give the remote institutions the sense that the politicians are paying attention to their gripes. But Widdecombe's visits to an institution were sometimes shorter than she would have liked. 'You're not bringing a genuine interest in them when you're only in a place for an hour,' grieved Tilt. 'Trying to knock off every one was a tactical mistake. She would have been better off to say, "I'm going to spend a lot of time visiting prisons," and then to get out and spend a lot of time in rather fewer prisons than she did.'

Such assiduousness meant that when the House of Commons debated the 'Holloway shackling' issue on 9 January 1996, Widdecombe was completely conversant not only with the Prison

Service's approach to security but also, most importantly, with every aspect of its practice. She told the House that there had traditionally been a policy of letting women who were travelling between prison and the hospital go unfettered. But this had had to be reversed when an analysis showed proportionately more escapes by women than men between prison and hospital. The present policy, which was the same as that applied to men, required the inmates to be brought from the prison to the hospital in shackles, and then released only when medical treatment had begun. In the case of pregnant women, this meant when labour 'was confirmed'. When the baby was born, and medical treatment terminated, the handcuffs were in due course replaced. In fact, the Channel Four film showed Ms Walker moving freely around the labour ward before and after giving birth.

Widdecombe further justified the policy on security grounds: twenty women had escaped from wards in the previous five years, a figure disproportionate to the number of women prisoners. She could not disguise her impatience when she explained to the ranks of incensed Labour members, 'Some MPs may like to think that a pregnant woman would not or could not escape. Unfortunately this is not true. The fact is that hospitals are not secure places in which to keep prisoners, and since 1990 twenty women have escaped from hospitals. The Prison Service has a duty of care to the mother, but this must be balanced against the needs of the service to keep all prisoners, including pregnant women prisoners, in secure custody.' The use of male warders to watch over pregnant women caused her serious concern, she admitted, but the principle of the overall policy was correct.

The debate on the policy was ferocious, with Jack Straw, the shadow Home Secretary, echoing much public opinion in calling the policy 'barbaric': 'In a civilized society, it is inhuman, degrading and unnecessary for a prisoner to be shackled at any stage of labour.' Straw said that gaol staff felt so intimidated by ministers that they were forced into decisions 'which defy both common sense and common decency'. Many concerned organizations, such as the Royal College of Midwives and the Howard League for Penal Reform, joined in the clamour. Gwyneth Dunwoody, a Labour MP, accused Widdecombe of seeming 'to show a frightening inability to understand the difference between a woman who is four and a half months pregnant, and a woman who is in labour'. This referred to the earlier attempted escape by the woman attending for ante-natal care; the inference was that, as an unmarried woman who had never had a child, Widdecombe knew little and cared less about the travails of women in labour. Widdecombe later said that this was false, and that medical decisions about pregnancy were taken not by ministers but by midwives.

The 11 January issue of the *Daily Mirror* was largely devoted to the story, and gave birth to Doris Karloff, the monster minister. Under the headline 'Loveless Life of the Woman They Call Doris Karloff', the paper wrote: 'No wonder some MPs have dubbed her Doris Karloff after legendary Frankenstein star Boris, because of her manner and her love of dark clothes.' The nickname had indeed been in circulation among Labour MPs for a long time. It originated from the period in 1993 when Ann was preparing to convert to the Catholic Church, and at the same time started to wear crucifixes. Paul Flynn, a Labour MP with a caustic sense of humour who also wrote a column for a newspaper, observed that the roots of Ann's hair were showing on the dark head in the shape of a star. Flynn said: 'She appeared to have been touched by the finger of God – or the Devil . . . She was a terrifying sight in mid-shriek and closely resembled someone from Hammer Horror films casting. She became familiarly known in the back benches then as Doris Karloff or more often, Doris.' Flynn was more than happy to resurrect the smear when the *Mirror* began to wage its campaign against the minister over her role in the shackling episode.

The paper sought to buttress its claim that Widdecombe was a villainous and harsh spinster by quoting 'one woman colleague': ' "She is as hard as nails and as cold a politician as you would fear you could meet . . . she seems to have little feeling for anyone, least of all women." "She has done nothing for women throughout her political career," said Labour MP Barbara Roche. "She has shown a total lack

of understanding of women and families." ' Relations between
Widdecombe and Roche, a friend from Oxford days, suffered as a
resulted of that quote, and remained distant for quite some time,
although Widdecombe would later be grateful for her support when
rumours alleging that Widdecombe was anti-semitic appeared in the
press. Roche, who is Jewish, told the press that Widdecombe 'used to
vote for her at Oxford', and that put paid to some of the charges.

Roche was the only female Labour MP who was willing to talk
to the *Mirror* for its story – many who had been asked for a quote,
including leftists like Joan Ruddock and Mo Mowlam, had declined;
so Roche's willingness seemed particularly disloyal to the embattled
minister. In the same article in the *Mirror* the maverick Labour MP
Frank Field, upset by the abuse and personal comments thrown at
her, came to Ann's defence. He told the paper, 'She is one of the most
talented ministers in the Government. It shows the mismatch of
talent that she remains outside the Cabinet.'

Doris Karloff would trample daily through the *Mirror*'s columns
for as long as the affair occupied newsprint, and the name was
picked up widely by other tabloids. Widdecombe turned the
offensive name into a joke, and took to answering the phone
'Karloff' to catch callers out. Role-playing and inventing nicknames
are part of Widdecombe's stock-in-trade as politician and writer, and
this served her well in defusing the abuse at this difficult moment. 'It
is the exact same thing as you would say to a child who is being
laughed at. Call yourself fatty, and don't look hurt because if you do
they enjoy it more.'

But the *Mirror* went further than merely throwing names at
Widdecombe. The paper also called for her resignation. 'She displays
not just a lack of compassion. She shows no sympathy for women in
labour. Her callous rejection of appeals to change this procedure will
have shocked every reader . . . it is better to risk a very occasional
escape than to treat women in childbirth so appallingly . . .
Widdecombe is clearly not fit to hold her ministerial post. She has
absolutely no regard for public opinion or human decency. Howard
should over-rule her. Better still, he should fire her.' The attack went

across the board, with even the *Daily Telegraph* containing an article
that said the policy was 'mad'.

While the opposition, the pressure groups and the media were
launching into their campaign of protest, another formidable woman
was preparing a barb to puncture Ann Widdecombe's confident
argument. This would hurt Widdecombe more than the earlier
appeals to emotion. Baroness Hayman, a Labour peer and chairman
of the Whittington Hospital Trust, targeted a statement by
Widdecombe in the House of Commons debate in which she had
claimed that no complaints had been formally submitted from the
Whittington about the shackling policy. On 11 January Hayman
wrote Widdecombe a letter which began, 'I am afraid you have been
misinformed as to the hospital's position regarding the effects of
changes in custody practice in April last year.' She then referred to a
meeting in November 1995 when hospital staff had met the Prison
Service to air their concerns about the shackling policy. The hospital
officials had suggested that one way to deal with the problems was to
have the hospital come to the prison, rather than the prisoner come
to the hospital, and so avoid the risky journey; but, Hayman said, the
suggestion that 'a group midwifery, obstetric and gynaecology service
be provided in the jail to avoid the practice' was ignored. She had
then tried another route, writing to Baroness Cumberledge, a junior
minister at the Department of Health. Her letter, dated 4 December
1995, had pointed out: 'There are grave professional concerns over the
effects of the tightening of custody policies towards pregnant women
prisoners. As the main hospital providing care for women from
Holloway Prison, we are much concerned with the dilemmas current
policies are posing for both clinical and custodial staff.' This letter too
had been ignored.

The evidence of complaints to the Prison Service and the
government was irrefutable and damning. As soon as she read
Hayman's letter, Widdecombe immediately called a meeting with the
director general of the Prison Service, Richard Tilt, to discover
whether Hayman's claims were true. 'Have we had any correspondence at all?' she demanded. 'Tilt said, "Yes, but they haven't

complained." So I said, "Will you go through the correspondence again just to make quite sure?" ' The Prison Service's outright denial was scarcely credible given the volume and authority of the complaints, and Widdecombe insisted on seeing the file. 'I opened it up, and the first letter was a complaint. I really went potty in a big way. I said right away, "This is personal statement territory." I had made an extremely clear and unambiguous statement to the House that there had been no complaints from the hospital.' Widdecombe now had to take responsibility for a simple mistake by the Prison Service's administration. It was one that she was convinced its former director general Derek Lewis would not have made, as he had never been reluctant to get involved in the most detailed administrative minutiae when the matter at issue was sensitive. Widdecombe had remained in close contact with Lewis since his departure. Indeed, they were probably closer after he left the Prison Service than before. So, as the shackling episode ramified, Widdecombe turned to Lewis for informal guidance on how to deal with it. He warned her that prison governors were the only reliable sources of information, as the Prison Service bureaucracy was cumbersome and untrustworthy.

The initial response of some officials to Prison Service bungling was to hush the episode up by clarifying the record in the Commons library, thus avoiding a full statement in the House. Howard had later sought to claim that the new shackling policy was nothing to do with him, and had been introduced by Derek Lewis. Widdecombe: 'We went back to the divide between policy and operations – it was nothing to do with us.' She recalls: 'I'm not saying he wanted to stand up and say he hadn't known. He wanted to say this was a Prison Service decision. And I said that we knew about it. And he said that he didn't think he did. I said, "Yes, you did," and I quoted the stuff that I had seen and said, "You must have seen this," and yes indeed he did, but he saw it a bit later than me for some reason. He was away, or whatever it was.'

Patrick Rock, Howard's political adviser, sought to distance the Home Secretary from the affair with some spinning in the media. But Widdecombe said the policy had been mentioned in correspondence as early as the previous summer, and Howard could not repeat the scapegoating of Lewis. 'We had seen it in correspondence, but we hadn't focused on it, it had never been an issue for us,' she said.

There was no alternative for Widdecombe but to face up to the onslaught. 'I thought, "If I try to slide out with some written answer there will be hell to pay." 'That judgement was eventually shared.

The answer to the Private Notice Question [PNQ] Widdecombe delivered was provided by the Prison Service, and she asked them to make it 'sympathetic'. She wanted it to include the possibility that the government was considering changing the Prison Service rules for handling pregnant women. She could not announce a change in the rules, as that was the prerogative of Howard and he was away, but she could at least indicate that it was being actively contemplated. But the Prison Service ignored this request, said Widdecombe, and the statement she was given was hard and unyielding. It was also delivered to her so late that she did not have time to 'tear it up and rewrite it', as she would have liked, before the deadline arrived when it had to be delivered to the Speaker. 'Out of ignorance, I felt pressured by this deadline, and sent the statement over to the Speaker. If I had my time again, I'd have taken it and torn it apart and told the Speaker she had to wait because it wasn't ready. It was the first time I had answered a PNQ and I felt obliged to do what I was being told to do by the Speaker's office. That was a big mistake. So I had this thing to read out.'

The personal statement she delivered to the House of Commons on 15 January which dealt with Baroness Hayman's complaint – flanked by Michael Howard (now returned from his trip abroad) and David Maclean, the other Minister of State – only served to inflame passions. It treated the matter solely as an administrative mistake: 'I deeply regret that the advice which I had been given about this correspondence, and which I in turn gave to the House in good faith, was wrong.'

The opposition exploited the government's discomfiture for all it was worth, and Straw later said the admission had 'blown apart her defence of the policy of manacling pregnant prisoners. I hope that today's embarrassment will lead to some long overdue humility by both Mr Howard and Miss Widdecombe.' Doris Karloff reared her head once more in the *Mirror*, which claimed credit for pushing the story. Its headline on 16 January read: 'Karloff Backs Off'.

The policy change that Widdecombe had earlier sought now seemed to be inevitable, as the hostility towards existing practice continued unabated. On 17 January Howard announced that 'no woman who goes into hospital to give birth will be restrained from the time she arrives at the hospital... no prison officer would be present in the delivery room...Women prisoners will be escorted by two female prison warders...all restraints will be removed while prisoners were in the waiting area.' Howard also insisted that while chains would continue to be used for other hospital visits, governors would have wider discretion to remove them. On the following day Baroness Blatch, the Home Office Minister in the Lords, said: 'It has never been the intention of the Prison Service to apply handcuffs or chains to women who are confirmed as being in labour... But the Royal College has asked for certain modifications to be made to the use of restraints on pregnant women and the Prison Service has accepted its modifications . . . In future all physical restraints will be removed from a prisoner on her arrival in a hospital waiting room unless she is judged to present a particularly high risk of escape.'

Jack Straw continued to make the most of the government's climbdown, describing it as a 'humiliating retreat' and a 'panic after an avalanche of bad publicity... Ministers believed they could brazen their way out of this appalling situation. This was exactly what they would have done, had it not been for *Channel Four News* and public outrage and ministerial bungling.'

No sooner had the situation calmed down after this episode than the accident-prone Prison Service administration caused another furore. When a large number of prisoners were released unexpectedly following a revision of the Service's manual, the press were incensed. Michael Howard saw a public relations fiasco looming, and another potential blow to his claim to be tough on security, and demanded a meeting with the director general Richard Tilt and his colleagues.

The Prison Service officials were unable to say precisely how many prisoners had been released; during the course of the meeting the number rose from 80 to 400, and Howard 'blew his top'. The discovery that the revised manual was flawed and some of these had been released prematurely compounded the error. Widdecombe later thought to herself: 'If this had been Derek, Michael would have been going ballistic.' He was going pretty ballistic as it was. And he turned round to me at the end and said (when we were on our own), "I still think it was right to get rid of Lewis." And that was obviously when he had severe doubts. Anyway, there was nothing we could do about it; we had just sacked one director general, we couldn't sack another.' To adapt Oscar Wilde's witticism, for Michael Howard, losing one director general might be seen as a misfortune, but to lose two would look like a very serious form of carelessness. So Howard's own appointee, Richard Tilt, was allowed to keep his job, albeit at the price of doing the penance of a media blitz to apologize to the public and promise it would never happen again.

While the Prison Service clearly lacked management, it also lacked resources to deal with the burgeoning numbers of prisoners the judiciary were sending into its care. This was the result of the policy implemented by Howard and shared wholeheartedly by Widdecombe, that 'prison works' and was a deterrent that should be used more actively by the courts. But the new approach had its drawbacks. It meant that more prisoners would be engaged in less productive work because the resources and manpower were not available to provide constructive employment. This was a blow to Widdecombe, who strongly believed that prisoners should spend their time doing something useful rather than mouldering in the cells. 'Purposeful activity fell off, and overcrowding went up, and all the things that we had so much achieved in the previous years went. That wasn't because Tilt wasn't competent, that was because of these enormous pressures that were suddenly piled into the system.' In fact, the Prison Service was so deprived of resources that it was forced to seek extra space to house its charges, including disused holiday camps and ships.

Another factor also served to demoralize the service. The government was discussing experimenting with the market testing of prisons. This meant that the Service would be pitted against private contractors for the job of running prisons, and faced the possibility of losing some of its control. The scheme had already been promoted by Lewis, but before it made headway, Tilt sought to rebuff it. He argued that transferring to the private sector would cause immense confusion and immense dislocation. In the course of the argument, Widdecombe went for advice to her trusted friend Derek Lewis. Lewis rebutted Tilt's argument, and told her it was not necessary to move prisoners out. In fact market testing was dropped by Howard as a result of this fraught internal debate, and not implemented until Labour took power a year later. The research Widdecombe undertook to understand it came in useful in her first opposition job as health spokesman, when she advocated much more active involvement by the private sector in the NHS.

The shackling episode was not the only controversial event during Ann's period at the Home Office. She was also in charge of immigration policy and instrumental in attempting to deport the Saudi dissident Mohammed Al Mas'ari. This got thrown out by the courts and brought the government some embarrassment. She also had responsibility for firearms legislation and introduced a bill outlawing the possession of certain weapons. This offended some of her own MPs to the extent that several voted against it. Finally, she dealt with a hunger strike by asylum seekers at Rochester Prison in which two people nearly died.

Constituency matters were not neglected even while Ann operated at a ministerial level. For example, she made a dramatic visit to Morocco — entirely at her own expense — to secure the release of a constituent, who had been imprisoned on a trumped up allegation of drug smuggling. She returned thinking that her mission had been successful when the Moroccan government fell and she was forced to take the case up again. This time she was successful.

In her seven years in government, Ann Widdecombe had risen from the relatively obscure junior ranks of the Department of Social Security to the highly visible and sometimes controversial fortress of prisons minister. She had also become identified in the public eye as a right-wing woman, who looked firm and fearless under pressure, or was heartless and immovable, according to one's position. The abuse, like the praise, hardly affected her. But the failure to obtain a Cabinet position did. For Widdecombe had combined a vice-like grip on her principles with a driving ambition for a seat at the Cabinet table. When John Major reshuffled his Cabinet in June 1996, there seemed to be a chance that this goal might be reached; but the Prime Minister found no obvious vacancy for his loyal servant. Major explained the decision to leave her out: 'It's not very long experience as a Minister of State in a senior department, which is perhaps why she didn't quite make it.'

As the 1997 election hove into view, Widdecombe saw that, for the time being, she would have to be content with the rank of Minister of State and Privy Councillor. The status of privy councillor is given to senior ministers (irrespective of rank) at the Prime Minister's discretion, and Major gave it to Ann Widdecombe in January 1997.

By this time, a sense of foreboding was beginning to overtake the Tory Party. The constant rebellions over Europe had damaged morale inside the party, while Norman Lamont's fiasco over the European Exchange Rate Mechanism damaged it in the eyes of the public. The result was consistently low opinion poll ratings and a near certainty that the revived New Labour party would win the general election. Widdecombe remembered well the moment the date of the poll was announced. 'I was in the House of Commons tea room at the time it was confirmed. There were some people there who looked very ill indeed. There was one chap there with his hand across his tummy. I knew there were people there who weren't going to come back. It was very difficult; all the time you felt, this is the work of nine people [the Eurosceptics who consistently voted against the government]. There was therefore a lot of personal angst around.

'On election night itself, obviously I knew we were going to lose. But not on that scale. I made one wrong calculation. The canvass returns did not reflect the opinion polls. The opinion polls were showing this huge gap, but my canvass returns were holding up remarkably well. I thought, "This has happened in by-elections that we've lost catastrophically." But of course in by-elections people stay at home. My assumption, which was wrong, was that in a general election people would not stay at home, they would actually go out and vote. They didn't, they stayed at home on a grand scale. Up and down the country they stayed at home, our people. I hadn't taken that into account. So the meltdown was much greater than I thought. I arrived at my own count, and the first news I got ironically was wrong. Somebody came up to me and said, "Gummer's just lost". I thought, "if he's gone we've all gone." He hadn't gone. It was nevertheless a preparation for the Portillo loss, for the loss of Tony Newton, which upset me much more. Gillian Shephard hung on by a whisker. It was a dreadful night in which you were just there and colleagues were going down everywhere.'

Ann Widdecombe attended her own count at Maidstone, where she polled 23,657 votes, with a 12.9 per cent swing to Labour. She stayed there for a long time, she recalled, to support her devastated party workers, before eventually going home. The next day, she appreciated the sheer scale of the disaster, and realized that the Tory party was staring at a long period of opposition. A stark choice was offered to her. She could either wallow in despondency like a lot of her colleagues – many of whom took a long time to cast off the assumption of eternal Conservative power – or accept that the landscape would not be the same for a long time, and start building a new life suitable to changed and straitened circumstances.

For the woman who had learnt to expect the worst and live with the moment, the answer to the choice was crystal clear. She would come out fighting.

FOURTEEN

Tory Feminist

Ann Widdecombe says that sex is irrelevant to politics. But she has risen to prominence in an age when sex and feminism are of compulsive interest. She cannot resist entering the debate. But her comments and positions tend to offend rather than placate.

Feminists regard her as a traitor to the cause of women because of her stances on abortion and pregnant prisoners. Homosexuals see her reservations about gay rights as verging on the medieval. Colleagues on both sides see her fighting to be more macho than the macho and terrifying as a result. Widdecombe, it seems, can never be right.

Widdecombe fights to appear aggressive, but is, in fact, privately very emotional. Some would even say feminine. In an age when women politicians are supposed to be cool, Widdecombe is involved at a very deep level, and has occasionally been moved to tears in the company of colleagues when events have gone against her.

When Widdecombe started in politics, her greatest problem was dealing with constituencies which were prejudiced against women in general, and particularly confused by one as individualistic as herself. She did not have the partner thought necessary to indicate a settled private life and she was not prepared to bluff. Her stridency made few friends while her looks attracted much negative comment.

Widdecombe did not change, but she did persist; and in the meantime, Tory attitudes to women changed. The arrival of Mrs

Thatcher, a much more conventional Tory woman than Ann, but possessed of a ferocity that was not typical of her sex, and the more impressive for it, introduced conventional Tories to the possibility that women could be winners, big time. The ground had been laid for Widdecombe to gain a foothold not merely in a strong constituency, but also in the senior ranks of the party. When Maidstone selected her in 1986 they were in part seeking to repair the error of many years earlier, when they had rejected a young Mrs Thatcher as their candidate. They hoped Widdecombe would become their Mrs Thatcher. She certainly had the intellect and commitment.

But both Widdecombe and her followers were disappointed at her rate of progress after she was elected to parliament. She made a great impression on the House with her campaign for a bill on abortion, but had to wait three years to get a toehold on the ministerial ladder. Even then, while her competence in social security was well proven, she was kept at the lowest level for almost another three years, while more conventional Tory women – like Gillian Shephard and Edwina Currie – were promoted up the ranks. The directness of her manner, the strength of her convictions and her lack of 'photogenic appeal' (as it would be described) seemed to prevent the wielders of power in the government from recognizing her ability.

Meanwhile, the public and the media had latched on to her apparent eccentricity and happily made fun of a woman who did not conform to images of conventional attractiveness. The party hierarchy saw this mockery and, for a long time, sought to keep her at arm's length. The 'Doris Karloff' label, used repeatedly after the shackling episode and the frequency with which she was described as a spinster, were just two of the more derisive names that have stuck to Ann.

These offensive slurs brought out the best in her stoical nature. She tried to make fun of the 'Doris Karloff' sneer, and began to answer the phone 'Karloff' or 'Doris'. She makes no secret of the fact that she is overweight and dumpy, and not a model in looks. She has said without any apparent distress, 'I am overweight. I am ugly, I am dumpy, I have crooked teeth. I am forty-nine. I am a spinster. So where's the problem? . . . Interest in physical perfection is an irrelevance. We have got image out of all proportion and that is not just wrong but evil. It shapes our attitude to disfigurement and disability and leads to the abortion of deformed babies in our search for perfection.' She later dealt with this topic in her novel *The Clematis Tree*, where the central character is disabled.

Given that a lack of conventional femininity has haunted Ann since she entered politics, some sympathy with women in a similar predicament might have been expected. But Ann has always maintained that she has no interest in women's issues or problems. She insists that she made it to the top of the Conservative party by her own efforts, and that all Tories should do the same, whatever their gender. 'I should hate to think I was only going to get into the Cabinet because I was a woman,' she said in 1998. 'I don't think positive discrimination has done us any favours at all. Some of the new women are good but they are the exception. Most of them first of all give the obedience of puppy dogs to Blair. They have always got their pagers out. They dress à la Follett (Barbara Follett, the Labour MP), who tells backbench colleagues what to wear, and they whinge when Madam Speaker tells them off . . . I'm not impressed at all. They're very poor, these versions of the sisterhood.' On another occasion, she described 'Blair's babes' as 'ghastly. All those pastel suits and that power dressing – and they're just clones.'

As her parliamentary colleagues got to know her, they realized that Ann Widdecombe was not the conventional woman MP. Michael Brown, a former Conservative member, noted that Ann wanted to be 'one of the boys'. 'Quite a lot of women MPs did not go into the members' smoking room, which was very much a male club. But she was very much one of the boys. When Mrs Thatcher came into the smoking room with her handbag, you made sure the gentlemanly banter would stop. But we would never make any of those concessions when Ann was in the circle. She was one of the boys.' David Amess, Ann's Catholic colleague, concurred: 'She looked a bit old-fashioned. She didn't really look like a modern girl. She was resisting change. Ann never went in for dressing very smartly, whereas some of our Conservative ladies would always be done up. That wasn't Ann, although she was dressed smartly from time to time, but she certainly never spent huge amounts of time cultivating her physical image. She wasn't into that. She was who she was and people admired her really for that.'

Ann went even further and denied the importance of her sex in her growing career. 'I don't regard myself as a woman MP,' she was quoted as saying on one occasion, 'I'm an MP who happens to be a woman, in the same way that I'm an MP who happens to be short and fat.' And, she added, 'I am elected for the people, not just for women.'

Her appearance also made a political statement. It told the electorate that you got what you saw, warts and all, and not an airbrushed image. Image consultants had been banned from her office as early as the Maidstone election campaign in 1987. Then she had been called by one such who suggested that, as there were four women candidates, she would be judged on her appearance. Widdecombe emphatically refused even to consider amending her image. In the election, she increased the Conservative majority by 60 per cent, and concluded that the electorate was not swayed by cosmetic presentation. 'When I entered politics,' she said, 'I did so because of my belief that I could make a serious contribution to the Conservative Party. Parliament is about making this country better, it is not a fashion show catwalk.' One observer noted: 'She is one of the very few women MPs to have achieved that fine old feminist goal: liberation from lipstick and thoughts of hemlines.' She herself said in 1997, 'I don't wish to set myself up as a role model for girls, but I do think the fact that I am short and fat and ugly is very helpful for women.'

As Ann became a more prominent figure in the party, some noticed she was quietly paying more attention to her looks and couture. She has now agreed to do 'makeovers' for magazines, but the fact is she has always worn large ear-rings, donned high heels, Miss Dior perfume and make-up – although she admits that it wears off in the course of the day and she always forgets to top up her lipstick.

She dyes her hair when the white roots become too obvious, and she also takes considerable trouble over her nails, always using a base coat to avoid discolouring them and applying an oily drying agent. She avoids using any varnish at all for four weeks continuously once a year, and conditions them every day during that time. 'I haven't a hope of being like Mrs Thatcher,' she admits, not particularly regretfully. 'I used to say that Mrs T could get off a train at five in the morning looking as if she'd stepped from a beauty parlour and I could step from a beauty parlour and look as though I'd got off a train at five in the morning.'

But Miss Widdecombe blithely continued to eat the chocolates. She did not try that hard to lose weight. She hated diets and continued to indulge her weight-adding fancies, enjoying a drink to unwind with a friend after the last red box of the evening, preferring whisky and soda to herbal teas, and using the well-worn failed-slimmer's excuses: 'I'd rather be round and jolly than thin and cross'; 'I may be roly-poly but I am happy and a diet would just make me grumpy.' Mounted on her office wall is a Garfield cat poster that reads: 'If you want to look thinner, hang around with people who are fatter than you.' Ann Widdecombe seems to have settled for that option.

She has also accepted that she will never marry. In fact marriage was never likely. As a convent schoolgirl, she was never afflicted with the adolescent obsession with the opposite sex. In the dormitory at night when the conversation centred entirely on boys, she 'used to get sick and weary and tired of it.' She preferred to go her own way and read Virgil. Later, when she entered the public eye, and reporters asked her about the subject, she has always said that ' "Mr Right" has never come along and it was never a high enough priority to go out looking for him.' As far as she was concerned it was a 'non-question'. Her brother Malcolm has said that, indeed, ' "Mr Right" did not come along. As far as Ann is concerned, there is nothing to worry about. There are some people who go through life bemoaning the fact that they are single, and they are always whinging about it; and there are others who get married and whinge because they can't have kids. I think that my sister takes the line, "Okay, I'm not married. That doesn't mean to say I can't have a satisfying and fulfilling life." I think my sister would simply say, "I'm satisfied. I'm living a fulfilled life." '

It is certainly a very full life, and one which she acknowledges leaves little room to fulfil the demands of a conventional husband. She works a punishing schedule, managing on about five or six hours' sleep, so she revels in the luxury of an empty flat when she returns at all hours of the night. 'I shut the door on the rest of the world and think, thank God for that. And I'm glad there's not somebody there demanding his supper or wondering where on earth he put his clean socks.' After making a whisky and soda and listening to the radio, she gets straight into her pyjamas and 'I scoot under my very heavy duvet with a hot water bottle – a childhood habit – and I'm dead to the world until that wretched alarm starts shrieking again at six-fifteen.' And if there were a Mr Right having cornflakes with her after that, he would have to put up with her early-morning bad temper. She is only ready to face the world when she has drunk her first cup of coffee, read *The Times*, listened to the *Today* programme and done a couple of hours' work.

Most husbands would find it hard to fit into this lifestyle. But Ann never even made an effort to find one. She discovered in the course of her romance with Colin Maltby that her feelings about sex and physicality did not coincide with most men's. Her principled opposition to sex before marriage was understandable, given her respect for the values of the past, as opposed to day's permissive society, which she abhorred. Her insistence on her virginity is logical in this context; she has been quoted as threatening to sue anyone who alleges that she has had a sexual relationship. But other statements show a positive aversion to the physical act, a revulsion voiced in almost schoolgirl language: 'Sex is yuk. I'm very grateful that when I get home at night there isn't a man making silly demands.' 'Ugh! That is one thing I don't miss. That sex thing is so over-rated. I prefer a bath and a detective novel. I really can't understand why people make such a thing about it.' 'Everybody is obsessed with the wretched thing. I think there is a gross over-rating of it and certainly a gross obsession over it.'

Ann was introduced to information about sex by her mother, who gave her a book on the physical details; she said she found the book boring and did not bother reading it. Later, when she was at university in Birmingham when the 1967 Abortion Act came into force and it was then that her inate horror of abortion gathered further momentum.

Widdecombe has never ceased to stress how much she dislikes talking about this and other personal areas. One frustrated journalist commented: 'She emphatically doesn't like inwardness, the modern therapy culture and its habits of nostalgia and agony.' Others have noticed the fact that she 'resists the search for meaning, ducks away from emotion and preserves her privacy well. She is an old-fashioned stoic.' She is horrified by the contemporary 'counselling culture', which in her view has undermined both traditional English reticence and the power of the priest in the confessional to absolve the sinner. She identifies the counselling culture as predominantly feminine, and has said that she feels happier in the company of men. 'I don't go in for long-drawn-out self-analysis. I take myself – and other people – as they are. I do not find talking therapeutic. Talking is a modern obsession and I think it's becoming totally out of hand. There was a time when reticence was respected. Nowadays people pour out their most intimate experiences and I find it horrifying. Maybe that's why I prefer the company of men to women. Men don't bother with all that self-agonizing conversation. They don't make emotional demands . . . I have to say that men tend to be nicer. The worst attacks on me come from women MPs.'

This admiration for men was evident as early as her Oxford days, when she admitted that had she been born a boy, she would like to have gone to Sandhurst and joined the army. Her admiration and love for Murray, her father, has never left her, and it has coloured her entire attitude to life and her sense of herself.

The women's movement was an understandable *bête noire*. She not only lacked sympathy for their causes and campaigns, she also believed that they were damaging the sacred structure of the family by advocating that mothers should go out to work. Widdecombe was in no doubt that caring for a family and working outside the home were incompatible. She also said that the secure family needed a full-time mother (just as she had had) and the full-time mother could not also work. She wrote in October 1997, 'Such is the emphasis now on women's economic freedom, that we have begun to place no value whatsoever on the woman who stays at home and brings up a family. To be a full-time wife and mother is one of the highest callings a woman can have. A life lived for others should not be despised . . . Today women who provide stability for their children, support for their husbands and care for their husbands and parents are dismissed as "just" housewives . . . it seems that pay, not worth, now determines a woman's right to be respected.' The column ended with a call to her 'sisters' to resist despair and depression. She comforted women who looked after their family and did not work that they were doing the right thing, however much it might be criticized. Ann did not think that mothers made good MPs. 'You cannot be a good mother and be a good MP at the same time'. She said it was hard enough work managing a constituency properly, and to give a family the love it needs as well would break anybody's back.

Ann herself had built up a political life that was so full-time that any great attention to domestic matters was out of the question. Indeed, some colleagues have expressed concern that her furious work rate might prematurely exhaust her physical resources. She certainly does not leave herself much time to shop or cook (she has described herself as very much a beans on toast, take-away fish and chips sort of person). At her constituency home she relies on Kay, her daily help, to keep the shelves stocked and the house in a state of good repair. She says Kay 'looks after me totally like a rather wonderful wife. I haven't been so well looked after since childhood.' For Ann was doted on by Rita throughout her childhood. Her friend Linda Seale, who was invited to spend the half-term holiday with the Widdecombes, saw how little Ann had to do around the house when she was a child, and was amazed. She noticed that Ann's 'mother would do everything for her. Her mother would cook the meal, then clear up, then wash up. She would do her washing and ironing and make the bed. It's not that she took her mother for granted; she just accepted that that's what she did.' Mrs Widdecombe was not only a full-time mum, she was also a full-time wife. Her husband, like men in general 'in those days', to use Ann's words, was the wage-earner, he 'wasn't meant to come home and change the nappies'. Ann took a similar view of life. Though she is very fond of children, she is quite happy being the very affectionate maiden aunt rather than the twenty-four-hour mother and carer. She pays great heed to her brother's children and grandchildren; Malcolm has three children who in turn have produced one great-nephew and one great-niece for Ann.

This fondness for children has shown itself in a close relationship she has built up with two young people, Nikos and Theodora Louridas, who lived above the local kebab shop, the *Royal Dolphin* in Kennington Road. She met them twelve years ago and became a frequent customer at the café, enjoying her favourite doner kebab and glass of retsina, her nose buried in a detective story. The children were quite small in those days, and she used to play silly games with them, and was introduced to their dog. As they grew older she helped them with their homework and taught them card games. One important lesson that Theodora owes to Ann is the importance of being a good loser, a good sport. 'I was a terrible loser, but Ann would never let me win. Today, Theodora says, 'We both love Ann to bits. She is one of the most lovely people you could hope to meet.'

The absence of a domestic life and a permanent relationship has meant that there is only the slenderest of barriers between Ann's private and public lives. This enables her to channel her huge personal energies into politics of the most committed kind.

Her campaign to win justice for Derek Lewis was one such commitment. Now she would fulfil it in a very public way.

FIFTEEN

Something of the Night

WHEN Ann Widdecombe walked to the House of
Commons on 19 May 1997, she was bristling with nerves
in a way that surprised even her closest friends. The
short, squat figure that usually made such decisive and aggressive
movements was hunched. She looked isolated and distracted. For
once, it seemed, this Commons warrior who could boast medals from
many unpopular campaigns was daunted by the task ahead.
Assassinating the character (her own words) of her former boss and
the former Home Secretary, Michael Howard was her duty; and there
was no escape.

'I cannot tell you how reluctant I was, even as I went into the
House of Commons. As the Speaker said, "Ann Widdecombe", I stood
up, and I thought "Uh." It was the last thing I wanted to do. I
profoundly did not want to do it right up to that moment.'
Widdecombe then took out an eighteen-page typed text from an
orange folder and started to read it word for word. Thirty-five minutes
of reading later her ordeal was over. Howard's had just begun.

She began the speech by lulling Howard into a false sense of
security by paying tribute to his work at the Home Office before
moving on to the core of her remarks. 'It is with considerable sadness
and considerable reluctance, which I have to overcome, that I turn to
the rest of my remarks. But for my utter conviction of their rightness
and of the imperative that lies behind them, I should not be making
these remarks at all.'

As a political occasion it was highly memorable. Widdecombe
seized the stage and forensically examined Michael Howard,
convicting him of misleading the House in his explanation of his
falling out with Derek Lewis which had led to Lewis's sacking. The
events had been picked over by the press for the whole of the previous
week, but the House listened to this speech in complete silence.

This was mandarin-style drama, played in the corridors of power
and for the highest stakes. Michael Howard had assumed he could
march through the corridors and all would bow before him. So when
a civil servant looked him straight in the eye, he threw a tantrum and
wanted him cleared out of the way. Widdecombe arrived on the
scene to find a duo of battered egos in headlong and inexorable
collision. Eighteen months later, when the issue had been played out,
she saw in the episode not just high-handed government, but
evidence of amorality at the highest level. She declared: 'We demean
our high office if we mistreat our public servants . . . we demean
ourselves if we come to the House to indulge in a play of words.' The
new Leader of the Opposition (at that time unknown) should 'clean
up Parliament's image in the eyes of the British people'.

In the course of her speech Widdecombe took on not just
Howard but the entire era of sleaze that had done so much to bring
down the Conservative party. 'It is urgently necessary for the House
to restore its reputation with the nation. Many of our great institutions are falling into disrepute. I was wretchedly aware of how many
people to whom I talked during the election uttered the sentiment
that politicians of all parties are sleazy and corrupt and principally
concerned with their own interest and survival.' By pointedly
detaching herself from that sleazy atmosphere, Widdecombe offered
herself as a guide to a new and better politics.

Widdecombe concluded:

> 'Courage and toughness are both more than instant law and instant
> dismissal. As hon. Members we demean ourselves if we come to the
> House to indulge in a play of words and make statements which,

although they may not be untrue – they never are in the House – may be unsustainable. My decision to do what I have done today was extremely difficult ro reach, and I have agonised over it for months. One of the worst moments was when I decided that I would do it. I knew how shocked, hurt and upset not only my right hon. and learned Friend but many of my colleagues would be, but I formed the view that I could do no other. I reached my decision in the interests of giving very belated justice to Mr Lewis...partly of clearing my own conscience, although that is my problem, because I should have resigned at the time and did not...I am aware that I probably will not be forgiven for my decision by some Conservative Members uintil the day I leave Parliament. If I had not done what I have done today, however, I would not have forgiven myself until I left Parliament and beyond.

'As I sat down I thought, "Thank God for that. It's done" – I'd delivered the speech,' she said later. 'Was it also a sense of delivering the justice? Yes, but I think that came a bit later. Never, ever at any time since then have I ever regretted it, or any part of it, or anything I said.'

She sat down to much waving of Order Papers on the Labour benches, and to silence on her own. Many Conservative MPs were shocked by her speech; her senior parliamentary colleagues in particular were left fuming at the public humiliation of a colleague. They had seen and known the ferocity of Widdecombe's evangelical belief in truth and honesty; her self-belief in some circumstances was an invaluable asset. But what many of her colleagues saw now was less self-belief than an uncontrollable self-righteousness which was overwhelming the conventions of party and personal loyalty to which politicians subscribe, and on which they rely. They had seen Widdecombe leading the pro-life crusade ten years earlier; now they saw her crusade for Lewis driving a battering ram through the (admittedly) unsavoury state of Westminster ethics. At that moment, she had very few friends in the House.

Gillian Shephard saw the speech as vengeful and harsh, not an act of the forgiving Christian she had known for a long time and liked. 'I was appalled,' Shephard huffed. 'It was the most dreadful thing to do to a colleague, shortly after we were all bleeding from our wounds after the election. It is not something I could ever have done. I really do believe in forgiveness. I do not think it was either a particularly tolerant or Christian thing to do. That's Ann. There it is. She's conviction, through and through. But by the same token, it was a very courageous thing to do.' Shephard's disapproval was short-lived. She went to Ann's fiftieth birthday party a few months after the Howard speech, and sat at the top table, next to Cardinal Hume.

Virginia Bottomley was shocked rather than offended by the speech. 'It's like writing a novel about your marital disputes; it's not worth the scandal. I think once people start speaking like that, it's challenging.'

Misguided but characteristically eccentric was the view of Michael Ancram, the chairman of the Conservative Party. 'I believe loyalty to colleagues is important. But then that is Ann. Ann is forthright. If Ann has a strong view about something, she expresses it. That is part of what makes her the very splendid figure that she is. Everybody knows Ann. Ann, if she believes something, speaks her mind.'

Widdecombe herself dismisses the accusation of disloyalty as absurd. 'I was the epitome of loyalty,' she asserts baldly. 'I was utterly loyal to the party and did not resign in October 1995, whereas some of my colleagues did resign over issues in that period. I did not. I kept absolutely quiet until after the election when the party was already divided over the leadership election and it was safe to speak. It was then, as far as I was concerned, an issue of justice.'

William Hague saw the speech as reflecting the stubbornness of the conviction politician. 'She will die in the last ditch to fight for her opinion. You have to respect that, but to me it didn't ring true. It wasn't something I would have thought about Michael Howard. It was quite convenient for me as a leadership contender!'

Sinister motives were at work, said seasoned commentators on party machinations. Phillip Oppenheim, the former junior minister in the Department of Employment turned political columnist, said

Widdecombe was 'unpleasant and opportunist over Howard. Howard was a good whipping boy. No one liked him. The press thought he was oleaginous. *The Guardian* thought he was manically right-wing. I thought he was silly to stand for the leadership. What she did was highly personal, highly unpleasant, very self-serving.'

Anti-semitism was at the heart of the speech, said some in the party: Widdecombe had succumbed to the influence of Tory anti-semites in publicly attacking a Jew. But while leading Conservatives have spoken of anti-semitism in the Party, there was no evidence that this was at work here, and Widdecombe has always robustly denied the charge, pointing out that she was once a member of the Conservative Friends of Israel group.

When Widdecombe sat down, Howard sought to make a defence. He argued that his statement to the House in October 1995 had been vetted by civil servants and they had not challenged it. He reiterated the grounds for sacking Lewis and insisted he had gone through proper procedures. He denied the charge that he had sought to overrule Lewis's decision on the suspension of the governor of Parkhurst. 'At no time did I cross the line between what I was entitled to do and what I wasn't,' he said. 'Every decision that I have taken in my career in government has been taken because I thought it was in the public interest.'

Widdecombe drew immediate blood. To her surprise and delight, Howard agreed to her request that the new Home Secretary Jack Straw be asked to publish the minute of a meeting with Lewis which showed how Howard had unsuccessfully tried to overrule Lewis in his decision not to suspend Parkhurst's prison governor. Straw agreed, but only after consultation with the Permanent Secretary, as ministers are never allowed to see the documents of a previous government. The minute was published during the debate and showed that Richard Wilson had asked Lewis whether the proposed form of wording relating to Marriott's move from Parkhurst, 'is today being removed as governor', was acceptable. Lewis replied 'or tomorrow'. At this point Howard had immediately jumped in, saying 'No, no, no, I want today.' The decibels are not recorded, but the

repetition suggested voices were raised. Howard was exposed as
trying to dictate operational decisions to the Prison Service, which
blew a hole in his persistent claim that he would never interfere and
undermined his reliance on the distinction between policy and
operations to exonerate himself from blame for the Parkhurst escape,
on the grounds that this was a strictly operational matter.

Widdecombe's speech may have been brave, but only time would
tell if it was also reckless. It was not clear at the time whether those
like Shephard, who found the speech morally offensive, would win
out over those like Hague, who found it merely wrong-headed.
Despite receiving many expressions of support, Widdecombe knew
well that there was a chance she could be ostracized by the cosy
Westminster club perhaps for as long as five years. 'When you're in
this place, the one thing you never do is attack a colleague. I had
never done it before, but this was the exception that proved the rule;
I didn't want to do this, but I was determined that I was going to do
it.' She was also prepared to take whatever pain might be inflicted as a
result. If colleagues ignored her or spoke ill of her, she would have to
accept it. In fact, of course, the Conservative Party was much more
forgiving than she had ever expected, and decided to overlook the
effects of her intervention just a year after it was made.

The speech had its origins long before the May 1997 election.
When Widdecombe saw Howard's cynical sacking of Derek Lewis in
1995 she knew she would have to make a stand at some point. That
point came when Howard started to build a campaign for the party
leadership in the run-up to the May election. Her mind was quickly
made up: he was not a fit candidate, and she had the evidence.

John Major's resignation after the Conservatives' election defeat
precipitated a full-blooded leadership contest. Howard threw down
his hat, initially making an alliance with Hague to seek to appeal to a
wider band of Conservatives beyond the hard right alone. When
Hague pulled out of the alliance overnight, Howard stood alone.
Widdecombe trained her sights on him.

She had two reasons to shoot early and hit hard. First, there was a
possibility that Howard would win the election, and that, in her view,

would be a disaster for the Tory party. Most party insiders, however, thought that unlikely, and said it was more likely Howard would be trounced and quickly disappear into obscurity. Second, she judged that at this point morale was so low in the wake of the landslide election result that her attack could add little to Tory misery.

She did, however, take some soundings. Close friends like the Catholic MP David Amess told her to watch out. 'When she said she was going to do it, I counselled against it. I just simply used the point that I was never in favour of Conservatives airing their dirty linen in public.' She went to her priest, Michael Seed, and told him: 'I've just got to do this, and it will be assassinating somebody's character, but I've got to do it. I don't think it's vengeance from my point of view. I've got no personal axe to grind because he was actually always quite decent to me when we worked together. It's an axe on behalf of somebody else.' In the end he did not dissuade me.' Her former colleague Derek Lewis was worried that she might hurt her career for his sake. He said later she told him: 'She felt she needed to set the record straight and also for her own conscience and she felt an absolute need to prevent Michael Howard becoming the leader of the Conservative Party.'

Widdecombe's initial plan was to set out the facts of Howard's behaviour in a letter to the leader of her party, John Major. That would get the matter off her chest; but it would most likely be hushed up by a politician who was out of the fray. Major would not have wanted either to interfere in the contest, or to be seen to be inciting conflict between two of his former ministers. He had 'effectively abdicated' from the leadership of the party, said leading Conservatives. According to one, 'not only had he resigned and he wasn't really doing anything, we were all left to muddle along.' Widdecombe later said, 'If I write to John Major, what is he going to do? He's not in the business of appointing the next leader – he can't do that.'

David Alton started the process which led to Ann's big stand, when he approached Michael Prescott, the political editor of the *Sunday Times*, on 10 May. Alton gave Prescott a summary of Ann Widdecombe's view of Michael Howard and the events leading up to

Derek Lewis's departure. The repercussions from this single phone call began immediately. Prescott called Widdecombe to check the truth of Alton's facts. She overcame some initial reluctance and quickly ran through the entire story. The material would be put into a letter she was considering writing to Major, she told Prescott.

She also uttered to Prescott the phrase that would subsequently enter the pantheon of put-downs. Michael Howard, she said, had 'something of the night about him'. The description had been in Widdecombe's mind for many months and she had asked friends whether they thought it fitted the man; now she was ready to expose it to the political daylight. The briefing to Prescott was off the record, but Ann repeated the phrase several times, and said that she was quite happy that those who read it should know instantly that it was hers. The phrase featured in the front-page splash article by Prescott that appeared in the *Sunday Times* the next day, although it did not make the headline, which read 'Howard Damned By His Minister As Dangerous'. Inside the piece, Widdecombe referred to Howard as 'dangerous stuff'.

The 'something of the night' soundbite rang true to the media, who latched on to it, and the public, who had long tired of Howard's ranting – although what it actually meant was obscure. One Conservative said he wished he had thought of it himself. Widdecombe said she took the phrase from the title of a thriller by a little-known American writer called Mary McMullen. That looks like coincidence. Religion is never far from Widdecombe's mind, and 'night' is associated with the dark and satanic. For Widdecombe, 'the further away you get from God and heaven the deeper the dark . . . my picture of hell is complete with devils with tridents and burning lakes and darkness.' Widdecombe was turning to the colourful language of evangelism to condemn her man, much as Alastair Campbell looked to the language of the mind to say that Gordon Brown was 'psychologically flawed'. Two politicians; two traditions of character assassination.

Widdecombe herself explained the use of the language of the night by alluding to common parlance. 'My image of badness is dark.

You hear a lot of people saying, "There is a dark side to a character." So if I'm saying somebody's been bad, yes, there is a dark image there.'

Colleagues had their own interpretations of the phrase. Baroness Blatch thought Ann was referring to a part of Howard's character that was 'not what it seems'. Blatch in fact thought Ann shared much of Howard's right-wing philosophy and his forensic skills, so his bad behaviour towards Lewis had puzzled her. Phillip Oppenheim said: 'I respected the soundbite she used, it was a well crafted soundbite. She carried it off brilliantly. She turned herself from being a fringe middle-ranking politician, whom no one had very much time for and who was considered a right-wing weirdo, into being a chatshow character, with something to her.'

Prescott followed up his phone call to Ann with one to Michael Howard to cross-check the details and elicit a response. Howard, by this stage, had put his name forward for the Tory leadership election and was hopping mad. Widdecombe was then contacted by Rachel Whetstone, Howard's political adviser, who wanted to check her story. Had she told Prescott that she considered Howard had dealt dishonourably with Derek Lewis? asked Whetstone. Had she written to John Major? Widdecombe said yes to the first and no to the second. She dashed any hopes Howard might have had that the matter would be quietly laid to rest by saying that she had 'not decided what I am going to do'. The conversation, the first of a number with Whetstone, was 'difficult'.

Widdecombe wished, with hindsight, that she had pre-empted Whetstone's call to her, and called Howard first. 'The only part of the proceedings of the whole week that I regret is that Michael found out from Prescott and not from me. I should have immediately phoned Michael. I didn't even think of it until it was a bit too late and I realized what I should have done. Events were moving too fast.'

That phone call would have been only a matter of politeness. Ann was bent on her course and would not expect a recantation by Howard; equally, there was no chance that Howard would give it. The two were now at war, and they were fighting for their political futures. She considered that Howard had behaved badly and deserved a scolding. He was also a bruiser who was quite capable of giving as good as he got. 'I knew he would be very hurt because he wasn't expecting it. I knew he'd be shocked. I also knew that he would defend himself with every last weapon that he had.'

The press had gorged on Tory infighting during the latter years of the Major government. Now this episode offered the promise of more talk of split, venom and embarrassment. So they pursued the story with alacrity. 'The whole world began to ring me up.' She had a stock line for newspaper and television reporters who asked her what she thought of Lewis's dismissal. She said that it 'was unjustly conceived, brutally executed and dubiously defended'. Reporters wanted her to go further and say Howard's defence in the House of Commons of his decision to sack Lewis was 'dishonest'. But she stuck to her script.

The national press and broadcasters gave the story massive coverage, and the Howard camp was damaged. But one more blow was needed for the knock-out. It was as yet unclear what that would be. Widdecombe considered using the parliamentary device of the 'personal statement' to make a speech on the subject, but was told that this was inappropriate as it was primarily used by members to make a resignation speech. Then she discovered that a law and order debate had been scheduled for 19 May, eight days later; a contribution by the former minister of prisons would fit in well here. That speech would deal only tangentially with the topic of prisons and law and order, and at much greater length with Widdecombe's highly topical matter. But such was the excitement that the Speaker was unlikely to be concerned. Ann would get her hearing.

The scene was now set for the showdown Widdecombe sought, and tension among MPs was building. But the script for this last act had yet to be written – and there were more twists in the drama yet to come.

When Ann Widdecombe came into her Westminster office on Tuesday 13 May her overnight case was packed ready for a trip to Scotland for a TV appearance. She was looking forward to the aeroplane ride and a brief break from the Westminster hothouse. In the hour to spare before her taxi arrived, she reached for the pile of newspapers. She read in the *Daily Mail* that she had been 'wooed' by Derek Lewis with 'flowers, chocolates and dinners' into opposing his dismissal. One insider was quoted as saying in the article that 'I think she fell in love with him. He flattered her vanity. He sent her flowers and took her to dinner. I don't think she was used to that, poor girl.' To heighten the sense of illicit romance, the story noted that Lewis was married with two children.

This black spinning sent her into orbit. 'Phshoo! It was lies from start to finish.' She cancelled her visit to Scotland and contacted every possible media outlet to deny it. Her story was consistent. She said that the 'only flowers sent were from me to Mrs Lewis on the day Mr Lewis was dismissed, for which kindly thought I was bawled out by Mr Howard.' She told one journalist, 'She would swear with her hand on the Book there was no chocolate, there was not a petal of a flower and there was not the slightest crumb of a dinner' while Derek Lewis was director general of the Prison Service.

The source of the 'flowers and chocolates' rumour was anonymous and the Howard camp sought to disown it as soon as it was published. 'If somebody who claims to support Michael gave that briefing, then he would denounce them,' said a source close to the former Home Secretary shortly after publication. Those close to the Widdecombe camp sought out the originator of the allegation. One candidate was Patrick Rock, Howard's aggressive political adviser. The 'Rottweiler' later said: 'Oh, I don't know about that! I am sure nothing improper ever happened. He is married. So leave that completely to one side. I just think she regarded him as a firm and close personal friend. And I think she still sees him. She felt passionately that he had been unfairly treated. She felt morally outraged.' Attention focused on Tim Collins, Howard's confidante who was responsible for his leadership campaign's liaison with the press. Collins, who became a colleague of Ann's in Parliament at the 1997 General Election, was seen by several journalists, including Andrew Pierce of *The Times,* talking at length to the *Daily Mail's* political

correspondent Paul Eastham on the Monday – the day before the
offending rumour appeared in the *Daily Mail*. Pierce wrote a story
saying that, 'all fingers pointed to Tim Collins' as the source of the
'chocolates and flowers' rumour. When Howard saw, in the first
edition of that day's *Times*, that the revelation was on the front page
'he went bonkers,' says Pierce. 'He rang our editing staff to demand
that the story be toned down or changed. We told him to get lost.
It's one thing when you're the Home Secretary and it's quite another
when you're the former Home Secretary.' Pierce did not flinch and
the story remained unchanged in the paper's later editions. Collins to
this day denies any role in the briefing.

The entry into the dispute of a hint of sex, however fantastical,
stirred up the public fight. The Howard and Widdecombe show led the
news. When the two gave separate interviews to *Channel Four News*
that day, Howard came over well. He was not a man who gave the
appearance of self-doubt so when he was asked to appear on *Newsnight*,
he agreed. The format for the two interviews was the same. The two
protagonists were interviewed separately – Ann first to make the
allegations and Howard following to give a refutation.

The earlier interviewer had given Howard a smooth ride. But
Jeremy Paxman had other things in mind. Derek Lewis had briefed
him in advance and he knew Howard's weak point.

Fourteen times Paxman asked Howard to deny the accusation
that he had sought to instruct Lewis to suspend Marriott, and
fourteen times Howard refused to do so. His fading reputation was
damaged beyond repair. Widdecombe's work had been done for her;
she later acknowledged that the Paxman interview was much more
devastating than anything she had done herself that week. She put the
following message on her answering machine: 'Thank you very much
for ringing this number. I'm not here, I haven't yet made up my mind
whether I'm going to make a statement or not, but meanwhile for
anybody tempted to vote for Michael Howard last night's *Newsnight*
should be compulsory viewing.'

The few limping leaders of the Conservative Party who had
survived the May onslaught tried to limit the damage. Alastair

Goodlad, the acting chief whip, who was caught in the crossfire between Howard's friends and foes, summoned Widdecombe to tell her that she could not make her charges from the front bench. She laughed out loud. Widdecombe had received no formal request to serve on a front bench. 'My big joke was I'd been thrown off the leadership campaign team of Peter Lilley I'd never joined, and asked to leave a front bench I'd never sat on – it was very funny. Interestingly, Alastair made no attempt to persuade me not to make my speech against Michael.'

Then John Major, Ann's patron from her days in government and a good friend, asked to see her. Howard had told Major that her assault on his character was damaging the party and that Major should appeal to Ann to stop. Ann sent him away too, but with more grace. She told Major she had shown loyalty to the party when it needed her most. He knew that better than anybody. But now that the party was washed up and in danger of electing a leader who she believed would further damage it, she had no qualms.

As showdown day dawned, the Howard camp got in touch again. By now it was widely known that a speech was imminent, Ann having seen to it that the media had been tipped off. To ensure a fair contest, they wanted some advance warning of the thrust of her speech. Howard would only argue over the 'issues concerned', and he wanted to be assured that Ann intended the same. It was a trifling request, and Ann gave that assurance. She would stick to what she knew at first hand. In fact, she had been given 'most vicious stuff' about Howard by his many detractors, but she was not taking risks as the slightest error would expose her entire charge sheet. 'I was very wise, I thought, no, I am going to stick to what I know. I have seen the documents, spoken to the witnesses and was present myself. I also knew my own detractors would be blackening me to him and he would have the sense to ignore it. Neither of us was an idiot.'

Then Whetstone told Widdecombe that Howard would like to speak to her in order to deny responsibility for the many rumours currently doing the rounds. She hesitated for a moment. 'I thought, "Oh God, what if he asks me not to do it?" So I was steeling myself for what Michael would say. Anyway, we had a very sort of brisk uneventful conversation. And that was it.'

Widdecombe planned to give Howard an account of her case on the coming Sunday, and journalists asked to film her delivering the letter at Howard's front door. But Widdecombe, who is not usually camera shy, said this was one shot too far. 'I said, "No it's a Sunday, I am not going to have hordes of people watching me put a letter through a letterbox, it doesn't add anything to the issue at all. It doesn't add anything to the veracity of the statement, it's just a photographic thing designed to embarrass Michael.'

In any event, Widdecombe was out of London at the time. She was visiting Derek Lewis's house in Essex to consult his papers and prepare her speech. He was an irreconcilable enemy of Howard, but she used his fax machine to send the document to Howard. The media had staked out Lewis's house as they expected Widdecombe's visit, but the two conspirators were amused, and perhaps disappointed, that by the time she arrived the cameras had left the scene.

Lewis provided Widdecombe with much moral support in the run-up to the House of Commons speech. He had also kept himself well acquainted with all the issues, as he had recently published a book, entitled *Hidden Agendas*, on his dispute with Howard. Appearing in 1997, this caused rather less of a stir than the author and publisher must have hoped, as Lewis was not much of a name outside his own immediate political and professional circle. It had also upset some people. Judge Stephen Tumim, the former Chief Inspector of Prisons and an observer of the affair, was quick to spot that it was 'a very bad-tempered book. If it was simply bad-tempered about Michael Howard I could understand it. But he's bad-tempered about almost everybody.' Lewis's bitterness was fuel for Widdecombe's frustration. He had lost a job he enjoyed doing, and resented being a political pawn, but she was incensed at the machinations of the case: Howard's politicking, manoeuvring and lack of transparency had got out of control. Westminster's ministers play games with Whitehall's civil servants every day, but she believed Howard's antics had overstepped the mark of decency and had threatened the unspoken accord that exists between the minister who lays down the law and is answerable to Parliament and the civil servant who obeys his minister and has no public voice. This breakdown had implications not just for the Conservative government, but for the workings of the British democracy. This was probably what she had in mind when she told Prescott that she considered Howard 'dangerous'.

Widdecombe had seen plenty of evidence of Howard's apparent machinations and double-talk during her own time in the Home Office. But Lewis had told her that the plotting went back to as early as 1993, and that helped persuade her to begin her own private investigation of the documents. Thus she set out to investigate the background to Lewis's unhappy saga, in the process unearthing material that would lead to the exposé of May 1997.

In early 1996, after Lewis had gone, she asked civil servants to dig out the old files that related to various rows Lewis had had with Howard. She was prisons minister and perfectly within her rights to ask for them, and she took care not to photocopy sensitive documents. The officials brought in the bundles of files over the months during 1996, and Widdecombe put them aside for spare evenings, as her non-stop round of prison visits was rushing her off her feet. As she worked her way through them, she became increasingly angry seeing a ministerial style that was characterised by an absence of frankness and a willingness to resort to scapegoating. She simply noted the documents and drew up a chronology and a narrative of events. At the time she didn't know if or how she would use them. Yet, given her hostility to Howard and the knowledge that he must not find out what she was up to, there was something subversive about the search. This unofficial investigation by the minister was not disclosed to the Secretary of State, with whom Widdecombe continued to maintain a professional relationship. They never ceased to be political soulmates, and in spite of the personal rift, worked together well to the end of the Major administration.

One set of minutes got more attention than most. This referred to a meeting which followed the major escape from Parkhurst in January 1995. At this meeting Howard and Lewis discussed how

Lewis planned to deal with John Marriott, the governor of Parkhurst Prison. Howard was worried about the loss of political face, and wanted Marriott suspended straight away. Lewis said the case had to be dealt with by the book, and Marriott should be moved to another job until the formalities had taken place. The meeting ended in a blazing row. Howard wanted to force Lewis to do as he was told. But civil servants and lawyers told him he did not have the authority to instruct Lewis. They said Lewis was responsible for operating the prison and managing the people, Howard only for policy; so Lewis decided what happened to the governor.

Lewis feels Howard never forgave him for winning out in this battle of wills; so when the publication in October 1995 of the Learmont Report criticized the management of the Prison Service it gave him the opportunity to get rid of Lewis and he took it.

But then Howard gave Lewis an opening for his own revenge. When Labour held a censure debate on Howard's treatment of Lewis and his running of the prison system, they raised the subject of the row between the two men. They asked if Howard had tried to force Lewis to suspend Marriott there and then. Oh no, said Howard, he had only wondered whether Marriott should not have been suspended. A gentlemanly disagreement had apparently taken place, with Howard happy in the end to concede to Lewis that moving the governor sideways into another job was more sensible than suspension.

Lewis's memory of the meeting was totally different, as he wrote in his book. When Lewis told Howard he wanted to move Marriott sideways, 'Howard exploded. Simply moving the governor was politically unpalatable. It sounded indecisive. It would be seen as a fudge... If I did not change my mind and suspend Marriott, he would have to consider overruling me. His tone was menacing and I was left with no illusions about the possible implications for me.' According to Lewis, Howard asked him to leave the meeting, and to reconsider his decision within an hour. Lewis went to discuss the matter with Richard Wilson, the Permanent Secretary. 'He looked grim-faced and said that things were getting "white hot" and in "danger of going nuclear".' Later Wilson told Lewis that Howard had said that 'If I did not suspend Marriott, he would go down to the House that afternoon and announce that he had sacked me.'

Howard consulted lawyers to see whether he could instruct Lewis to suspend Marriott. They said this would be blatant interference, as Marriott's future was a decision for Lewis under the agency agreement. Howard was forced to concede the point.

As recounted in Chapter 12 above, Widdecombe had seen Lewis in the latter days of his period at the Prison Service and backed him staunchly. She preferred his version of events and did not trust the arbitrary way in which she felt Howard excercised his authority. She also knew that the former Home Secretary was extremely clever with words. To nail him down, she wanted the exact transcript of the meeting made by a neutral civil servant. But Howard had always refused to publish it. When Jack Straw, then shadow Home Secretary, demanded it in the censure debate in October 1995, Howard was prepared only to produce a typed-up and desiccated civil servant's summary of the meeting which lacked much important detail. Widdecombe wanted that detail for her attack on Howard in May 1997, and in pursuit of it made some informal visits to the Home Office. Civil servant friends (of which she has many) told her that an inquisition was in progress to find out what documents she had seen while in government. The mandarins' greatest concern was for the contemporaneous minutes of Howard's dramatic bust-up with Lewis. Eureka! This was the proof she needed that the smoking gun existed. All she needed now was to prise it out of the heavily secured official filing cabinets.

The full-frontal attack she planned for the House of Commons in May 1997 was her best chance of showing Howard and the House that his description of the meeting with Lewis twenty-one months earlier had been completely false and misleading. When Straw yielded up the contemporaneous account of the meeting after her big speech, Lewis had been vindicated, Howard exposed from his very own mouth. Indeed, when Lewis heard that the minute contained the phrase 'No, no, no, I want today,' he told Widdecombe: 'Thank

God for that! I was beginning to wonder if I was going mad.'

Ann Widdecombe's speech certainly put paid to any hopes Howard might have nurtured of gaining the Conservative leadership. Howard's henchman Patrick Rock admitted: 'It rebounded on Michael in the sense that if he was going to be the leader of the party, the question would arise: "Is he good at getting on with colleagues?" That led to subliminal worries in some of the constituencies.' More than this, it transformed Widdecombe herself from a little-known middle-ranking minister to a star who could take the big stage. Indeed, as Tory MPs considered the mediocre list of candidates for the vacant position of Conservative leader, some may have wondered if they were missing the real winner. But Widdecombe herself showed her usual talent for backing losers in leadership elections and chose not to back Hague. In past elections she had backed Heath against Thatcher and Hurd against Major; now she was supporting Peter Lilley, her former Secretary of State at the department of social security, and then (on Lilley's elimination) the equally doomed joint candidacy of Kenneth Clarke and John Redwood. Hague she considered 'too youthful'.

In the same month as the Tory old guard was vanquished at the polls, and a new and untried leader was elected, a new personality was born. In due course Conservatives would also appreciate that Ann Widdecombe was not merely a belligerent debater. She was also a thoughtful ideologue whose politics were not quite what many would have expected.

SIXTEEN

Retro-Tory

ANN Widdecombe brings a moral voice to a Conservative Party which for twenty years has embraced the amorality of the market and the pursuit of the rights of the individual against the collective. It is a message which is both subjective and hard to categorize. A term such as 'Christian Conservatism' describes it as well as anything. Others have chosen to call Widdecombe a 'social authoritarian'. Her harshest detractors, from within the Conservative Party rather than without, have boiled the abuse down to 'Nanny Wid'.

Many of Widdecombe's policy thoughts are derived from her own experience and inner truths, so they neither fall in with accepted party policy nor fit any one philosophical framework. Indeed, some colleagues have said Widdecombe lacks a philosophy and is overly subjective. She says she is predominantly right-wing but, using the analogy of 'dry' and 'wet' that pervaded the Thatcher years, 'A desert has oases and an ocean has desert islands.'

Widdecombe looks back to Britain in the 1950s, the period when she grew up, for her model of a well-run society. There she saw generally accepted standards of public decency and behaviour contributing to harmony. The paradox of that view, from a Conservative viewpoint, is that Britain was also a heavily class-ridden culture and Margaret Thatcher's push for enterprise was responsible for removing many of the consequent barriers. The consequence of those dramatic changes, with their underlying message that the individual was king and there was no such thing as society, was the end of deference, and the introduction of a brasher approach to both public and private life.

Widdecombe answers this critique by asking another question: 'Are we a happier society today than we were fifty years ago? No, with divorce and abortion higher than ever, society is not happier, it is sadder.'

The pursuit of desires and individual convenience has created a selfishness which, in her view, undermines social harmony. Widdecombe regards the degree of freedom allocated to the mother to choose an abortion as a primary indication of today's irresponsible society. Society's greater good requires its members to subordinate elements of their individuality. This concept is very relevant to Widdecombe's own insistence on reticence about personal feelings.

Widdecombe is no less disapproving of selfishness in public life, as she showed with her attack in May 1997 on the lax moral standards of parliamentarians in the latter part of the Major years. While she regarded Michael Howard as the primary culprit, she cast her net much wider. She railed: 'It should alarm us all that the House is now so comprehensively viewed as devoid of honour and a sense of service.'

Values based on religion and decency that once held good need to be reasserted. The most important of these is the sanctity of the family, which has been undermined by record rates of divorce – it afflicts 40 per cent of marriages, she reminds us. She laments the loss of belief in life-long marriage (such as that enjoyed by her parents) with many young people living in relationships, but not marrying. The legislation of the 1960s in the fields of homosexuality and abortion began a process of liberalization which has spun out of control, she says. Society has always accepted some degree of permissive behaviour, but the pendulum, as she puts it, has swung to an extreme and the unconventional has become the norm.

The remedies proposed can be harsh, the prescribed changes severe. She says society needs to put a cap on the tolerance it shows to homosexuality. The 1968 law that legalized homosexuality opened a Pandora's box. Decriminalization was necessary because illegality was cruel, but permission given to a tiny minority has become the maxim for the many. She accepts that the stigmatization of the unmarried mother that forced pregnant women into the hands of back-street abortionists in the 1950s was heartless. But the pendulum on abortion has also swung too far. Widdecombe would like to revert to the situation pre 1967, before abortion was made legal but under strictly limited conditions primarily governed by the risk to the mother's life, not risk to her social well-being or respectability.

Bringing back capital punishment will also look cruel to the new relativist Britain, but Britain without capital punishment was actually crueller, she says. Widdecombe produces figures to show that more murders (for which capital punishment would have been the penalty prior to 1965) were committed after the removal of capital punishment than before; so, she argues, it did serve as a deterrent. Widdecombe has voted for hanging on a free vote, but she is resigned to the fact that capital punishment has gone off the British penal agenda and 'It's not coming back.'

To some, Widdecombe's moral universe looks harsh but real; to others, it is repressive. Her colleague Alan Duncan says abortion is murder, but the clock cannot be turned back. Duncan belongs to the libertarian wing of the Tory party who advocate untrammelled individual freedom, and minimal state intervention in personal affairs. When he wanted to publish a new edition of *Saturn's Children*, a book he had co-written – before joining the government – with Dominic Hobson, which included a section calling for the liberalization of laws on the distribution of hard drugs, he knew that Widdecombe, by now his boss on the Shadow Health team, would not approve. He was right and decided to delete the offending chapter.

Widdecombe says the state has a role in protecting the individual from the most severe threats to freedom and health. But the state has no such role in the marketplace. Here she believes the individual needs freedom to run his material and economic life without inter-ference from bureaucracy or Brussels. Competition between individuals in business is natural and healthy, and government should allow free rein to instinct and allow those with ability to thrive. Her distaste for large impersonal machines (and perhaps her family history in enterprise) leads her to support the small businessman in his campaign against bureaucracy, rather than the largest multinationals. But she has freely admitted that she is not gifted in business of any sort, and says she is better at 'earning money than making money'.

Can Widdecombe remoralize the sad society she sees around her? As she sees the individual looking more and more inward, as the family disintegrates and as society seeks security in the irrationality of cults, contrived TV soap operas (TV is a particular *bête noire* of hers) and global markets, what chance has a single politician, however aggressive, however opinionated, of changing opinions that have moulded the minds of two generations?

Her support in this crusade is the God she worships as well as the electorate and country she serves. 'Arguably every decision that I make should be inspired by Almighty God. Nobody is that perfect. I'm not.' Similarly, while Widdecombe believes in Conservative government, she does not believe it has more divine right to rule than any other party. 'If you want God to work through government then He has to work through all mainstream parties in a democracy,' and there can be no one valid answer in these circumstances, 'otherwise you would get one party making exclusive claim to Christian virtue which, in my view, is perfect nonsense.'

Her tireless efforts to raise Westminster's standards of probity have won some acceptance as well as much hostility. But Widdecombe is unbowed. She will judge her success by seeing how the country responds. For this is not a message on her own behalf, but one that, she may consider, speaks from a higher being to a greater world. It is a message that is out of tune with many modern Conservatives, but as Widdecombe looks at their legacy, she may feel her answers deserve a hearing.

Ann's Conservatism took root early, when as a child she heard how her grandfather's small but thriving bakery had been forced to close when a new Co-operative store set up next door and took away its business. Socialism had not only curbed enterprise, it had also snatched the family fortune. No member of the Widdecombe household shopped in a Co-operative from that time on, and socialism and Labour became dirty words. Murray Widdecombe, the baker's son, was a strong supporter of the Conservative Party – although his career prevented him from being politically active – and he taught his young daughter about the divide between capitalism and communism: 'There was a very stark choice to make when I was growing up. You were one or the other. You could not be a mix of both. I believed that individuals had to be free to grow economically, to make the most of their talents, to let children grow tall, some taller than others, and that the state should interfere minimally.' Ann Widdecombe demonstrated her choice at the age of fourteen by joining the Young Conservatives.

Religious parables were part of her daily discourse then, and she has never ceased to use them to explain her fundamental political as well as religious views. Christ's exhortation to the rich – 'Ye who have two coats give unto him who has none' – shows how socialism and conservatism differ. 'I would say that, if you have two coats and you meet someone without any, you have an individual duty to help. A socialist, on the other hand, would say that you should confiscate the second coat, cut it up through taxation and redistribute it in bits.'

The liberal aspects of Ann's Conservatism are best demonstrated in her approach to prisons policy. She gained first-hand experience of the failures of penal policy through her visits to many prisons as prisons minister in the Home Office, and has used her time in opposition to devise the new 'prisoner centred' style. To some, this can seem more liberal than the approach taken by her Labour opposition, let alone by her harder-line Tory colleagues. She regards prisons as a crucial tool for social protection, rather than merely a means of social control. Widdecombe believes that rehabilitation within prisons is an imperative to improving the employment skills and qualifications of ex-offenders: 'Unless the chap that you let out of the prison doors is better than he was when he went in, you haven't protected the public. I don't care how many people you stick in prison but I do care what you do with them when you get them there, and that is not mutually exclusive as most people still think it is. I wouldn't mind the prison population rising way above where it is now, providing prisons aren't warehouses. They should be seen as places with constructive purposes.'

Rehabilitation is seen as a humane if not generous method of bettering both the individual prisoners and society as a whole. She says the costs involved in care and retraining, together with the costs of housing ever-rising numbers of prisoners, should be met by using prisoners to work for private contractors and perform real, economically useful work.

Private sector solutions are always preferable to public sector answers, says Widdecombe, indicating her innate suspicion of the state and big government. As opposition health spokesperson, she pushed for the application of private sector skills and funds to the public sector through the expansion of the Private Finance Initiative, admittedly in a manner not materially different from that being exploited half-heartedly by the Labour government. 'You have to have a mixed economy in health as you have everywhere else; but you need a deliberate mixture, not one that happens by accident in some haphazard fashion. We should recognize that we need both sectors, and that both have a role to play. Then you work out how to share the costs of health. You should not have to wait until the NHS fails, and then opt for private practice.' So wouldn't it be better, she asks, if the mix were openly acknowledged and planned for? The state 'is no longer the sole provider of prisons but why should it be the sole provider of education, or of health? Why does this big wall exist? Is there some rule that says that health and education services must be provided either by the state or by the private sector, and we must never mix the two? The two sectors should be working together. The state should not be the sole provider of anything except, conceivably, in defence of the realm.

'It is my view that the private sector actually brings both efficiency and higher standards to the delivery of public services. Individuals should be as free as possible, businesses as free as possible, to innovate and expand. If you stifle business with regulation, you drive out the little dinky businesses, and big business becomes disillusioned and looks elsewhere.

'No employer should ruthlessly be able to exploit his workforce, but it is right that an employer should be able to come to terms and conditions with his employees, and not have it forced on him by the state. I don't believe that the state should provide everything.'

Visceral distaste for anything that smacks of state control or socialism permeates her economic policy. 'It is the idea of a state monopoly that offends me, emotionally offends me, the idea of the state having a monopoly over anything. The state as a sole provider.' Hence Widdecombe emphasizes the need for lower taxes as part of a moral crusade for a freer country. 'Lower taxes make for a stronger economy and I am a great believer that if you cut taxes that you create a lot of incentives in the economy and if you raise taxes you do the opposite. And if you take things to the extreme, when we cut the upper rate of income tax from sixty to forty per cent, there was a hugely increased take for upper rate taxpayers. Suddenly tax avoidance schemes no longer had very many charms; it was actually worth doing the extra hours' work because you got to keep the money at the end of it, people were willing to work and weren't so concerned to get round the tax.'

Yet Widdecombe is prepared to use language on the distribution of tax revenues from which the Labour Party, in its New Labour incarnation, has shied away. 'I agree that taxation is primarily redistributive: you must take more from the rich and less from the poor. But ultimately, the purpose of the fiscal system is to maximize the tax intake without creating disincentives. And if that means you must take a bit less from the rich in order to do so, and you've got more money at the end of it, you can put it into your big state services such as health and education. It lowers morale just taxing the high earners just because they earn high. Rather, you tax in order to get an income in order to supply the services which are not going to be able to be supplied any other way.'

Taxation is essential to this argument; a competent state presence is essential and indeed a moral necessity. 'The individual must, as far as possible, take responsibility for himself. If there comes a point where he can't, then it is perfectly moral – indeed, obligatory – for the state to intervene; it absolutely should intervene at that stage. Mind you,' she adds, 'I came from an extended family which took care of each other, and that I think is the first port of call.'

The individual who works hard deserves his rewards and that earns him the opportunity to enjoy material comfort. But there are moral issues here too: he also has a duty to support his family, as well as those in the society who are disadvantaged. Prosperity should not be a licence for indulgence. Widdecombe: 'I make no apology for talking about the moral fibre of the nation. You are always better off working, you are morally better off working. People sometimes say to me in my surgery, if I take this job, I will be no better off than I will be on benefit. But I say: You'll be earning your own money, you'll be independent, you won't depend on the rest of us. Once there was a social stigma to taking what was then national assistance; some people who actually needed it wouldn't take it. We started to move away from that but have now gone too far in the other direction. People are now taking it when they don't actually need it.'

The poorly performing system was also at fault in the asylum seekers crisis that occurred in the third year of the Blair government and in which Ann participated so powerfully as the Tory home affairs spokesperson. 'The asylum system is meant to provide a haven for people who are in genuine fear of persecution,' she says; and that, to her, is a very moral and proper thing to want to do. If the system is widely abused, one of the biggest sufferers, as Widdecombe said in her party conference speech, is the genuine asylum seeker: 'He comes to this country, he is not only legally, but also morally entitled to a quick and settled haven. He can't get it because he's held up with thousands of others from whom he is indistinguishable, and eighty per cent of seekers have no claim to be here at all.'

Widdecombe sees the protection of 'asylum rules' as essential because they have been established to help people fleeing from persecution, death and torture. About twenty per cent of all asylum seekers will make a case to stay either because they comply with the rules or else on compassionate grounds. The other eighty per cent abuse the asylum-seeking rules: 'All those whom we send back or should send back or say we're going to send back because they have no claim to be here, they are actually positively damaging the genuine asylum system.'

Critics of Widdecombe's approach suggest that it 'blames the victim', or even indicates 'guilt until proven innocent'. They argue that it assumes all asylum seekers are bogus before they have been interrogated and the question determined one way or another. Universal detention of all asylum seekers, advocated by Ann Widdecombe, will, she says, ensure full and quick interrogation followed by decisions within weeks, not months, about who can stay and who must go. Widdecombe's priority, of course, is to ensure that only *bona fide* asylum seekers gain entry to Britain.

On matters of conscience, where party whips do not apply, Ann has maintained and exercised her right to hold independent opinions. In recent years her opposition to hunting has become clear, and she has spoken most powerfully on the subject. 'Eight of us go in on the anti-foxhunting side whenever there is a vote, and all the rest of us go in pro. So it is very clear where the sympathies of the parliamentary party lie, but it just doesn't matter.' The stance puts her at loggerheads with the 'Countryside' lobby whose influence in the Conservative Party, and the country, has grown dramatically. There is a larger issue here. Hunting, and countryside issues generally, are part of an emerging political agenda for Conservatives in today's Britain – concerned with the environment, personal rights and so on, rather than trade union block votes and devaluation, as in the past. Tories will have to work hard to seize this ground from New Labour.

The pursuit of issues of conscience has been a Widdecombe hallmark since she entered Parliament and her positions on both abortion and foxhunting conflicted with the established view of her party leadership at the time. Europe is not an issue which Widdecombe regards as one of conscience. But while she supports the party's new Eurosceptic line, she appears tolerant of those who want to reject it. 'I am always completely relaxed about there being two views on Europe in our party. Now there are two views within Labour, two views in the country, two views in business, and every way you look there are two views... To deny this reality, in the face of a referendum or free vote, is absurd. True, significant people, like Ken Clarke and Michael Heseltine, disagree with the official line. They have made a huge contribution to the party and the country, and deserve to be heard, but we must remember that theirs is not the policy of the party.'

She says Europhile leaders of major departments would have to accept the policy line of the party. They should decide whether their reservations were more important than holding office. 'I can belong to a party which has no view on abortion,' she explains, 'but I could not be the Minister for Health and actually license abortion clinics.'

Widdecombe's reservations about European monetary union echo with a curiously old-fashioned Tory rhetoric. 'If you lose control of tax and spend, then you've lost control of the right to govern and that is what I think would happen,' she says. But she also believes that no decision should be taken on the single currency until it has been observed, economically and politically, through an economic cycle. Until then, she says, it is best to reserve judgement. 'Ruling out entry now forever would be grossly irresponsible; yet rushing in at this stage would almost certainly end in disaster.'

'But,' she says, 'the politics matter too. It may be that the British people in a referendum would decide that losing control of taxing and spending would not be a major tragedy. But Britain must know it is a possible consequence and I firmly believe that if Britain loses sovereignty by joining the single currency, then that would be wrong.'

What of the argument that Britain will lose out in the meantime – as it arguably did by not joining the old EEC? 'You make judgements at the time, and this is one on which I would rather defer judgement,' she says. Remember, she adds, back in 1975 there was a cross-party line with Harold Wilson, Jeremy Thorpe and Ted Heath all backing entry. And there would still be a cross-party line today. By having a free vote you are not coercing anyone, as she explains. 'We

(Tories) are saying, this is the policy, we stand on a manifesto, and will enforce this policy; but if you have a conscientious private view then there will be time in which you can deploy it.'

Widdecombe's long political memory enables her to bridge the gap between the 'One Nation' of Macmillan and today's harder-nosed entrepreneurialism. The recipe might appear eclectic and random, without her own passion and moral belief. But those qualities would underpin much of Widdecombe's contribution to the Conservatives who now found themselves in opposition for the first time in eighteen years.

SEVENTEEN

Bouncing Back

WIDDECOMBE attacked Michael Howard in the full knowledge that it would consign her to a period on the back benches. To her frontbench colleagues this looked like a double whammy, as she would be giving up government without having any power in opposition. But Widdecombe was riding on a wave of fame. That buoyed her for the inevitable exile. She later said, 'I lost the habit of government on the first day I became a backbencher. I think that was a huge advantage.'

Such a move enabled her in time not merely to return to the middle orders of the New Tory front bench, from where she had come, but eventually move to the very front of the team. While many former Tory ministers slipped quickly and with varying degrees of bad grace into the obscurity of opposition, Widdecombe cemented a reputation for being both outspoken and authoritative. This worked in two ways. First, she had had considerable experience of government, and that would distinguish her from the pack of inexperienced newcomers. Second, her speech against Howard, while motivated by principle and loyalty, also served to distinguish her from the valiant (but in many cases disillusioned) old guard that peopled William Hague's first team.

The Howard speech had required her to quit the chaotic opposition front bench even before it was formed. In the week before the speech, she had told Alastair Goodlad, the Chief Whip, that she did not want to be considered for a frontbench job. She thus not only had a free hand to speak out against Howard, but could use the back benches as a springboard to develop an independent identity.

The length of this self-imposed exile would be determined by events. Some colleagues told her that a fitting punishment for the disloyalty of the Howard speech was five years' solitary on the back benches. But those sounded to Widdecombe like the words of Howard's hanging judges and she hoped for remission. In any event, she knew she would have to fill the time with some 'purposeful activity', and she went back to the novel writing that had been squeezed out of her life by the demands of ministerial work. She also signed up to do a six-part television 'courtroom' series, appropriately called *Nothing but the Truth*, in which Ann appeared as a judge. presiding over a court where moral issues were debated. She also became a regular guest on the game show *Call my Bluff*.

In fact, the period in the wilderness would be much shorter than the jeremiahs predicted. A year after her exile began, the expellee would be invited back to a front bench which had failed to make the slightest connection with the public. Within eighteen months even greater glory would follow, when Widdecombe would rouse the massed troops of the Tory party with a conference speech which showed not just that there was life after Howard but also that she might just be the face of Tory politics after Hague.

Such glory was the last thing on Widdecombe's mind as she contemplated the best way to win back the affections of her party. She found her route forward by returning to her roots. Just as she had become the scourge of modern morality with her abortion law reform some ten years earlier, now she would be the scourge of parliamentary sleaze, the standard-bearer of an ethical crusade. The legacy of the so-called 'cash-for-questions' affair continued to besmirch Parliament, and she saw a niche for some moral leadership. Her speech on 19 May 1997 had trailed her thinking when she said, 'It is urgently necessary for the House to restore its reputation with the nation. Many of our great institutions are falling into disrepute. I was wretchedly aware of how many people to whom I talked during the election uttered the sentiment that politicians of all parties are sleazy and corrupt and principally concerned with their own interest and survival.'

Shortly after going on to the back benches, Widdecombe successfully bid for a place on the Select Committee for Standards and Privileges – a watchdog of parliamentary behaviour was set up in the latter days of the Major administration as a response to the series of financial scandals that culminated in the 'cash-for-questions' episode. The experience was less edifying than she had hoped. Instead of a committee composed of ever-so-experienced members of the House like herself, she faced across the table a group of young new Blairites, many of whom had just entered the Commons. The committee had a massive Labour majority – reflecting the balance in the House – with just three Conservatives, and it was chaired by Robert Sheldon, a solid but undistinguished Labour Party stalwart. The committee's first major case after the 1997 general election resurrected memories of the sleaze that had overwhelmed the last government. Before the election, the committee had asked Sir Gordon Downey, the Commissioner for Standards in Public Life, to investigate Neil Hamilton, the MP who, as a minister at the Department of Trade and Industry, had allegedly taken money in brown paper envelopes from Mohamed Al Fayed in return for asking questions in the House and making representations to ministers about Fayed's application for UK citizenship. The case had been exhaustively examined by the media and also been the subject of a libel action which Hamilton had brought against *The Guardian*. Downey's report was highly critical of Hamilton, and the committee had to decide how to deal with him. Hamilton had, of course, already lost his parliamentary seat to Martin Bell, the broadcaster who had stood at Tatton as an Independent candidate. But Downey's report still stood.

The Tories on the committee argued that if they were to pass judgement on a fellow MP, the committee should have the procedures and safeguards of a courtroom, rather than just a parliamentary talking shop. The committee, they said, was equipped to deal with the minor infringements of MPs who forgot to declare a benefit or the like, but a case as complex as Hamilton's needed much enhanced powers and procedures. Widdecombe: 'I thought the whole procedure was chaotic. And indeed it was common ground that the procedures were inadequate. Certainly inadequate to that sort of major investigation.'

The select committee did not have the power to call witnesses, nor to allow the defendant to answer questions and call his own witnesses. Widdecombe, who had wanted to call Mohamed Al Fayed as a witness, sought to press the committee to change its rules. Considerable disagreement followed, and the committee refused. In the end Hamilton was allowed to address the committee. His lecture lasted two and a half hours and could not be interrupted, bringing ridicule on the exercise and humiliation on the committee.

The same sort of row occurred over Hamilton's right to challenge the committee's verdict as the committee's rules provided for no right to appeal. Widdecombe saw this as a kangaroo court and became more disillusioned. Even Martin Bell, Hamilton's recent conqueror, made public his view that Hamilton was being treated unfairly.

Bad temper had permeated the committee's proceedings from the start of the Hamilton case, and continued into its discussions of how the evident disagreement among its members would be presented in the report to the House of Commons. Committees of this kind make every effort to present a united front when they report, and Widdecombe wanted to go along with this convention. So she agreed a form of words which read 'the committee could neither add to nor subtract from the Commissioner's earlier report.' This was intended to give the impression of an abstention. As the committee had not had a chance to examine the facts fully, Widdecombe was saying, it could not make a judgment on them. When Sheldon reported back to the House that the committee had in fact accepted Downey's report *in toto,* Widdecombe felt 'grossly betrayed'. 'I had made it very clear throughout that I did not support it because I could not support it. This was not because I rejected it but I had no basis on which to accept it.' Sheldon said later that 'the Commissioner's view was one that was not opposed. I interpreted her failure to put in an amendment as not opposing it. She may not have agreed with everything, but she did not oppose it.' Widdecombe: 'We have left a man with no clear verdict and no right of appeal on the major issue which in most people's eyes is the one on which he has been condemned. Now, if that is natural justice, I don't recognize it.'

The fact that Widdecombe would be associated with the report's conclusions, from which she had sought to detach herself, coupled with her hostility to the committee's procedures, prompted her eventual resignation on 18 November 1997 in characteristically dramatic style. She went into a meeting of the committee when it was in private session, placed her resignation letter on the table in front of Sheldon, and departed. She wrote in her letter: 'I now regard the shambles which have characterized the handling of this report to be deeply shameful to the committee and something with which I no longer wish to be associated.' She later attacked the Committee's procedures in a debate.

Her position on the committee equipped Widdecombe to ask pointed questions of the government about the Ecclestone affair, which raised the damaging possibility that the squeaky-clean New Labour government was no more immune to sleaze than its predecessor. Bernie Ecclestone, the head of Formula One racing, had made a million-pound donation to the Labour Party in what looked like a naked bribe to have rules on cigarette sponsorship relaxed for Formula One events. These questions were seen to test the Prime Minister and attracted the attention of her party managers. She later said: 'I had an extremely lucky run in which I kept coming up with questions for the Prime Minister.'

The decision to support the efforts of Michael Foster to ban hunting with hounds showed Widdecombe at her most passionate. Pets, especially cats, had always been part of her family tradition, and while she would not go all the way with her father's view that 'the more I see of people, the more I love my animals!', she certainly did love having animals around and caring for them. The issue was of such concern to her that she used her backbench passport to show dissent and broke ranks with most of her colleagues. Widdecombe looked forward to getting stuck into work on the first private member's bill she had been involved with since the Abortion Bill of the 1980s. She was supported by her long-time friend, fellow stalwart of the abortion debate and Catholic soulmate David Amess, and six other Tories.

She argued in the debate, 'Hunting is not a pesticide, so we must ask what it is. It is cruelty. I am not against killing foxes or culling deer. I am against the chase, the cruelty involved, in prolonging terror of a living, sentient being that is running for its life . . . Yes, the scenes of a hunt are splendid, so splendid that they are all over my dining room curtains, but they are colourful scenes of olde England, and in an olde England, not in modern Britain, they belong.'

The style of the speech and the ease with which it was conceived came to be a hallmark of Widdecombe in opposition. Its argument was reduced to simple devices, even to absurdity, while the language was clear and direct. She dealt with the claim that stopping hunting would cost jobs by producing a witty *reductio ad absurdum* straight from her classical education: if that were true of stopping hunting, then eliminating illness would put doctors and nurses out of work, and stopping crime would put the police out of a job. The success of the speech apparently took her by surprise. 'It wasn't a structured speech. I sat there writing notes from the points in the debate and I had a collection of about six odd things. And when I actually stood up to speak I thought, "This is going to be rather pedestrian." It became a fiery one as I tackled these five or six points that I had written down.'

The debate, and her work on the committee set up to look at Foster's bill, re-ignited memories among the longer-serving MPs of Ann as a rebel in an earlier era, while the many newcomers to the House saw a different and, for many, more impressive side than they had expected of the politician who had for so long been dubbed a right-wing bigot. The House of Commons voted 411 to 151 in favour of Foster's Wild Mammals (Hunting with Dogs) Bill, but it was lost through lack of parliamentary time.

Towards the end of 1997, her impressive parliamentary interventions as well as the speech on hunting started to bring Widdecombe some plaudits. Winning a 'woman of the year' poll lifted her confidence that she had turned the corner. 'Suddenly it went just whoosh! I don't know why, life went whoosh!' She did not know where the celebrity came from: 'It's one of those things that suddenly hits you before you realize it's happening.' Ann Widdecombe may have been knocked sideways by the fame, but she certainly was not knocked over. Conservative morale at the end of 1997 was at its nadir, but Widdecombe saw the first signs of hope. However much the Tories feared her, and in some quarters even despised her, they could not do without her.

Around the middle of the following year, a quick return looked likely when Widdecombe was sounded out by the whips' office to see if she would 'have any problem' working with Michael Howard. There would be no feud, she hastily confirmed, but equally no question of a recantation of a single word of her speech. Practical but uncompromising to the last, she told journalists that she and Howard 'did not have to be lovey-dovey' to work together. There seemed little chance of that. But she later acknowledged the man's intellect when she said that Conservatives sat up to listen to Howard's expositions on the world scene as Conservative spokesman on foreign affairs, although his role in opposition carried minimal clout.

William Hague needed to hear no more. Widdecombe had given her word that she would not rake up the Howard issue ever again. Hague: 'She had said her piece about Michael Howard but she wasn't saying any more about it. So that wound began to heal at least with other people in the party. A lot of people felt bad on Michael Howard's behalf and that would have made it quite difficult to include her in the first round of Cabinet. But that had largely resolved itself by a year later.' One colleague added: 'She was one of the few senior Conservatives people could actually trust. She was in the minority because of the legacy of the last government and the scale of the last defeat. The thing with her is you get just what you see.'

As the reshuffle of 1998 came closer, the issue for Widdecombe was not whether there would be a job for her on the front bench, but which one. There was some suggestion she would be asked to take over from Angela Browning, who had just left the post of second in command at the Department of Education. If that had happened, the doubters would have won the day – and Widdecombe was not sure she would have given them the triumph of putting her on probation. To her relief, 'young Mr Hague', as she had called him since the two had known each other in government – he in social security, she in employment – had got his way.

The timing of Hague's first major reshuffle caught Widdecombe by surprise. She had the usual full diary, but was told to make herself available and duly cancelled all appointments. This was a big event not to be missed. Hague called her in to Conservative Central Office and said he was giving her responsibility for health. She could not have hoped for more. This was resounding proof that the party's new establishment had decided to put the unhappiness of the past behind them. For Widdecombe, the job offered her a chance to take the lead in developing party policy in one of the most sensitive possible areas. She also relished the task of shadowing Frank Dobson, the avuncular 'Old Labour' Secretary of State for Health who had made a minimal impression on the Commons.

Shortly after Widdecombe went dancing out of Hague's office to begin Dobson's demolition, she was asked by the media to reconcile her strong ethical views on abortion with the Health Secretary's responsibility for licensing abortion clinics. She said the two were incompatible: 'So long as licensing abortions stays with the Health Secretary, I couldn't do that particular job.' Duty to God and religion clearly preceded duty to politics and career, so there was no question about loyalty. When William Hague was asked his view he merely said that the person who holds the job on one side does not automatically transfer to the same job. But one journalist, Mary Riddell – an experienced Widdecombe watcher – accused Widdecombe of 'cherry picking parts of her portfolio that accord with her private credo. If her party's strategy is coloured by her traditionalist Catholic brand of moral theology, we might as well have policy direct from the Vatican Press Office.'

Any concerns that the Conservative health team would be overly religious or moral were dispelled by Hague's appointment of Alan

Duncan as Widdecombe's deputy. This rich oil trader and author, who had managed Hague's election campaign, held extreme libertarian principles. He had gone so far as to co-author a book which advocated a completely free market in illegal drugs and had talked about liberalizing laws on homosexuality – views that were a complete anathema to Widdecombe. The two were diametrically opposed on large areas of policy, but on health policy they were relatively close. Duncan said later that 'on issues of conscience, we respected the difference, and on the health portfolio we got on famously.' In fact colleagues of the two said Widdecombe had occasionally to 'slap down' some of Duncan's more extreme plans for dismantling the NHS's 'monopolistic state structure', but the liberal economist took it in good part.

The priority was to develop a Conservative health policy, and Widdecombe set the tone by driving a cracking pace. Members of the team who thought that opposition should be more relaxed than government were caught off guard. Earl Howe, the Conservative health spokesman in the Lords, recalled meetings in 'the very early part of the day! She called meetings at eight o'clock or quarter past eight in the morning, and none of us really thought this was necessary – except Ann herself. When you're in government you certainly expect to work very long hours and have meetings at eight o'clock in the morning. But when you're in opposition, some of us felt we didn't really need to do that! But this is Ann.'

The team were fiercely loyal to her because she did not 'crowd people out. She included them,' said Duncan, who liked how she distributed the work around the team, and did not hog it for herself or favoured colleagues. The two had a relationship which relied on teasing as well as respect. He recalled an occasion when Ann overheard him speaking to a journalist who was 'being obnoxious. I said to the journalist something like, "Why don't you just fuck off?" She said, "You've just used a man's word!" I said, "I'm sorry, I'm just defending your honour." She said, "Maybe that's just OK then." ' The jousting continued when Widdecombe visited Duncan's house in Rutland, saw a stuffed budgerigar and fox head in his study and wrote in the visitor's book: 'What did these poor creatures do to deserve their fate?'

Colleagues who were daunted by Widdecombe's formidable manner found teasing 'quite a good way to approach her', said Howe. 'You might think she has very fixed views about everything, but I don't believe that is always the case. Her views on private beliefs, especially where they relate to religion, are very strong. But otherwise she is very willing to listen to others, and if convinced, change her opinions. She may state her views at the beginning of a discussion, and you then say, "Ann, have you thought of it this way?" You expect to get your head bitten off, but she doesn't do that. She goes away and reflects, and very often will come to your point of view: "I've been thinking about this, and I think you've got a point." That is wonderful – you don't feel you're talking to a brick wall.'

Ann made straight and honest speaking her hallmark as she targeted the hapless Frank Dobson, who was repeatedly bogged down in allegations of rationing, hospital waiting list crises and under-investment in the NHS. These themes resurfaced when Widdecombe prepared her speech to the Tory party conference that year. The address would be a landmark for Widdecombe, to whom it gave a chance to address her legions of fans in the constituencies. This was her debut as a ministerial-style speaker at conference, and she wanted to celebrate her return in style. She was determined to make the most of it.

Widdecombe wanted not only control over content but also control over the way she would present her speech. She decided to abandon the standard podium address, and instead to pace the platform without a script. 'For a very long time I had decided that my Party Conference speech was going to be different. I was going to move around and talk – a bit like the crazed Evangelist. It wasn't going to be the standard.' Widdecombe had seen how evangelist preachers used this approach to inspire the faithful and persuade the doubters. She also knew that she had the presence of mind and memory to speak dramatically and without notes. The evangelist in her would lift the members out of their slumbers: 'I knew that it was so unusual. I knew I could rouse them, and that we desperately needed it. We were all in a shocked and demoralized state then. The purpose was to re-ignite the party, and I was utterly certain that that would happen. And what I envisaged did happen. Other people had different visions when they heard what I intended to do, but I said "I'm doing it this way." '

Some among the Party's leadership were not so sure this was a good idea and tried to dissuade her. Michael Ancram, for example, one of its more traditionalist members, was particularly worried that it might go wrong. Her own team were concerned that she would forget her lines, while the Party's policy wonks were anxious lest she misphrase policy and embarrass the party. These doubters did not understand the formidable Widdecombe memory or her capacity for rising to the occasion. But the Party's administration was in such a chaotic state that no one would have dared to argue with one of its liveliest wires, even if they had wanted to. So, with the encouragement of William Hague, she pressed ahead, with carte blanche to write and present the speech as she wished.

The stage was set for a conference event that would go down in the annals. The night before her speech, Widdecombe went to the conference hall to look at the stage. She saw that the designers had been given a free hand with a redesign and had produced a minimalist effect. She had hoped she might be able to prop up a few notes on a pot plant, but none was to be seen. She had also decided to wear a dress without pockets, so the possibility that she could refer to some notes secreted on her person was ruled out. Memory would be her only recourse.

Widdecombe did have a speech structure and a text written out in advance. But she did not memorize it as an actor memorizes the lines of a play. Rather, she adopted the approach which comes naturally to her – and which she had practised and perfected since she harangued the Oxford Union some twenty-five years earlier – and worked from a very few key words and phrases. 'I had a speech structure but I did not learn it because I knew if I learnt it and I forgot it, I wouldn't be able to move fluently. I merely read it about twelve times, slowly. I decided what it was I really had to say: "We're going to spend, we want a free NHS, but we need this additional private finance" – and some rude stuff about Frank Dobson.'

The speech would not only be a remarkable feat of memory; she was also determined it should be a dramatic occasion. She would walk round the stage, and seek to address the audience directly. This would need some rehearsal. 'I practised roaming round so that I didn't fall off the edge. You've got to have a sense of how much space you've got. You're looking out at them – you're not looking down. I didn't rehearse the speech. I did rehearse movement and all the rest of it.'

The effect of the speech was stunning. An audience that came into the hall downcast left it elated. They had seen that at least one member of their Party's leadership had more spunk and panache than they could have known. 'The audience roared and cheered after Miss Widdecombe did her business. She upstaged William Hague in the same way that Mo Mowlam stole the show from Tony Blair at last week's Labour Party conference,' wrote Peter Oborne in the *Express*. 'Her fists went up and down like pistons when she spoke, her huge ear-rings jangling and the silk lace peeping out of her stern blue dress.' The press interpreted speaking 'off the cuff' as speaking from the heart and having confidence in yourself. Peter Riddell described it as an oratorical *tour de force,* but one that had substance as well as style. He said Widdecombe's view on breaking down barriers between the public and private sectors to enable the public sector to benefit from private funding showed that the Tories had 'started to think'.

The speech not only broke all the rules of presentation, it also broke the time barrier, overrunning the slot allowed to the health spokesperson. But that was a fault on the right side, given the euphoria it had aroused. 'I threw out the entire programme; nobody minded. Apparently William was standing behind the platform waiting with Cecil Parkinson who was going to go on to speak after me. Apparently he was saying, "Got to have her on every day." Nobody minded that the whole thing was thrown. The whole place came alight. It worked; it was terrific. Everybody went completely gaga.'

The new thinking embodied in the speech would be demonstrated in an intense media assault in the months following the conference. Widdecombe concentrated her fire on Labour's double talk and double countings. For example, she told Jonathan Dimbleby in an extended television interview, 'I want to recognize rationing is there, which is why I tell the truth and use the word itself.' Rationing, she said, existed for operations on varicose veins, lypomas and certain drugs – she mentioned interferon, and treatments for Alzheimer's Disease – were not prescribed 'as widely as they might be'. She called for a more open debate on rationing. Widdecombe's period at health coincided with the announcement in July 1997 of the launch of a new body for examining the value and effectiveness of drugs used by the NHS; now she dismissed the National Institute for Clinical Excellence (NICE) as 'a posh phrase for rationing'.

Her attack widened out to include 'double counting' in Labour's claims on health spending, later a substantial campaign of assault that did considerable damage to the government's reputation. This issue brought her into a brief but vitriolic conflict with Adam Boulton, the political editor at Sky TV. The interview, which followed the 1998 health statement, had got off to an unfortunate start. Boulton wanted to interview Widdecombe, who was standing on College Green outside Parliament, from the local Millbank studio. But this would require Ann to use an earpiece to hear the questions, and this she refused to do, citing health grounds. So Boulton was forced to come to the interview in person. She said he arrived flustered and contested vigorously her claim that the government had presented an £11 billion spending increase as £21 billion. When Boulton said that the figure was a 'misprint', Ann went 'potty'. 'He had not let me make the argument I wanted to make,' she said. The two subsequently had another flare-up when he considered that Widdecombe had impugned his professional judgement by accusing him of being a Labour Party supporter. An exchange of letters followed; but Widdecombe later said that relations with Sky and Boulton had since been repaired.

Her own strategy for fully funding the health service involved an expansion of the private sector. She advocated the widening of private medical insurance to remove pressures on the NHS. 'If certain burdens are removed from the NHS, then the NHS can do more and your rationing becomes less. I am after getting the minimum degree of rationing by sharing the burden.' Rules on tax relief available for individuals using private health care, whether they bought it direct or with an insurance policy, should also be changed. 'Those who are getting private health care are paying taxes towards a health service that on the whole they are not going to use, and they are therefore subsidizing the others. We are all in this together. What I do not want are Berlin Walls between those who go private and those who go public. . . I want to acknowledge that taxation alone isn't going to solve the problem. I want to look at ways of getting total spending on health up. Therefore I am looking at ways of exploiting private sector resources.'

The claim that Widdecombe planned to privatize the NHS was rebutted by her insistence that she 'did not believe in compelling people to take out health insurance, and that I thought the NHS must continue to be available to all. And free, at the point of need.' She told Dimbleby, 'It doesn't matter whether the private sector provides it or the public sector provides it, if it's under the aegis of the NHS it will be free at the point of delivery. It will be available to all regardless of means.'

The party was also committed to spending more on the National Health Service in real terms 'year on year'. 'If you don't give that promise, people will see the private sector as a substitute, not as an addition. I'm talking about additionality. My line was, "Until you can promise that you will spend more in real terms year on year, you can't then get on to the next stage." But if you get that promise out of the way, then you can get on to the next stage.'

The commitments to the public service cheered moderate members of the old Tory guard like Virginia Bottomley, herself a former minister of health, who saw a parallel with Widdecombe's internal battles at the Home Office. 'When she was a minister at the Home Office she was somebody who had recognized and respected the public sector and public servants. That was the whole point – she stood up for Derek Lewis. I felt the NHS managers were being

kicked about by the new political politburo, and they would respond
to a Conservative spokesman who hadn't been part of health before,
but was evidently committed to the health service and the public
sector and felt that a politician should treat officials fairly.'

Battles with two groups of opponents had preceded the twin
commitments to maintain spending on health and advance the
interest of the private sector. Some colleagues had told her they didn't
want to commit themselves to the increased spending she proposed,
while others had said they didn't want to risk talking about the
private sector 'because they thought it would alienate the electorate'.
In the end, the mix she proposed chimed not just with the party, but
also with the government, which, in a backhanded compliment, itself
went on to work in the direction she had outlined.

She could take similar pleasure from the government's change of
tack two years later over waiting lists. For a long time the Labour
government had targeted the reduction of numbers on waiting lists
for medical treatment as a policy goal. But Widdecombe had insisted
that numbers were less important than the length of waiting time and
the severity of the illness. Earl Howe later said: 'It's no good knocking
numbers off the waiting list, then proving you've done something for
the nation's health, when all that has happened is a lot of people who
are less seriously ill have been treated because they are easier and
quicker to treat. And the more seriously ill are left on the waiting list.
And that, I am afraid, is what's been going on. And she was very
effective in exposing that.'

Widdecombe's success at the 1998 Party Conference and her
subsequent media activity had placed her more firmly in the public
eye than any other Conservative frontbencher. She had even
overshadowed her leader, and her case for a further promotion at the
first available opportunity was unanswerable. This would be demonstrated the following year.

The Conservative period in opposition, meantime, had provided
Ann Widdecombe with the spare time to prepare a manuscript which
would not be delivered at the podium but read on the page. Her
career as a novelist was about to begin.

EIGHTEEN

The Making of a Novelist

Like Gaul, Widdecombe has three compartments to her life. The first two are politics and religion; the third is writing. This has hitherto been the least prominent of the three, but Widdecombe has said that when her parliamentary career comes to its natural end, writing could become a primary activity.

Her desire to express herself through stories as well as in Parliament or the confessional has never been far below the surface. Writing gives her the opportunity to explore the first two areas of her life and have some fun with words as well. Fun does not come easily to Ann, but she thinks she can have some without anyone looking when she has characters through whom to filter her ideas. So her creative work offers a window into her private concerns about political roles and individuality which she would rather not display publicly. She is, of course, quite happy for others to look through that window and make what they will of what they see; but whereas she would regard a speech as failing if the message were not crystal clear, she sees her writings as mysteries intended to entertain rather than persuade. A comparison with Graham Greene may seem wildly exaggerated, but in the sense that both authors write to entertain while tackling very large religious and political issues, it is not wholly far-fetched.

No one had to teach Ann how to write or what to say. She wrote from a very early age, without prompting or guidance. She was as individualistic about her writing as she would later be about her politics. Already at age seven she spent hour upon hour writing stories, modelling them on the authors and books most popular among English children of her time and background – Rudyard Kipling, Enid Blyton and her *Famous Five* series, and the stirring adventures of Captain W. E. Johns's wartime pilot *Biggles*. Later, when school life required creative writing to be confined to curriculum topics and Ann and her classmates were expected to write fact rather than fiction, she continued to produce stories at home. Writing of all types was never something that had to be forced upon Ann. She always loved 'essay day' at school and was as enthusiastic about writing on whatever subject her teachers set as she was about trying to match her favourite childhood authors. Her ability to write and enjoy writing, and her continuing desire to write, have been lasting features of Ann's private life.

The most monumental of Ann's childhood writings was created when she was aged ten or eleven and attending the La Sainte Union Convent preparatory school. Entitled *The Love of Lord Douglas*, it was her first and only play and it had a big impact on her parents: 'It was a bit of a swashbuckling thing, set in some unspecified time in history with people rushing about trying to marry against their parents' wishes because the bride was poor, and there were sword fights and God knows what else. But my parents were quite impressed and this is the first time I remember my parents stopping and taking notice. My father actually suggested that I try to get it published or enter it for a competition. It was a vague sort of suggestion and we never did much more.' For many years this play was the highlight of the family's Christmas entertainments: a tiny theatre was created by stringing up old curtains across the playroom and the cast of three – Ann and the two neighbouring Davies children – played out their roles to an admiring audience.

By the time the Widdecombe family had moved to Guildford and Ann was in her early teens, her love of the *Famous Five* and *Biggles* and swashbuckling movies had evaporated and the likes of Jane Austen, Sir Walter Scott and Agatha Christie had taken over. In competition with this mixed bag of authors were the high adventure and masculine action of popular war films. This action-packed form captured Ann's imagination and inspired her first serious attempt at writing a book. 'It was written in my school holidays and grandly known as *My Book*. It was made up of three or four exercise books stuck together. Divided into chapters, it was good stuff; every chapter ended with something that made you want to read the next. It was called *Forest Trek* and all over the front cover I drew forest trees and orange snakes and goodness knows what other horrors of the forest. It was a story of a plane crashing in a forest and there were some survivors who were all men, and it is about their trek through the forest and what happens to them. All I remember is the hero is named Paddy and everybody died including the hero. They all met the most ghastly fates. It was the most utterly gloomy work.'

Except in the realms of imagination, the young Ann never aspired to become a real adventurer. During her primary schooling she was a member of the Brownies but never moved on to the Girl Guides. Even as young as fourteen, Ann knew the advantage of confining adventure to the imagination of her literary life: 'I certainly did not aspire to the sort of adventure I was portraying. I joined the Brownies but the Guides were never for me, which was all about going to camp and that sort of stuff. I liked my creature comforts too much, my hot bath and my cocoa.'

A second book, called *Mountain Climb*, in the same action-packed style, followed hot on the heels of *Forest Trek*. Like its predecessor, *Mountain Climb* was kept away from school and written by Ann during weekends and holiday periods, and sometimes read to her mother's friends while she sat up in bed. Ann recalled the second book as a more mature piece than the first: 'There was much less action and much more character and I actually had the grace to allow a couple of people to survive at the end of it. It wasn't all gloom, doom and destruction. It was a much better work and I wish I had kept those two, as the growth from one book to the other would be an interesting thing to look back on.'

Things changed dramatically during Ann's secondary schooling as a boarder at the Convent in Bath. Through her favourite teacher,

Sister Evangelista, Ann developed a deep interest in Latin and Roman history, and this was to have a profound influence on her writing: 'I was absolutely spaced out on Roman history. I read serious books on Roman history, day in and day out.' Ann's love of this historical period coincided with a fashion of the time, which Ann embraced with enthusiasm, for books and Hollywood blockbusters set in the period of the early Christians and their struggles with the Romans.

In the final year of her schooling, now deeply inspired by these historically powerful themes and images, Ann embarked ambitiously upon what she called *My Novel*: her third fully fledged book, entitled *The Fish and The Eagle*. 'I wrote screeds and screeds on this book by hand. The fish was Christianity and the eagle was Roman, and it was a theme I was terribly interested in.' Ann borrowed heavily from popular books and films set in the time of the early Christians and the crucifixion, such as Henryk Sienkiewicz's *Quo Vadis* and Lloyd C. Douglas's *The Big Fisherman* and *The Robe*. 'The book went quite out of control because things were always happening and I could never bring the darned thing to an end. But it wasn't a bad attempt at a really rather basic, not terribly intelligent, historical novel – not bad at all.'

Only remnants of this work remain in Ann's possession, although seven much smaller gems constructed around the same subjects still exist. Written in pen and ink in her bold and sharply cursive personal hand as entries in a short story competition, two of these moral tales are also named *The Fish and The Eagle*. Both present different versions of the same parable: a Christian wages a moral battle within himself between cowardice and courage. As in a number of her other stories, Ann introduces a sting in the tail centred on a moral dilemma: if you are a Christian you face dying courageously in the name of truth or surviving as a coward, knowing that you have falsely upheld the values of Imperial Rome. In effect, Christians must suffer in the name of truth, in the name of Christ; indeed, they have the duty to suffer honourably, just as Christ suffered for humankind.

In places the stories show flashes of a vivid imagination, as in this passage from the end of her favourite version of *The Fish and The Eagle*:

Livius gazed around at the half-starved beasts wondering in which he would meet his death, and as he did so his eyes fell on the lifeless body of Crispinus, mangled beyond recognition. One thing, however, was recognizable, the only thing so it seemed to Livius – the peace in his eyes, the peace which Livius had once loved and which not long ago he had so feared. As he gazed on these eyes they disappeared and a cross took their place – a bright glorious cross. Then the brightness vanished and he was once more looking on Crispinus' eyes. At that moment he felt a calm, steady peace diffuse over his whole soul. He believed and he loved again. He fell on his knees to pray and, at that moment, he felt the lion's teeth.

Of all the stories from this period, the one that Ann looks back on with greatest satisfaction is *Before Philippi,* another competition entry, handwritten on six pages of a school exercise book. The story's themes are truth and retribution; it presents the ideas that appearances can belie the truth of a situation and that, ultimately, justice prevails. Ann claims that her writing at this time was aimed at nothing more than producing a good yarn: 'I don't think I was trying to say anything in *Before Philippi.* I think I was just indulging my love of Roman history and the fact that I was very pro-Julius Caesar, really very pro-Caesar. Those wretched people with their knives and their stabbings and all the rest of it.' She admits that as a storyteller 'I try to spring surprises, twists in the tail. It was obviously a form I was attracted to at that time.' But she also admits that she was using these depictions of the persecutions of Christians in ancient Rome, 'when the Romans were really just the enemy of the early advance of Christianity', to represent 'the prevailing of faith over all manner of temptations', a recurring theme in much of her writing.

A well-remembered tale from Ann's Convent days is *The Huguenot,* which won a school competition. It portrays a struggle closer to Ann's own experience: that between Protestantism and Catholicism. Set in the religious wars of sixteenth- and seventeenth-century France, it tells of the concealment of a Huguenot hunted by Catholic persecutors. Throughout the story the reader assumes that the sheltering household is Protestant. Then, in the last line, comes the twist, in which the falseness of the assumption is revealed:

> 'Goodbye,' said the Huguenot. Then, before he could say thank you, the door was shut. He walked slowly away and as he did so he repeated his prayer of thanks that he had been guided to a Protestant house. Suddenly he remembered the object in his pocket and took it out. In the dim light of the stars he looked at it. Then he stood still. The object in his hand was a rosary.

An obvious theme of this powerful story is that not all Catholics were persecutors of Protestants during the Huguenot period, nor were they without feeling for their fellow humans, no matter what their faith. In retrospect, we can see the young Ann's story of *The Huguenot* – if not her predilection for all things Roman – as unwittingly foreshadowing her eventual empathy with the Roman Catholic Church. But, as Ann says in warning to any would-be literary sleuths: 'I always remember our English teacher saying, "I'm sure Shakespeare wouldn't recognize the analyses we write of his plays today," and I'm not going to pretend I was doing more than I was doing which, I think, was writing good copy at the time.'

After leaving school Ann spent three years at Birmingham University and another three at Oxford. She stopped writing fiction at university, and it was not until 1974 that she took up her pen again, in a four-year period she calls her 'big splurge'. Certainly, by the time she was living at Ottershaw in 1974 Ann had embarked on her first adult novel *The Long Winter*, had returned to her short-story writing, and was chasing hard to get her work published in women's magazines and by the Arts Council.

Ann admits that *The Long Winter*, her first story with a contemporary setting, was an ambitious piece owing rather too much to Susan Howatch, an emerging blockbuster writer of the time. The theme, however, is familiar: personal conscience as the final arbiter of truth and justice. Three young boys dress in tiger outfits and cause a car crash in which the occupants of the car die. The children manage to keep their part in the tragedy secret, grow up and go their different ways: Nicholas becomes a politician, Christopher becomes a nervous wreck and Charlie becomes a criminal. In middle age Charlie decides that the other two are good targets for blackmail. Fortunately for Nicholas and Christopher, there is another car crash, and this time Charlie dies and they live. Readers are left to imagine the burden of guilt weighing down on the survivors.

Ann never quite finished *The Long Winter*. 'I knew the end but I only got as far as the end crash, no further. There was a large chunk of Charlie that hadn't got written. It was the only book that I didn't write in strict sequence. Bits of it never got written and I reckon it's wherever *The Fish and The Eagle* is, in a dreary attic somewhere, covered in dust.'

While at Ottershaw, Ann also wrote at least seven short stories. Of these, *The Knugle* is perhaps the most psychologically interesting. Ann's readers can only guess at the source of the finer details of this tale, for she is unprepared to explore its content herself, or, indeed, the personal source of any of her stories. She does, however, concede one point: '*The Knugle* describes a situation I knew terribly well. It is a real, genuine autobiographical piece. I didn't have a babysitter who came up with that sort of stuff, but the actual situation of being left alone and a bit afraid of something in the wardrobe was real.'

Submitted to *Woman's Own* magazine in 1976 but rejected for publication, *The Knugle* traces a young boy's inner struggle with loneliness and fear. When his parents go out, the boy goes through a range of emotions, before finally resolving his anxieties by means of a mental game. The boy's initial feeling is a desperate hope that his parents will not leave him alone, which turns to resentment that they can be happy while he is not. When he is absolutely certain that he has been abandoned, a deep-seated fear materializes in the shape of the Knugle, a malevolent creature of his imagination which lurks in his wardrobe and can reach out and grab him in the dark. But the babysitter manages to divert the young boy's fear into something positive: the unseen Knugle becomes a large, clumsy, furry, playful creature, who is lonely too and longs for the child to be its playmate. Although the boy is unable to stay awake and play with the Knugle himself, his many stuffed animals do this for him. The Knugle is no longer lonely or afraid, and the child can now distinguish between illusion and reality, and has a useful game with which to chase away his own fears.

In the final passage of *The Knugle* the child has carried his learning from this fearful experience into his adulthood. The mind-game by which he learnt as a child to overcome his fears still provides him with a valuable psychological tool: 'for in later years when the child was a man with his own version of Goldilocks in tow he knew how to cope with things which frightened him by convincing himself he was stronger than they. When human knugles threatened he remembered to pity their weakness and to avoid feelings which might otherwise have been resentful or cowardly.'

The Knugle may reflect experiences from Ann's early childhood years in Singapore, a high social time for her parents during which their daughter, then aged between five and nine, was often left in the charge of household servants. The sources of the details are not important. What is relevant is that the story invokes memories of bouts of fear, especially fear of the dark, familiar to many children. The challenging resolution – the act of turning a negative situation into a positive asset – seems to have echoes of the strategies and stoicism for which Ann Widdecombe, the politician, has become known. The themes, too, are familiar: cowardice and courage, and how to face them, are central to the *Fish and Eagle* stories and others written nearly twenty years earlier, and appear again in later stories such as *The Shy Girl* and *The Dissident*. When cowardice is pitted against courage, courage wins every time! It is a theme dear to Ann Widdecombe's heart.

There is a second story relating to a boy from Ann's 'big splurge' period. Perfectly typed in double spacing by her own hand, *The Pupil* is barely three A4 pages in length. The story tells of a male teacher's inner struggle when faced with a recalcitrant student named Frapsell:

> I could cope with the disobedient, the idle, the bullies and the bored, but not with Frapsell. Frapsell's bad behaviour, carefully designed to

be obvious, was nonetheless elusive. I would never have sent him to the Head because I would not have known in what terms to report him. How does one report half-suppressed irony in a tone of voice or a mocking expression in a face which never seems to change?

For the teacher, the problem of how to deal with Frapsell is both mental and emotional; the child's behaviour deserves punishment, but the teacher prevaricates, unable to decide what to do. The teacher is aware that the child is the innocent victim of the inadequacy of his parents' relationship with each other and with the child:

> It was the parents' fault. It nearly always is. They expect teachers to keep control over children who have been brought up without control. They blame large classes but Frapsell would have been no better in a class of one. Individual attention at school will not make up for neglect at home.

The twist comes in the last line of the story, when the reader learns that the teacher is paralysed and cannot act because the child is his own son.

The fundamental themes in *The Pupil* are those of rebelliousness and discipline, recalcitrance and retribution, and cause and effect in social behaviour. They are contemporary forms of the parables and moral dilemmas that dominated Ann's teenage writings. They are also themes which derive from her Anglican childhood and convent schooling; they form the basis of her personal beliefs, colour all her literary work and have become part of her political *raison d'être*.

Of Ann Widdecombe's fourteen short stories, only two have female protagonists. It is remarkable that in both these stories the heroines reflect an unaccustomed degree of lightness. *The Shy Girl* alludes most directly to personal experience and is the only story of Ann's that is, ultimately, joyful. It contains two interesting autobiographical details from Ann's personal life around the mid-seventies. First, the Victorian choker in the story is clearly based on the one worn by Ann at a social event she attended with Colin Maltby in

Oxford, as featured in a much publicized press photograph; and secondly, there are the hot pants: they, too, were real and were the cause of Colin's first noticing Ann at an Oxford Union debate in 1971.

The Shy Girl follows a young woman's inner struggle to overcome her lack of self-confidence. Alone and preparing for a social event to which she will go unaccompanied, she is comfortably appreciative of her physical appearance:

> The girl sat in front of the mirror examining the result of the infinite pains she had taken with her make-up and dressing. In the soft light of the bedroom lamp the result was perfection! Her skin, normally blotched with clusters of faded freckles, was radiant with a gentle peach colour; her eyes, skilfully highlighted, were bigger, brighter, more remarkable. Her dark hair which she had wasted many hours wishing blonde curled softly over her high forehead and puffed out at the sides toning down the contours of her face. The overall effect was gentle, soft and appealing, with the Victorian style choker adding just the right final touch.

The shy girl tries to build up positive illusions of herself as being the central attraction of the party, popular, vivacious, warm and sought after. In reality, she is nervous, alone, someone people strive to avoid. She goes over in her mind the ploys she has used at parties in the past for circumventing her aloneness – hovering around the drinks table, helping people to carry their drinks, pretending to be looking for things to eat or for some friend, washing up, seeking companionship with young women like herself and disappearing to the Ladies. Once, she recalls, 'her efforts had been even more drastic. She had worn hot pants when the fashion had not yet really caught on. Oh, that had produced interest!'

Finally, the girl's determination to attend the party outweighs her misgivings. The evening gets off to the usual start, but then things become different. She meets a boy from her Do-It-Yourself class. They are joined by others with DIY problems to be solved and the shy girl is able to contribute practical advice. Later she goes on to argue about Women's Lib and to discuss dressmaking. She discovers that she is managing on her own and is asked to dance, several times. Indeed, the next day many young men seek her out. The shy girl reflects on the outcome of her contribution to the evening:

> She was laughing aloud, joyously, ecstatically happy. They had found her interesting and been gratified by her interest in them. Instead of a tense, self-conscious girl evidently wanting the status of a companion they had found someone with an independent interest. And she had been interested in them because she had been keen to help...
>
> Looks and brains helped. Hot pants might even help. Effort could pay off. But these things were preludes, it was what they found afterwards that made people stay to hear more or go away again. Of course, it had been so easy with her DIY classmate – he had known what came afterwards because it was all he had ever associated her with. It would help if she met him at all her parties.
>
> It would help but it was no longer essential. She could manage alone now although something told her she probably would not have to. 'Yes,' she giggled to herself as the phone began ringing, 'I've learned to do it myself.'

The moral of *The Shy Girl* is that 'doing it yourself' – having courage, helping others, being interesting in one's own right – reaps its own rewards. This attitude appears to have served Ann Widdecombe well over the years, for, as she has made publicly clear, and as the press have continuously emphasized, privately she remains alone. Certainly, living her life alone and on her own terms has reaped its own rewards politically.

The only other of Ann's short stories with a woman as its main character is *Rejuvenatae*, which, she insists, is to be seen as nothing more than her first and only 'stab at sci-fi'. Again set at a party, it centres on a female physicist engaged in an inner struggle between her desire to maintain the appearance of youth and sexuality, the result of an elixir of youth, and her deep physical tiredness and wisdom that belie this youthful appearance. After much deliberation, the physicist tells her story to a young male biochemist she meets at the party. On her twenty-first birthday she was presented with a bottle of rejuvenating tonic, a 'passport to a second youth'. The bottle contained two doses, the first to be taken between ages forty and forty-three, the second twenty years later. The tonic supposedly has the power to regenerate the whole person – body, heart, brain and other parts – but she is unimpressed by its creator's lack of 'any sense of greatness for himself' or concern for the 'effects of his work on the world, ethics, religion, humanity and all its hopes and aspirations'. Scientists working with the tonic's creator have exploited the secret of the elixir purely for monetary gain.

The young biochemist thanks her, because from now on, with her story in mind, he will be 'a careful biochemist'. Even though, now aged sixty-two, she feels more tired than ever and looks forward more to ageing than to youth, she takes the second dose: 'I am more tired but here I am at a party talking to a man and he is wondering if I am Juvy.'

The story presents Juvies – those who have used the tonic – with a number of personal dilemmas: the tonic benefits only women, not their older husbands; the body looks young to others but feels old to its owner; the mind is wiser than the body looks; ambition is wearisome because there is so much time in which to fulfil it; people and their unending petty complaints, falsenesses and envy become tiresome; even goodness becomes cloying; youth battles with disillusion; and, finally, the mind can be made to forget but the spirit cannot. All these problems stretch ahead into the future. The physicist resolves them by rationalizing the contradictions. She thinks of tomorrow as something unseen and pretends not to understand its essence; she tries to be hopeful and eager, ignoring the voice inside her that scorns her efforts; and she reinforces the pretence of her life by refusing to reveal any of its secrets.

When questioned about *Rejuvenatae* – a story she calls 'my juvenilia' – Ann denies that it has any biographical content. She prefers to say that, as far as she can remember, she was simply trying to produce a tale like many of her others that twisted things around for her own enjoyment. But it is possible to view the resolutions that the physicist arrives at, with their suggestions of personal hopes and ambitions put aside, as holding true for Ann Widdecombe, fortifying her in the real contradictory choices she has had to make. Most of all, like her protagonist, Ann keeps her inner life a secret.

Three of Ann's later short stories deal with male protagonists striving to reconcile conflicting ideals and hang on to their hopes. In these tales, personal life is invariably sacrificed for political or moral principles. *Sower, Upon What Ground?* charts the political education of a boy growing into adulthood, set within a family at personal war within the wider politics of Northern Ireland. It is an ironic story, in which the young man rejects national politics in favour of personal development in the land of the enemy. But he pays for his political reconciliation by forfeiting his private life:

> That was a year ago. I left England six months later. Christie would not come. She could not contemplate, she said, bringing up her children 'in such a place'. She said she would wait for me a year but I shall not change my mind. To come was difficult but to go would be impossible.
>
> The troubles are far from over and the children still throw stones but I am not alone in my work – Priests and Padres, teachers and mothers, peace workers and others are looking for a common harvest. Too much seed still falls on stony ground, and on thorny too, but some falls on good ground and grows and spreads; it all falls on Irish ground and some day that ground will be covered with a gold harvest, a harvest of love and hope and peace. Rains will still fall but they will give strength to the harvest and help it to grow more fair and more abundantly till all men are of one faith – the faith of the seed they have sown.

The Dissident tracks a man's mental and political struggle to remain true to himself after he has lost faith in the political regime for which he works. In the end he reveals his loss of faith to his political masters, because to suffer for the truth is preferable to compromising his beliefs. Quite mercilessly, he promises himself that

he will be less charitable to his oppressors than the dissidents he has
punished have been to him:

> It is Tereshkovic [his superior officer] who has decided me. I shall
> hand in my resignation tomorrow. There are limits to what one
> human being can do to another and I have reached my breaking
> point. I shall have one more night amidst the order and comfort of
> home and then I shall join the dissident on the wrong side of the
> desk. He knows my decision. I can see it in his eyes and his face
> changes from taut determination to gentle sorrow. I have seen the
> same look between dissidents as they pass in the corridors of Unit B.
> I have seen him pitying me for some time. I shall not be as charitable
> when I face Tereshkovic.

After the Russians explores the mental anguish among the
members of a political group centred on a single family when one of
the group is presumed to be under arrest. As they await news of their
missing comrade each member has a different response, ranging from
abject despair to spiritual hope. Then they discover that the arrest is
imaginary: their comrade Michael is safe and their personal and
political doubts are reconciled. Or, rather, this is what they think, and
what the reader thinks too, until the very last line of the story:

> 'But why should I have telephoned?' Michael looked puzzled.
> 'Because of the men. Oh, of course as you didn't go out you
> wouldn't have noticed. They were all there at the wrong time. Your
> man, Peter's man and mine. So I rang up to see if Peter was okay and
> he was and then we didn't hear from you.'
> Throughout Mary's explanation a change had entered the room.
> Peter was sitting rigid, Sarah was staring at Michael and he at
> Victoria. Mary herself suddenly heard her own words.
> 'I was so glad to see you I'd forgotten,' whispered Peter. 'If it
> wasn't your arrest they were warning us of, then what was it?'
> 'We must separate.' Michael's tone was urgent but more urgent
> still was the knocking and ringing which now began at the door and
> imperiously resounded through the house.

These stories present life as a matter of contradictory, ironic personal and political choices centred on moral values. The need to live by one's truth, to trust in hope and reconcile one's moral choices is paramount, even if it means self-sacrifice. The correct choice is always based upon a moral principle. These are the same moral dilemmas we find in Ann's teenage parables, where the conclusion is that the ultimate truth is Christ suffering in the name of spiritual truth. They are serious stories with twists in the tail: life is concrete, purposeful and rarely flirts with gaiety.

By the end of her 'big splurge' period, at the time she moved to Barnsbury Road in Islington and began working at London University's Senate House, Ann had almost completed one novel, written seven short stories and received nothing but rejection slips. She had also filled some fifteen volumes of personal diaries, all written in the same blue, hard-backed books. Together with some bits of diary-keeping from her school days, she discarded the lot: 'One day when I started re-reading the diaries I thought, oh no, this really is too awful, and threw it all away. I didn't ever want anybody peering into them, so I'm afraid that volumes of Widdecombe's thoughts and reflections and all the rest of it went.'

As Ann's political life developed, her literary life fell by the wayside. It was work by day and politics by night. 'And the writing just went. It went right out the window. I can't remember writing at all at Fulham and I can't remember writing at all at Kennington – until *The Clematis Tree* – and I was there thirteen years by then. Every holiday I was in Burnley or Devonport. I did research for The Bow Group and wrote an awful lot of research pamphlets during that time. I was carving out a political career and there was room for two things in my life but there wasn't room for three.' Ann's yearning to write lay dormant for twenty years.

Curiously, the only records we have of Ann's literary ambitions during this period relate to a play. To be called *The Happy Spinster*, it was to be a comedy, and an 'ode for independence'. The idea stemmed from Ann's distaste for the contemporary 'vogue' for women's rights, exemplified in the Equal Pay Act of 1970 and the Sex Discrimination

Act of 1975 and the resultant setting up of the Equal Opportunities
Commission – matters with which she became intimately familiar
during her time as a reluctant minister for women's affairs. The plot
centred on a young woman barrister and 'examined male resistance to
the emerging women's liberation, not in the sense of emancipation
but in the workplace'. Ann says that it was something she 'carried for
years in my head' but never found time to get down on paper.

Things were not to change until 1997 when Ann moved to the
opposition back benches and seized the opportunity to make time
for herself to write: 'The red boxes went, I had time on my side, and
I was wise enough to know two things: first of all, the time would fill
up and, secondly, if I didn't write now I was never going to break into
this magnificent world of writing. And so I put public pressure on
myself, absolutely quite deliberately, by announcing I was writing a
book because I thought that would make sure I did do it.'
Widdecombe announced publicly in May that year that she was
writing a book and quickly produced what she calls 'slam down',
getting the whole story down on computer without taking too much
care about the details. She worked on it while on train journeys and
on holiday in Singapore, and with one revision *The Clematis Tree* was
ready for the publisher.

At first glance, *The Clematis Tree* (published by Weidenfeld &
Nicolson in 2000) seems slight compared with Ann's earlier literary
efforts. The short stories written more than twenty years before are
rich in dramatic moral choices and religious dilemmas that end in
suffering in the name of truth. The right choice based upon a moral
principle is paramount. By comparison, *The Clematis Tree* appears
quite an ordinary contemporary tale of woe and private dilemmas,
thinly disguising a personal political tract. At least, this is what her
literary critics say. In fact, there is a much bigger parable at work
within *The Clematis Tree* than at first appears. Uncovering some of the
content of Ann's early writing provides insights into the fuller
treatment of her favoured themes that we find in *The Clematis Tree*.

The 'clematis tree' itself had always been a central symbol within
the novel, but Ann had not planned to use it as the title. While she

was actually writing the book it was always called *No Light To Die*, from a line of Dylan Thomas's, 'Rage, rage against the dying of the light'. Ann's agent, Caroline Dawnay, had hated this title from the start and enlisted her publisher, Ion Trewin, to 'get her off this terrible title'. It was Trewin who suggested *The Clematis Tree* and Ann immediately appreciated the possibilities. The clematis is a woody climber, the only native British variety having the botanical name *Clematis vitalba* and the popular name 'traveller's joy'. In homoeopathy, people who benefit from the clematis are 'wanderers between the worlds', attaching little importance to physical reality as they withdraw from a painful present to live in a world of dreams. This dreamlike state aptly describes the life of Jeremy, on whom the clematis parable focuses, and is also the context in which the pain of his life and death are reconciled.

Bel Mooney in *The Times* was one of the few critics to appreciate the clematis tree of the book in the way that Ann intended. Mooney called it a 'metaphor for the lives of those like Jeremy, not empty or meaningless but a focus for love and selflessness in others'. To Ann, the clematis vine growing up and over a dead tree is a parable for the way in which Jeremy's life is imbued with a purpose not immediately obvious in its apparent futility: 'Jeremy is like the tree: passive, but giving beauty, and the clematis is all that love which embraces him and grows stronger and more beautiful. That tree will always have a purpose now until the last bit of it is dead, and its purpose is to light up its surroundings.'

The idea that Jeremy's disabled life serves a spiritual purpose for others closely resembles themes in the stories which Ann wrote as a teenager describing early Christians who sacrificed their lives in the name of Christ. In *The Clematis Tree*, however, the symbol of the clematis becomes broader and deeper than a mere metaphor for the role of Jeremy and his sufferings.

The story itself opens in a beautiful garden where Mark and Claire are celebrating the christening of their new daughter, Pippa. The happiness of family life is shattered when their young son Jeremy is knocked down by a speeding car. Nothing is ever the same again:

Jeremy is left severely brain-damaged and wholly dependent; his parents are forced to cope as best they can with catastrophe and a crumbling marriage; his little sister adores him but resents all the attention he receives. Family roles and dynamics are played out within an army of Claire's determinedly helpful relatives. Most notably, there is Claire's MP sister, Sally, who, faced with the slow and painful death of their mother, introduces a euthanasia bill before Parliament, a measure which imposes its own set of ethical and emotional pressures.

Under the strain, Mark undergoes adulterous temptations and Claire spends her time self-indulgently buying Jeremy all sorts of things he will never be able to use. Their self-absorption is shattered when Pippa is feared killed in a school coach crash. Pippa's survival, the death of Claire's father, Sally's falling in love, and eventually Jeremy's death by drowning gradually bring Mark and Claire to a better understanding of themselves. But Mark's disillusion with his marriage remains. He asks for a divorce but Claire counters by announcing that she is pregnant; so Mark resigns himself to marriage and the burden of responsibility. Mark finds spiritual peace and reconciliation with his son in a dream:

> As Mark watched, other children surrounded Jeremy and he recognized Christina Bright and the others who had died on the coach. They were happy, reaching out to Jeremy, and beyond them he knew there were others, many, many others. The children of Dunblane, of Aberfan, of famine, of strife. Mark . . . saw his son give him one last smile. Mark waved and, singing 'Love, perfect love, is the gift of Christ our God,' the small ghosts faded from his dreaming sight forever.

Over and above its portrayal of contemporary life, *The Clematis Tree* attempts to present an overall parable of birth, suffering, death and reincarnation, the spiritual cycle of regeneration that is at the heart of life itself. Metaphorical links with the moral and religious themes of Widdecombe's earlier stories abound. The story begins with a christening, a celebration of new life, and centres on the suffering of Jeremy as a vehicle for the love and compassion of others, in the same way as the suffering of Jesus Christ. In some ways, Jeremy's life and its meaning parallel those of Christ himself, and much of the imagery draws on a secret, sacred world that is an integral part of Ann's private life. For instance, the Christian name of Jeremy derives from Jeremiah, the name of a major prophet of Judah and his Book of Oracles, and the dead Jeremy surrounded by Christina Bright and the other children in the passage quoted above surely presents an image of Christ's ascension in a blaze of angelic light. Mark is inspired and supported morally and spiritually by his meeting with Smith, the widow 'with that lovely serene face'. Smith serves as a Mary Magdalene figure, inspiring Mark's understanding of the clematis tree as a parable for Jeremy's suffering, an understanding which supports him through the trials and tribulations of his daily life. The parable concludes with Jeremy's death coinciding with Claire's pregnancy – an 'immaculate conception', given its lack of sexual evidence – suggestive of reincarnation. Mark, an atheist Jew, guilty but repentant, represents ordinary man, an Everyman worthy of the forgiveness bestowed on him, just as Christ forgives humankind its sins: 'Peaceful, forgiven, reconciled, he woke and stared into the darkness. Beside him his wife stirred and gently moaned as the child within her moved, proclaiming its life.'

Though unimportant when set against the broader moral and religious themes, the book also contains a number of autobio-graphical fragments. The spinster Aunt Isobel is perhaps in part based on Ann herself: 'poor Aunt Isobel', as she is known within the family, has never married owing to some unspecified 'disappointment' in her youth, which may reflect how Ann's own family viewed her never having married. Mark's meeting with Smith takes place at Estoril, where Ann and Colin Maltby had the first of their two holidays together. Even more personal is Mark's statement to his daughter Pippa: 'You're the sex we wanted, you're healthy and you complete our family.' Here perhaps Ann is exorcising a ghost from her own past; she retold the story on her fiftieth birthday that her mother, brother and grandmother had all wanted her to be born a boy, and her father once said to her that she, rather than her brother Malcolm, ought to have been the boy of the family.

As Ann Widdecombe observed of the reviews, 'If you read them all as a batch, they divide up into those that address the book and, on the whole, are either favourable or mixed. Then there are the critics who address the writer and overall they're bad.' Many found *The Clematis Tree* rather preachy: Rowan Pelling in the *New Statesman* called it 'a thinly disguised moral tract', while Sally Weale in *The Guardian* found it 'heavy on duty, responsibility and endurance, the central tenets of Widdecombe's personal philosophy'. One senior editor allegedly turned the book down because, though reasonably well written, she found it overly moralistic and propagandist.

The reviewers – like Ann's mother, who 'thought it quite miserable' – also remarked on its gloominess. Ann Chisholm of the *Sunday Telegraph* wrote that there is 'too much darkness and not enough humour or light in the story'. Many found the style heavy: Boyd Tonkin in *The Independent* spoke of 'a stodgy meat-and-potatoes prose' and Bel Mooney in *The Times* considered it 'a clunky addition to that tradition of didactic fiction which runs back to the moral tales of the eighteenth and nineteenth centuries'.

But many were impressed by Ann's moral insights. Rowan Pelling spoke of 'the neat correlation of cause and effect' and Boyd Tonkin called *The Clematis Tree* a 'compassionate novel'. Ann Chisholm gave Ann credit for trying to be fair to both sides of the euthanasia argument, and Bel Mooney praised her for 'setting aside her own certainties to show that people may do right unwillingly, and that the fallibility and resentment of her hero are a part of the human condition'.

Perhaps the most interesting review appeared in The *Sunday Times*, by Ruth Rendell, the writer of psychological thrillers. Rendell gets stuck into Ann's abounding clichés and old-fashioned adjectives and the fact that the characters are 'imbued with moral rectitude and are undisguisedly proud of it'. But she concludes that the novel is 'full of dull things yet, paradoxically, it is not dull. You want to go on reading, you want to know what happens, it isn't easy to put down.'

Playing on Ann's famous description of a certain Home Secretary as having 'something of the night' about him, Rendell claims that Widdecombe 'has something of a Sunday afternoon' about her.

The Clematis Tree is the first of seven stories that Ann Widdecombe has waited years to turn into books, and she is now at work on her second novel. Set in France during the Second World War, it tells of the love between a young French woman and a married German officer. Her family are Catholic resistance workers and the treachery and morality of war affects all around them. Ann now relishes the way in which her characters take on lives of their own, like some in *The Clematis Tree*, who 'suddenly appeared' and 'just wouldn't do the things I had originally planned for them'. She works quickly and with an open mind, producing as many as 4,000 words in one go. It is meeting characters like Bernadette and Cecile in her new book, people who were not planned, that Ann calls 'Great fun! It's huge fun!'

Of her future writing plans, Ann says: 'If I am going to do anything apart from straight novel writing, it will either be detective novels or it will be historical novels – not bodice rippers, please, but historical novels. It won't be plays – you might one day say, ho ho ho, you were wrong here. But I don't think so. I don't think I'm talented enough. You need a special talent to write plays. I think I have found the niche.'

The prospect of a full-time literary career excites Ann Widdecombe: 'Just as when I switched from working at the University of London to become a Member of Parliament I said, "This is absolutely wonderful. I am now doing full-time what I used to do as a hobby, and being paid to do it," on my retirement from politics I think I shall say that it was "absolutely wonderful, now I will be doing full-time what I was doing as a hobby". I'm quite certain of it.'

But retirement could not have been further from her mind in June 1999.

NINETEEN

Home to Home

When William Hague offered Ann Widdecombe the position of Shadow Home Secretary on 15 June 1999, her joy was unconfined. 'I am going home to Home' she told journalists waiting to hear about her posting. She had achieved her long-held aspiration. 'Just leave me here for the rest of my time,' she thought as she wallowed in the pleasure. Hague saw that she fitted the job: 'She is a round peg in a round hole now, she really is. She's suited to that job; she'll be very suited to being the Home Secretary in government. You can see it in that job much more than say, being Chancellor of the Exchequer. She would really like to be the Home Secretary. She is genuinely hungry to do the job in government.'

The job of shadow Home Secretary had three attractions. First, it was clearly a promotion from her former job as the party's health spokesperson. The Home Office is one of the three great departments of state, alongside the Treasury and the Foreign Office, and the shadow Home Secretary is likely to be a close confidant of the party leader. Second, it offered the prospect for developing policy and speaking on subjects dearest to her heart and on which she was particularly authoritative, namely, law and order and the penal system. Third, there will have been a quiet pleasure in the fact that she was supplanting the former boss whose career she had destroyed. What she had not achieved in government, she would now achieve in opposition.

The promotion also enabled Widdecombe to build on the good

working relationship she had begun with Hague since her re-admission to the front bench in June 1998. From the moment he had taken office, she had liked the way he had kept a cool head while the Tories languished in the polls. Some even talked about blaming him for the problem, and whispered that he ought to be removed. But Widdecombe strongly disapproved of such talk, and stayed loyal to him.

Hague's support for Widdecombe was based on respect and a shared ideology. Hague said later, 'We are a very similar type of Conservative really.' He said they had similar stances on law and order, which combined 'toughness with pragmatism'. He also valued her work in the constituencies. 'It takes a large share of the burden, at a time when most people who are promoted are not yet national figures. Only a few people in the shadow Cabinet bear a large proportion of that burden and she never complains.' At a time when the party in the country was despairing of the parliamentary party after the landslide electoral defeat, Widdecombe raised their spirits.

Widdecombe's capacity to attract and manage publicity had been evident at the time she had delivered her speech against Michael Howard. She had used the media then to great effect, and had since built on her higher profile. When she ran the opposition health department, she had shown she was able to manage public unease on waiting lists; and as soon as she took over the Home Office brief, she showed herself able to manage the press and the issues with a sureness of foot many of her opposition colleagues lacked.

She had an early success in exploiting the computer system problem that caused delays in issuing passports. Widdecombe saw here not just an emotive issue which reached to the voters' deepest fears about their holidays, but also an opportunity to dump the blame on an individual opponent. Widdecombe had seen computer foul-ups discomfit many politicians when she was in government herself. At the Department of Social Security in 1991, she had seen how computerization of the benefits system delayed payment of benefits, landing her Secretary of State, Tony Newton, in severe embar-rassment. So when she saw queues of would-be holidaymakers at

Petty France in London at the end of June, Widdecombe arranged for
the cameras to escort her as she cheered up the anxious crowds.

Her target was Jack Straw, the Home Secretary, who, she said,
should have known that trouble would arise as the computer system
was being changed at the same time as a new law came into effect
which required babies to have their own passports. She was greeted
by what one commentator called 'an opposition politician's dream.
There were queues for tickets, queues for forms, queues for
information, queues for passports, queues for extensions. There were
even queues for the drinks machine.' Widdecombe's parade up and
down the queue in the rain was a photo opportunity which
celebrated her arrival at the visual centre of British politics. Hague
recalled: 'She was very good at cutting through the waffle and the
rubbish and the excuses when the government got into a muddle
over the passport agency last summer. She just ripped them to shreds.
In those situations she can immediately put forward the two or three
things the government should do to sort out the mess, she does it
with great authority. It's usually absolutely on the nail, and it's very
hard for ministers to cope with that.'

But this was only the very beginning of a summer when
Widdecombe put her stamp on British politics. Widdecombe had no
plans to leave the country that summer, so William Hague gave her
the job of covering for him if any story ruffled the newspapers
during the tranquil month of August, when most politicians are out
of the country, or at the very least have switched off their bleepers
and have not the slightest wish to be disturbed. Blair had given the
same covering job to his deputy John Prescott. At the time, he could
do minimal damage, and was unlikely to come under any great
opposition attack.

Widdecombe quickly attracted attention thanks to a piece of
Labour research which purported to show that she was the most
extreme member of the Tory party, using quotes that included her
view that most of the BBC's output was 'filth'. Widdecombe – the
erstwhile 'Doris Karloff', the shackler of pregnant women – had had
too much experience of demonization to be undermined by this, and

called it 'an absolute joke'. This was supposed to be the silly season, and one commentator thought he was being funny in calling Widdecombe 'a Tory Jo Brand'. The two women did indeed have physical characteristics in common, and both had strong political convictions – albeit at opposite ends of the spectrum. Widdecombe (like Brand) was used to being the butt of repeated comments on her physique and appearance. She had long accepted that those who made them were probably deliberately trying to divert attention from her message. Her usual response was to rebut the remark with a joke and shrug it off.

One issue arose that summer that was not just serious at the time, but came to dominate British politics for the best part of the following year. This was the growing concern over people coming to Britain to claim asylum. As each month's figures were examined, it became clear that the numbers were rising; by August, it looked as if the total of those seeking asylum would be 50 per cent greater in 1999 than it was in 1998. Widdecombe saw a potent political target. She defended the use of the word 'flood' to describe the new wave of asylum seekers. This was greeted with hostility by her enemies, who saw resonances of the famous speech by Enoch Powell, an early hero of Widdecombe's, in which he had used a classical reference to warn about the growing number of Asian immigrants to Britain. Powell said in the spring of 1968: 'As I look ahead, I am filled with foreboding. Like the Roman, I seem to see "the River Tiber foaming with much blood".' Edward Heath, then leader of the opposition, condemned the speech as 'racialist' and sacked Powell from the Tory shadow cabinet.

Widdecombe blamed the increase in numbers of asylum seekers on Jack Straw's decision, shortly after Labour entered government, to give an amnesty to the 20,000 asylum seekers who had waited longest to have their cases examined. This, she argued, made Britain appear 'a soft touch' and willing to admit those seeking asylum for 'bogus' economic reasons as well as those who came for genuine reasons of persecution in their own country. Her contention that more than 80 per cent of all asylum seekers were 'bogus' became part of the lore of the debate, but she also claimed that the system was so disorganized that relatively few of those shown to be 'bogus' would be returned to their country of origin. Disturbances in towns where asylum seekers disembarked, like Dover, and complaints about begging contributed to the tension and unhappiness surrounding the question.

Widdecombe: 'Labour came in and said they were going to reverse several of our high profile deportation decisions and abolish the primary purpose rule in immigration. They said they were not going to implement our provisions against illegal working, and the net result of all that has been that it sent out a message saying, "It's okay, forget what happened last year, the system's open again." Now, are they surprised that it's gone through the roof? It went through the roof very quickly when they did that. As far as we're concerned you've got to get back to a deterrent message.'

Widdecombe advocated detaining asylum seekers on their arrival in reception centres, which they could not leave until the validity of their cases had been examined. This would keep the visitors out of the community, so they would not go underground and escape. It would also enable the bureaucracy to work more simply, as the visitor would be available at all times for questioning. The time taken over the process of examination would be reduced from many months to a few weeks, while deportation would be much simpler with the bogus asylum seeker on the spot. Such a system would also take the asylum seekers out of the towns where the residents resented them, and put them in centres which were locked and guarded.

Widdecombe: 'I always wanted universal detention for asylum, which I thought was the only way you actually got full control of the situation. Initially it was believed to be far too expensive. It was only when the asylum system went very badly out of control that it was seen that if it provided a deterrent effect, it would, in the medium term, produce savings rather than costs.'

Widdecombe's campaign won considerable support, and in due course the government, which had sought initially to deny the problem existed, was forced to act. The decision to stop giving asylum seekers social security and replace cash benefit payments with food vouchers was the first evidence of a response to public pressure. They later accepted that detention needed to be imposed more widely and were said to be preparing sites as 'reception centres'.

One critic of Widdecombe's policy on asylum seekers was David Alton. Now Lord Alton, he has remained a very close friend and confidant, but on this subject their minds did not meet. Nevertheless, he defended her against accusations of extremism: 'I don't regard her as an "extremist". If I thought she was, I don't think I would really have travelled this far with her, in our own friendship, or in collaborative work. I disagree with her position on asylum seekers and refugees, but I would never call her a racist, because she is not.

'I think she has always been more in the middle ground than anyone has accepted. That is why I don't go along with the use of the word "extreme". Actually, her tub-thumping, oratorical style, her good use of language and her forceful argument − all this is sometimes confused with the assumption that she is mouthing a lot of Mosleyite sentiments, which she is not. Perhaps we have just got unused to people deploying their arguments with passion − sadly.'

The conviction Widdecombe exuded in the course of the campaign on asylum seekers produced either respect bordering on love, or contempt bordering on hatred. Some noted that media reactions were comparable to those that greeted Mrs Thatcher when, as the minister for education who removed free school milk, she was called 'Milk Snatcher'. One journalist quipped that Blair had complained that he lacked an opposition: well, now he had one. Widdecombe had started the summer as a 'bit of a joke figure', said another, but now dominated the airwaves because she is 'prepared to say what she thinks, even if it makes other people in the party a bit uncomfortable'. Widdecombe had always taken great pleasure in upsetting complacency, especially in her own party, and would have seen the last part of that comment as a great compliment. Her energy and sure touch contrasted with that of John Prescott, who looked 'bumbling', reported the *Daily Telegraph*. Her success in bringing the Tory message to the media was bound to be compared with William

Hague's performance, and the general conclusion favoured Widdecombe. The *Telegraph* again: 'She has done herself a lot of favours while in charge. Ann was only meant to be minding the shop, but you could say that sales have gone through the roof while Hague was away. Miss Widdecombe', it went on, 'is to the Tories what Mo is to Labour. Millions of voters are sick of seeing slick male politicians in dull suits delivering the same old lines on TV.'

The impact of the Widdecombe blitz on the media contrasted with Hague's inability to move the polls. But Widdecombe repeatedly stressed her loyalty. She later said, 'I enjoy the flattery of people saying that I may be the next Tory leader, but my head is not turned. The back benches of both sides of the House are stuffed with people who want to be the next PM.'

Her prime media foe was the novelist and critic A. N. Wilson, who had a column in the London *Evening Standard*. Referring to Widdecombe's summer media campaign, he wrote on 23 August: 'Something must be done to get rid of this ghastly woman. It would take a small swing to the Tories in some marginal seats and we could have Doris for PM. Anyone who is as embarrassed by her as I am would see what a calamity this would be.

'Why should we suppose that it is a virtue in some insufferable bossyboots if she has given 138 interviews in the space of three summer weeks? Should we not think it is a sure sign that she is deranged, a deformed personality. . .?' On another occasion, he wrote, 'Sensible people go on holiday in August. They do not give 150 interviews.'

But the Widdecombe bandwagon was rolling, and William Hague appeared ready to climb on board. The time slot she was given at the Tory party conference that autumn had once been the preserve of Michael Heseltine. While the two politicians differed greatly on ideology, they could both rouse an audience with fiery rhetoric and a well-turned phrase. This time, Widdecombe used the platform to explain a policy on young offenders which looked to some to be dangerously liberal. The audience was ready to follow a politician who had flair or colour, and gave her a long standing ovation. Her policy demonstrated both her familiarity with the failings of the youth penal system and an understanding of the lot of the young and disadvantaged. She later described it:

'We fail the young, if they come to the courts, get a slap on the wrist and go straight back into the same society which had caused the problem in the first place. Most of them are coming from the big council estates. They've never seen a stable male role model. They either have no father, or they have a series of people called "uncle". There's very low parental supervision so they truant. The overwhelming majority of people who come into prison have very low numeracy and literacy skills. They learn very early on that the law does not take seriously all sorts of petty offences, so they commit them and they escalate to greater ones.

'If a young person is making the neighbours' lives a misery, you don't let him carry on doing it, you take him out of that neighbourhood. You only have to do it once or twice in the area and you get the message over – "If you do this you get taken away." You take that person (and I'm talking about twelve- to fifteen-year-olds) out of the neighbourhood into secure training.'

The secure training centre should give those young offenders who had not been accused of the most serious offences of rape or murder the chance to meet academic and behavioural targets without the disorientation of repeated change of venue, sentence and guidance. She said the system of secure training as it was then structured was flawed because it required young offenders to make repeated visits to court to answer each of their previous charges, and this made nonsense of the attempts by staff to use the youngsters' stays in detention for rehabilitation. Offenders should also be given a variable sentence, according to which they would be released when they had achieved a set target. Once outside prison and subject to good behaviour, they would not be prosecuted for any earlier offence. 'The slate would be wiped clean, and they would enter the world free of any convictions.'

The Guardian's Simon Hoggart said the speech 'achieved something close to genius' in that it was given a standing ovation without mentioning capital punishment. Matthew Parris, *The Times'* sketch writer, was equally amazed. 'Some astonishingly liberal ideas were belted out with such belligerent swagger that Tory backwoodsmen found themselves applauding an enlightened programme of rehabilitation.' Both commentators were rather less complimentary about her get-up. Hoggart said her 'dazzling tartan jacket all made of colours not found in nature' looked like a 'picnic rug'.

When Widdecombe had finished her oration, she made a bid to embrace her leader, but missed his face. He sought to put his arm round her by way of an embrace but, as Parris described it, 'ran out of arm'. Relations with Hague seemed otherwise cordial.

The swashbuckling confidence she displayed over the summer, and again at the conference, allowed Widdecombe to be regarded as the 'unacknowledged deputy leader of the Conservative Party'. For a time, she appeared to have the platform to herself as the darling of the party and the toast of the country. But her claim to pride of place beside Hague at the opposition's top table would quickly be challenged.

Her rival was Michael Portillo, the Secretary of State for whom she had worked, somewhat uneasily, at the Department of Employment. Portillo had lost his seat at the 1997 election. Had he won, it was assumed he would have replaced Major as leader; his absence from the Commons enabled Hague, and indeed Widdecombe, to flourish. Hague's failure to rescue the party in the first year of opposition persuaded some that Portillo would have done better, and there was great pressure to have him returned to Parliament. Widdecombe, staunchly loyal to Hague, commented in early 1999, while Portillo was still in the wilderness, that although he was able, there was no promise he would be a 'prince across the water' who could transform Tory fortunes. Asked in that year for her attitude to Portillo, she responded: 'People don't see the larger picture. The media is so focused on Michael as a potential leader, but look, he'll come in and have to acclimatize himself being on the back benches and then presumably he will move to the front benches and then . . . Truthfully, truthfully I would welcome him back. He has force, brainpower, personality – especially since he lost at the last election. We need our big assets. Welcome back Michael, I say ... That is where William is so level-headed. He knows that he needs to be surrounded by bright people who could do his job if they had to. He can't keep the good people down. Bring them in. I am a competitive mortal. Of course I am competitive. But you do not win by wishing away the competition. You win by beating the competition.'

The need for Portillo's return to the Commons grew more pressing as the party's fortunes languished. So when Alan Clark died and a by-election was called in the ultra-safe Conservative constituency of Kensington and Chelsea, Portillo was front-runner to be the Tory candidate. His success in the by-election, on 25 November 1999, returned to the scene a potential leader – and one whose ideology and style were some way from Widdecombe's. Observers then began guessing how long Hague would keep Portillo on the back benches. His stay there was shorter than many expected: Portillo returned to the top table on 1 February 2000, as shadow Chancellor. The removal of John Redwood from the shadow Cabinet in the same reshuffle appeared to strengthen Portillo's position as the Tories' leading monetarist.

Since this promotion, observers have seen the makings of an uncomfortable rivalry. Relations between Portillo and Widdecombe are not as cordial as they may have been when their party's position was more precarious. Hague accepted an element of difference, but insisted that they could combine their talents effectively: 'They've got different styles. They're not natural soulmates. In some ways, in social issues for instance, I haven't noticed any difficulty in them working together.'

In truth, a number of factors have made Portillo's return to prominence in the Conservative parliamentary party rather less smooth than he and his supporters might have hoped. First, there is no doubt the party has taken longer than he probably would have wished to accept the revelation he made in the summer of 1999 that he had had homosexual relationships in his earlier life. He explained them by saying that they were an aberration and he had ceased to practise as a homosexual. But the party's fundamentalist Christian wing found such a statement at odds with their beliefs and are unlikely ever to regard the politician in the same way again. Portillo's second problem was his credibility in Parliament and the party. Conservatives struggled to understand his apparent switch from the caring and inclusive Conservatism he advocated when he was outside Parliament, and desperate to return, to the hardline positions he took when he was back on the front bench. Finally, Portillo has made less of an impact as shadow Chancellor than many had expected. His adversary Gordon Brown has been on a roll with a booming economy at his fingertips, and his position within the government has strengthened. Brown, with all the cards in his hand, has shown himself the master of the floor of the House of Commons. One observer commented that Portillo 'has not laid a glove on him'. Another said: 'Hague has got Portillo tied up as Chancellor.'

While Portillo has struggled to match Brown in the Commons, Widdecombe has shown herself at least the equal of her opposite number Jack Straw. Her attack on Straw's claim, made at the 1999 Labour party conference, that he was increasing absolute police numbers when he was only returning them to base levels, won her points. She said his statistical gyrations had 'rivalled Houdini'. She also effectively exploited Straw's delay in acting against football hooliganism. He had refused to support an earlier Conservative backbencher's bill making many of the same changes that he subsequently introduced; so when she and Straw joined forces to expedite the bill's progress at the end of the parliamentary session in July 2000, she had the moral upper hand and could dictate aspects of its contents.

The seemingly inexorable rise in crime figures – especially violent crime and crime against the person – that occurred throughout 2000 played towards Widdecombe's hardline stance on law and order. The Labour government's retreat from its early ideals on crime and law and order towards many Conservative positions has again strengthened the hand of the shadow Home Secretary. But whereas it was generally accepted that Widdecombe terrified Frank

Dobson into submission when she had the health brief, she has not had quite the same triumphs in her run-ins with Jack Straw. Michael Brown, a former MP and now a newspaper columnist, has observed, 'She doesn't get it quite all her own way. Very often, privately, I have the suspicion that she agrees with Straw's tough positions. On some occasions, he leaves Ann struggling a bit to outdo him. She doesn't usually beat him – he doesn't usually beat her, but she's got a big break with this job in that she's right up there with Hague and Portillo.'

Widdecombe would assert that rivalry between the crown princes was irrelevant so long as William Hague was at the helm. Hague: 'Every general needs a colonel, when they say they're going to go and advance to take that hill – they jolly well advance and take that hill! She is exactly like that. You know if she's told you she's going to do something, she will then do it, hell or high water, she will go out and do it. She's not afraid – she doesn't buckle under pressure.' But he also said that the new shadow cabinet is a team rather than a collection of stars, so some pressure may be placed on Widdecombe to curb her tendency to grab the limelight.

John Major is convinced that Ann will be 'a senior minister. Which position? She's a very able girl. People think the Home Office because she's doing very well there now. She might do well in other senior jobs as well, so I wouldn't exclude any of them.' But a facet in her character could still hold her back. In what must be seen as a reference to that agonizing period seven years earlier, when she was seeking his support to act against Howard, Major has said: 'There are two sorts of politicians: there are those for whom nothing would make them resign and there are those for whom events would make them resign. Ann falls absolutely in the latter category. I think she will be a very senior figure for a long time, unless that tendency to resign forces her to resign because something happens that she cannot personally tolerate. There is always that risk for someone with strong convictions like Ann, that could happen . . .

'People still tell you with affection Willie Whitelaw stories. I predict that in twenty years people will still be telling with affection

Ann Widdecombe stories – they will not be telling you stories about Jack Straw.'

The former Conservative minister David Hunt says he had 'always seen her as a potential leader of the party, and a potential senior member of the Cabinet who will leave her mark in history. I think progress is due to the unreasonable people and Ann is the archetypal unreasonable woman. She's not prepared to accept platitudes, she's not prepared to accept even the inevitable, because she believes that you can, even out of the most impossible situation, achieve something. So she never gives up.'

The public saw a different side of Ann Widdecombe in early 2000 when she published her first novel. *The Clematis Tree* showed a degree of sensitivity towards personal and family problems that surprised many commentators who had set out to rubbish the expected right-wing rant. In fact the novel showed how religious belief and family and political life were inseparable. Man without God is a hopeless case, was its pessimistic conclusion.

Widdecombe without God – politician as much as person – is also inconceivable. She has strong Christian beliefs, and pro-life views which are at odds with contemporary practice. Her stances on homosexuality and family values appear far out of touch with what happens in contemporary families and contemporary homes, and in the minds of modern men and women. The selection of Widdecombe as a leader would require a considerable leap of faith for a country and perhaps a party that has exchanged God for Mammon.

EPILOGUE

Widdecombe has said she hopes to win the next election. Well she may. She hopes to make the Government look so bad, that the electorate give her her wish. Well, the show is not over until it is over. But the prognosis, as of September 2000 when this is written, does not look good.

All eventualities have to be considered, and the next set involve a Conservative loss at the 2001 General Election which is kept within such limits that William Hague retains his job. Opinions differ on this, of course, but there is a consensus around the view that that would require the Conservatives to reduce the Labour majority from its present 180 to a majority of at the very most one hundred and probably 80.

Ann Widdecombe has always stated categorically that she would not run against an incumbent leader. So there would be no question of her challenging William Hague for the crown. But another massive Labour majority after the election would likely indicate to Hague and his youthful followers that their solutions, or their faces had failed to win appeal.

Hague would have the option of soldiering on, and forcing his parliamentary party to challenge him. If fifteen per cent of Conservative MPs sign a motion of no confidence a vote has to be held. Or Hague could voluntarily step down. Conservative MPs then vote on leadership candidates until all but two have been eliminated. Those two names are put to the entire membership of the country and the leader is elected through a postal ballot.

Ann Widdecombe has made no secret of her ambition to rise to the top of her Party – as we have seen, she has 'dreamt' of being Prime Minister – so she would most likely stand for leader. Some have doubted her ability to produce the party organisation to win through in the parliamentary machine, but MPs would be bound to take into her account both her popularity with the constituencies and her high profile in the media and with the electorate more generally.

Few Conservatives have a better understanding of the way constituency parties and officials tick than Widdecombe and few members of the party hierarchy have more assiduously courted the local members. For as long as she has been a Member of Parliament her evenings and weekends have been filled with speaking engagements at remote outposts of the Conservative empire. Tory backwoodsmen – many of whom feel Westminster is a long way away both physically and culturally – have warmed to the optimism and home truths of this unstuffy parliamentarian. Her 'evangelistic' speeches at party conferences since 1998 have consolidated her support in the constituencies.

But while Widdecombe is a favourite to win the hearts of the constituencies, she has also to persuade them that she can win over a majority in the country, where she is widely regarded as a character who stands out from the crowd of grey nonentities, even if she is seen by some as out of touch with prevailing beliefs. The range of activities in which she has engaged since 1997 should substantiate her claim to be able to speak with authority and objectivity on a wide range of issues and answer deep national concerns.

Widdecombe will be asked about her leadership credentials and style in any future campaign. Here, she has shown the capacity to raise morale. She has proved herself to be a doughty fighter for causes in which she believes and, while in office, it was acknowledged she was a particularly diligent administrator who cuts out the 'crap' (her own word) and gets to the meat of an argument.

But the hardest test for Widdecombe, were she elected, and one where her capacity is unproven, is showing the decisiveness, even ruthlessness, that leaders must exercise to form the best teams and sift out the chaff. Her preference is to be consensual rather than dictatorial. But while her sense of fairness and fair-play is innate and well-proven, the strong conscience may not serve her at the crunch moments. The fact that this personality component has not been demonstrated, does not mean that it is absent. Leading the Party would merely provide Widdecombe with a further and harder challenge, and it is one she would undoubtedly relish.

The constituency parties may of course feel that the Conservative Party needs a more cerebral and less emotional leader than Widdecombe to win a general election. This would lead them to support the candidacy of the evidently ambitious and competent Michael Portillo. William Hague has said elsewhere that Portillo and Widdecombe are 'not soulmates', and neither party would dispute the accuracy of this statement. Respect between colleagues is particularly important for Widdecombe and that would become a key issue were Portillo elected. But there is no higher priority for Widdecombe than the electoral success of the Conservative Party, so colleagues would hope that a *modus co-operandi* could be devised to allow Portillo's analysis and Widdecombe's colour to cohere. Friends of both point out they worked together in harmony at the Department of Employment, and subsequently in the Shadow Cabinet, so it can be done, the relationship can be made to work.

There will of course come a time, when Widdecombe chooses, or conceivably is forced, to consider a career or work outside Westminster politics. Some have speculated that she would make a dynamic chairman of a charity concerned with prisoners welfare and others see her joining the ranks of the 'Great and the Good' and a possible head of Royal Commissions and the like. She might even take a more active role in the Church of Rome she joined in 1993, or even build on her burgeoning media career.

She would have no difficulty choosing her title for elevation to the Upper House, as she once said (perhaps more in jest than earnestness) that she would enjoy being Baroness Widdecombe of Widecombe after the town in Devon, Widecombe-in-the-Moor from where her father's family may have originated.

Alternatively, she could leave the highlights of politics behind, and revert to her original childhood passion for writing, becoming a lady of letters and noted novelist. Predictions so far ahead are almost bound to fail. But Ann Widdecombe is unlikely to be far from controversy for a very long time. The energy in this fireball has a very long way to go to be expended.

INDEX